THE
AENEID

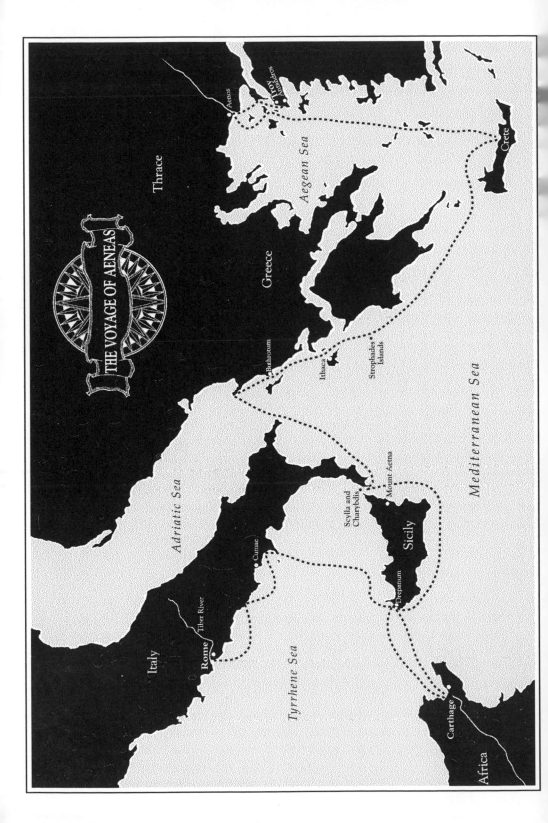

THE
AENEID

VIRGIL

Translated by
Edward McCrorie

With a Foreword by Vincent J. Cleary

Ann Arbor

THE UNIVERSITY OF MICHIGAN PRESS

Library of Congress Cataloging-in-Publication Data

Virgil.
   [Aeneis. English]
   The Aeneid of Virgil / translated by Edward McCrarie.
      p.   cm.
   ISBN 0-472-09595-1 (hardcover : alk. paper) — ISBN 0-472-06595-5
   (pbk. : alk. paper)
    1. Epic poetry, Latin—Translations into English.   2. Aeneas
   (Legendary character)—Poetry.   3. Legends—Rome—Poetry.
   I. McCrorie, Edward.   II. Title.
   PA6807.A5M38   1994
   873'.01—dc20   94-24222
                                                CIP

for Robert Bly

sator vatum

On Reading the *Aeneid*

"What is a classic?" is the title of the Presidential Address given to the British Virgil Society by T. S. Eliot during the dark days of World War II in 1944. For Eliot the key idea is maturity: "A classic can occur only when a civilization is mature, when a language and literature are mature; and it must be the work of a mature mind." The poet who for Eliot possesses these qualities is Virgil, and the epic poem that embodies them the *Aeneid:* "Our classic, the classic of all Europe, is Virgil."

Fifty years after Eliot spoke these words, I would expand his definition to include America, particularly the United States. I suggest too that this same quality, maturity, is essential to understanding the poem. Finally I argue that maturity is the quality of Edward McCrorie's fine new translation that most recommends it to readers. It is mature in a way that other American verse translations of the poem are not.

Poets of course, even those breaking untraditional ground like Walt Whitman, Allen Ginsberg, and Jack Kerouac, to name three poets very different from Virgil, work with or against a tradition and when they sit down to compose a poem, a long line of poetic predecessors sits just behind them, peering over their shoulders. The would-be poets in turn constantly glance through rear-view mirrors at their artistic forebears. Virgil did so and so does Edward McCrorie.

In my town, Amherst, Massachusetts, for example, Robert Francis, a poet of the first rank, was heir to two other Amherst poets, Emily Dickinson and Robert Frost. Frost's poems often recall Virgil's *Eclogues* and *Georgics,* and Dickinson, Horace's *Odes,* among other poets who influenced them. The two Roman poets in turn look back to and continue, again, not exclusively, the Greek Lyric and Bucolic poetic traditions.

In epic poetry, our subject here, a straight line runs from Milton to Dante, through Virgil, back to Homer. The challenge for the poet working in the epic tradition is to work within this tradition, discretely calling attention to his own literary predecessors, those a literate reader would recognize, while at the same time working fine, subtle variations on the stock themes and language of epic in order to make his own distinctive voice heard. This is less a contest to establish who is the better poet than to say: "My verse reflects and is a continuation of yours but is different from it, is in fact uniquely mine, not a mere imitation of yours."

The *Aeneid* is a work that establishes the Roman accomplishment—its tradition, history, and culture—as in every way equal to that of the Greeks; it is also, because of the universal themes it contains, a poem that resonates with what is essential to larger human issues and experiences, including our own American experience. It is not only a poem about Rome. Eliot's dictum needs to be enlarged upon. Our classic, the classic of the entire West, is Virgil.

Maturity. To understand Virgil's poem, its relationship to its Greek predecessors, as well as the importance of the *Aeneid* in interpreting Augustan Rome and our own American immigrant experience, a different kind of maturity is required. In addition to the kinds outlined by Eliot, the *Aeneid* requires maturity of its reader. A mature reader will bring to the *Aeneid* a set of experiences—those acquired in life and vicariously by reading—against which to compare Virgil's words. Where this is not the case, for example, among young readers who are deficient in terms of life experiences, if they are able to bring to the poem a literary imagination, one based on good prior reading, the very act of coming to terms with the ideas and language of the *Aeneid* can be a maturing experience in itself.

Ambiguity provides a good test of a reader's maturity for it is present in Virgil's poem in a way that it is not in Homer. Perhaps nowhere is this more evident than in the final scene of the *Aeneid,* the climactic confrontation between Aeneas and Turnus. After Aeneas takes Turnus' life, and in a most brutal way, readers rightfully ask whether this death is justified, whether Aeneas goes too far, whether Turnus might have been spared. The *Aeneid* ends in this haunting, perplexing way and it is left to the reader to ponder the resolution.

In the Homeric poems by contrast, similar questions do not linger in the reader's mind. In the *Iliad* and *Odyssey* it is more a question of *when,* less of *why* or *if. When* will Achilles return to battle to avenge his friend, Patroclus' death? *When* will Odysseus and his son Telemachus slay the suitors, all one hundred plus of them, the slaughter itself being a foregone conclusion?

What Virgil asks of his readers is above all an imagination that does not view the poem, and life, in narrowly defined, shadow-free terms. The *Aeneid* introduces readers young and old to a world very different from Homer's, one however that an imaginative mind, even without a knowledge of Homer, can enter into and enjoy. The *Aeneid* does not presuppose a knowledge of Homer, but with such a knowledge, the experience of the *Aeneid* becomes an even richer one.

In my experience as a teacher, the *Aeneid* initiates adolescents into the varied levels and complexities of the adult, Virgilian world. Young adults, on leaving Virgil's poem, should be better prepared to understand their parents' world and the adult world they themselves will soon be entering, for it is this world that Virgil's poem explores.

Virgil's hero Aeneas is a complex character. Compared to the decisions and choices he is called upon to make, Homer's heroes Achilles and Odysseus inhabit more circumscribed moral, social, and intellectual worlds. Achilles' sense of honor has been violated by the Greek general Agamemnon. Achilles' prize, a slave woman, has been taken from him and he will be satisfied with no other. The best of the Achaean warriors therefore refuses to fight. He retires to his tent and the tide of battle turns against the Greeks. Achilles returns to battle only when his best friend, the beloved Patroclus, dies in his stead, and wearing Achilles' own armor.

Odysseus, after a ten year's absence fighting at Troy and a decade of dalliance and delay in making his way home, uses every trick and stratagem his cunning Greek mind can devise finally to reach Ithaca. There, with the help of his son, Telemachus, and two faithful retainers, the swineherd and the cowherd, he slays the suitors and, with Athena's assistance, once more establishes his right to rule as king in Ithaca.

Two tests remain: the secret of the marriage bed that only he and Penelope possess—eventually he passes this test—and his recognition as son by his father, Laertes, in the final book of the *Odyssey*. By showing his scar to his father and by exactly describing the orchard that Laertes had planted when Odysseus was a boy, the son proves his identity to his father. It is his last, and perhaps most difficult, test. Note that Odysseus *reestablishes* himself as husband, son, father, king in Ithaca. He returns to that which he was before setting out for Troy. His odyssey, as we shall see, is very different from Aeneas' journey, in almost every respect.

The *Iliad* and *Odyssey* are each brilliant masterpieces in their own right, finely honed epics, the products of over five hundred years of oral storytelling in the Greek tradition. They are the

time-tested predecessors of the *Aeneid* and themselves the beginning of the Western epic tradition, yet they portray very different
worlds from that of the *Aeneid*. The *Aeneid* begins where the other
two poems end. Where Achilles is faced with three major decisions, Aeneas has manifold choices to make: to leave or defend
Troy; to return, placing his mission at risk, and search for his
missing wife, Creusa, in the burning city, Book 2; to help Dido to
found her city or to leave her, Book 4; to accept the Roman
mantle his father, Anchises, metaphorically places on his now-
Roman shoulders in Book 6 (does he understand what took place
in Book 6 or was it all a dream?); in Book 8, to lift to his shoulders
the Shield and to accept the Roman future depicted there as he
had carried his father from the destroyed city in Book 2; to slay or
spare, first, Mezentius, then that enemy's loyal, devoted son,
Lausus, in Book 10; to make a similar choice of his Rutulian
opponent, the great Italian leader Turnus, in Book 12. As his
father had ordered him to do in Book 6, "spare humble men and
war on the prideful," so Aeneas again and again is confronted by
difficult choices.

While by contrast, the *Iliad* and *Odyssey* offer less ambiguous,
more clearcut decisions, Aeneas is faced with a series of grey-
colored choices, where conflicting demands sway him now this
way, now that. The world of the *Aeneid* is less a clearly defined
world of precise choices required in a more primitive, heroic
society, choices of an earlier, less complex, Homeric civilization.
Rather, the *Aeneid* involves multidimensional, agonistic choices,
often between greater and lesser degrees of good and evil. Such
choices exist in the more advanced, developed civilization of the
Aeneid, a world of history and politics, philosophy and literary
tradition, assimilation and mimesis, spheres almost entirely absent from the Homeric poems, as intricate, detailed, and sophisti-
cated as each of these poems is.

Books 6 and 8 of the *Aeneid* provide good examples of such
differences. At the end of Book 6, Anchises identifies for his son
the individual Roman heroes parading past them. These heroes,
descendants yet unborn, begin with the Alban and Roman kings
and end with Virgil's own time, with Julius Caesar, Gnaeus Pom-
peius, and Marcellus, Augustus' adoptive son and heir apparent.
The son of his sister, Octavia, Marcellus died young, age nine-
teen, in 23 B.C., a few short years before Virgil's own death in 19
B.C. Similar historical references are absent from the Homeric
poems.

Aeneid 8 concludes with the Battle of Actium, 31 B.C., the defeat of Cleopatra and Antony—the order is significant—by Augustus and his naval commander, Agrippa, effectively bringing to a close the civil discord and chaos that ensued after Julius Caesar's assassination in 44 B.C. Augustus is now the sole survivor, the new *princeps* of the state. The Republic has ended; the Roman Empire is born.

Historical references of this sort are foreign to the Homeric poems—an important distinction—and effectively define the *Aeneid* as a poem about time, about history, about tradition and the historical process, how Rome and the Roman Empire came to be:

> . . . Juno's fierce and remembering anger
> caused him to suffer greatly in war while founding a city,
> bringing his Gods to Latium, leading to Latin
> and Alban fathers, to high walls of the Romans.
>
> (1.4–8)

The *Aeneid* contains more differences than similarities with its Homeric predecessors. It represents an essentially different poem from the Homeric accomplishment.

Why is this so? The Homeric poems reflect earlier aspects, some eight hundred years prior, of the continuing western tradition that form the basic groundwork of Virgil's poem. Virgil had to create a different kind of epic. With the *Aeneid,* the epic tradition takes a cyclopean step forward, one that requires a more advanced level of understanding, maturity, on the part of its readers. It is a maturity the poem itself helps readers to achieve.

My first exposure to the *Aeneid* was as a high school teacher in Delaware in 1959 at a private boys' high school. I was in my late twenties, married, the father of one son. I had lived away from home after college doing postgraduate work in upstate New York, leaving home for an extended period for the first time in my life. In my last year of college, I had also lost my father and sister within a six-month period. Finally, after a number of false starts, I had determined on a life's work, to teach Latin and the classical humanities, something I have done ever since.

The main events of my life described here, as I learned from teaching the poem for the first time, had parallel analogues with events of Books 1–6 of the *Aeneid.* It was a revealing experience for me as I worked through these books with my class for I felt as though my own life were being described in the poem, as though Virgil were speaking directly to me, so closely did I identify with the events portrayed in them. I was not aware of it at the time, but

the poem was also indirectly preparing me for events, as yet un-
foreseen, later in my life. Best of all, as I now realize, it was doing
the same thing for my students.

They were young, seventeen- and eighteen-year-olds, high
school seniors, younger in years than I but equipped, many of
them, with solid English and Latin reading skills—they were
fourth-year Latin students—and they had received a good ground-
ing in literature from their English and romance language courses.

Here was the great thing about the *Aeneid* that I and my
students discovered that year. While the *Aeneid* is the defining
story, at one level, of how Rome and Roman civilization came to
be, the poem is above all a highly human story, one that reflects
and foreshadows moments common to all of us as we make our
way through life. Like every truly classic work, the *Aeneid,* while
recalling past events, was also preparing me and my students for
events in our lives as yet unknown, events most of us eventually do
experience.

This, I can now say with assurance, is an important reason,
perhaps the main reason, for reading this work. It calls upon our
mature selves, and in those areas where we are lacking in maturity
it helps us to become more mature: it is itself part of this process.

When we are young, the *Aeneid* shows us what being an adult
entails—it partly helps us to grow up; and when we are older, the
Aeneid recalls those experiences we have already had, offering a
yardstick by which to compare how we responded to significant
moments in our lives.

The *Aeneid* is a poem that treats of human nature and the
human condition, and what it means to be adult, a mature person. It is a poem of parents and children, particularly but not
exclusively fathers and sons, of love won and lost, of suffering and
sorrow, of hope and achievement, of facing obstacles and over-
coming them, of confronting the demons without and within us,
of showing us how to live and, by implication, how to die. It is a
classic for these reasons too.

The *Aeneid* is also an "American" style poem. People emi-
grate, they follow religious or economic destinies, they travel far,
westward, in ships, they take on the journey only their most precious objects, sacred and familial, to a new world as yet uncharted,
to an undefined future, and to the obstacles encountered and to
be overcome there. This is a story most American immigrant
families, like Aeneas on his journey, can echo event for event.

And yes, the *Aeneid* also reflects the American story of confronting indigenous peoples and presents a study of the assimi-

lation of foreign culture with the native traditions. To Virgil's credit, this assimilation is unlike the American experience, which is more the shameful story of imposing foreign traditions upon the native cultures and destroying the native tradition in the process, traditions we brought with us from the foreign cultures.

The *Aeneid* also presents the story of the subjugation of native peoples, but with an important difference: instead of destroying the native traditions, assimilation took place, that of the invading people with the native culture. The result is a culture neither Italian nor Trojan but a Roman blend of the two. This fact helps to explain, at least partially, why native people like Camilla and Turnus are portrayed so sympathetically in the poem.

In the light of such subjugation, Virgil's poem raises the age-old question: does the end ever justify the means? and if so, under what conditions? In Aeneas' opponents one can limn many a Native American, just as one can see parallels to modern concerns in the conflicts between the Trojans and Rutulians, on one level, and between Aeneas and Turnus on another. Since both sides in the Italian conflict trace their lineage to Greek-speaking ancestors, one can also see the theme of Civil War experiences, brother fighting brother, carried out by the poet.

Here then are two ways to read the poem, ways that help to define it as a classic work. Experienced readers and imaginative younger readers alike can each read and reread the *Aeneid* at important junctures in their lives. The poem presents new opportunities for growth and understanding at each of these stages, at each rereading. Very few works of literature can pass this test. The *Aeneid* can, it does, and it corroborates Eliot's idea that maturity is the key to understanding Virgil's poem.

Maturity of the translation. Edward McCrorie's new line-for-line, verse translation of the *Aeneid* is also characterized by the word *maturity.* The work before you contains these qualities of a mature, readable translation: fidelity to the original, musicality, modernity, and movement. A word on each.

Fidelity. This translation provides for Virgil's poem what the translator Richmond Lattimore has supplied for the *Iliad* and the *Odyssey,* a rendering of the original text into English that is faithful to the language and spirit of Homer, in this case, Virgil. McCrorie does this for Virgil's poem. So closely does Lattimore follow Homer's language that students of Greek find it a most helpful tool to use in their own translation of the poem. To their amazement they discover the Lattimore version to be so true to

the original that it is almost a word-for-word, line-for-line translation, often retaining the very order of the Greek words, a difficult
feat given the differences between the two languges. McCrorie's
translation shows these same virtues.

In Lattimore's Homer, nothing is omitted, every metaphor is
translated, nothing is glossed over. Yet—and here is the astonishing part—the result is a highly readable and poetic work in English. McCrorie matches this accomplishment. He slights neither
his obligation to Virgil's text nor the responsibility he has to his
second-language readers, a fine line to walk—and he does so
gracefully. Finally it can be said: we possess a Lattimore-quality
translation of the *Aeneid,* true to the letter *and* the spirit of the
original.

Musicality. Choosing a five-, sometimes a six-beat poetic line,
one which mimics the dactyl-trochee rhythm of the last two feet of
the Latin line, using harsh consonants to suggest harsh actions,
and softer, more euphonic sounds to portray less harsh moments,
often too with enjambement or run-over lines as in the original,
McCrorie has given us a highly musical reading of the *Aeneid.* The
poem begins:

> Arma virumque cano, Troiae qui primus ab oris

which he renders:

> My song is of war and the first man from a Trojan
> coast . . .

Note the use of *cano;* "I sing" becomes "my song." The *Aeneid,* as
with all Roman poetry (or for that matter, most later poetry that it
inspired), is meant to be sounded out, read aloud, sung. Certain
kinds of Latin poetry, lyric, for example, are meant to be accompanied by a musical instrument, a lyre, again with emphasis on
how one hears the poetry. How else explain all the care the poet
and his translator lavish on the precise way the language sounds?
Put this present translation to the reading-aloud test. You will
discover it to be melodious, rhythmical.

Modernity. McCrorie's choice of poetic language is modern
without being solipsistic or slangy, is idiomatic yet formal and
majestic, is neither stilted nor pedantic. Other translators, in order to make Virgil more up to date, have opted for less formal
language and a faster moving line. Taken with other omissions
and glosses, this produces a quickly moving line but one that is not

quite true to Virgil. The slower paced, more majestic rise and fall
of the original, its sonority and mellifluousness, its operatic qualities—all of which we get in McCrorie—are sacrificed in these
other translations to a quicker pace, a faster reading. The result,
it may be argued in these other translations, is perhaps a more
colloquial translation, but less the formal poem Virgil created.

Again McCrorie achieves a delicate balance between language
attuned to a late twentieth-century ear while maintaining the eu-
phony and cacophony, the consonance and dissonance, stateliness
and symphonic cadence of the original. Here too fidelity to the
Latin text is not sacrificed to a more modern rendering.

Movement. Together with the orchestral-like music and the
elevated tone produced by it, the reader experiences the passion
and emotion of the *Aeneid* in this translation. It affects readers,
involves them in the story, makes of them active participants. One
cannot be a passive onlooker in this tale. Each reader will have
favorite passages once the book is read, but one that I would cite
to show movement in the translation is in the last scene of the
poem, what McCrorie describes as "Single Combat." In the following passage, note how closely the Latin word order is retained
in English, including the run-over, or enjambed, lines and how
rapidly the lines move:

> Cunctanti telum Aeneas fatale coruscat,
> sortitus fortunam oculis, et corpore toto
> eminus intorquet. murali concita numquam
> tormento sic saxa fremunt nec fulmine tanti
> dissultant crepitus. volat atri turbinis instar
> exitium dirum hasta ferens orasque recludit
> loricae et clipei extremos septemplicis orbis:
> per medium stridens transit femur. incidit ictus. . . .
>
> (12.919–26)

> While he delayed, Aeneas kept flashing the deadly
> spear. He spotted a chance: he threw from a distance
> with all his force. Stone from siege-slings have never
> roared or smashed at a wall, nor has lightning and
>   thunder
> cracked so hard: appearing dark as a whirlwind,
> bearing its grim conclusion, the spear went flying and
>   broke through
> the corselet's edge, the seven-fold shield at the bottom,
> grinding, and tore through thigh. Turnus was buckled. . . .

McCrorie, like Virgil, spent many years on this work, and it shows.

The story is told of James Fenimore Cooper, 1789–1851, author of the Leatherstocking Tales, whose best known work is *The Last of the Mohicans.* Cooper's father founded Cooperstown in upstate New York, near the Finger Lakes region where many of the son's novels took place. The future author liked to read aloud to his family and one day, when he was thirty-one years old and at the exact midpoint in his life, not yet having published any novels, he is said, according to his daughter Susan, to have thrown aside the book he was reading and declared: "I can write you a better book than that, myself!" Whether or not this story is apocryphal, Cooper went on to write fifty books, including thirty-three novels during a thirty-year writing career, travel books, political works, and a history of the U.S. Navy. (He had joined the Navy after being dismissed from Yale.) A not undistinguished record, and his daughter started it all.

The translation before you has a similar genesis. My friend Ted McCrorie tells me that his daughter Jeanne was unimpressed as a high school student with two or three English versions of the poem and asked him: "Why don't you do one?" This translation, many revisions and 10,000 lines later, is the result. Will it be as long-lived as the Cooper novels? It deserves to be.

Above all, as both of these stories indicate, literature, especially Latin literature, is meant to be read aloud. Family reading-aloud is fast becoming a lost art in this country. Read this poem aloud, to yourself, your family, your friends. I believe it is a version of which both Susan Cooper and Jeanne McCrorie (now Jeanne McSweeney) would approve. It sings.

Vincent J. Cleary
University of Massachusetts at Amherst

Contents

A Selective Glossary

Very obscure or relatively unimportant names, like **Acidalian** and **Lyaean**, are not included here, nor are all those names which the poet himself clearly identifies, like **Juno**, the **Tiber River**, and **Turnus**.

Achaean: a synonym in Virgil for **Greek**

Acheron: a river in the Underworld

Achilles: the greatest warrior on the Greek side during the Trojan War; the hero of Homer's *Iliad*

Aegaeon: a hundred-handed monster who warred with the gods

Aeolus: god of the winds; also the name of a strong Trojan warrior killed in Italy

Ajax: a powerful Greek warrior during the Trojan war; he profaned the temple of Pallas at Troy

Alba or **Alba Longa:** a city to be founded eventually by Ascanius, the son of Aeneas, in Italy

Amasenus: a river in Latium in central Italy

Amata: queen and wife of Latinus in Italy, mother of Lavinia

Androgeos: a warrior on the Greek side during the Trojan War

Andromache: the wife of Hector, a prince of Troy, the greatest warrior defending the city during the Trojan War

Anubis: an Egyptian god usually pictured with the head of a dog

Apollo or **Phoebus** or **Hyperion:** the sun god and god of the arts, often associated with the nine **Muses**

Arcadia: a mountainous area of the **Peloponnesus** in Greece

Argos: an eastern central sector of the **Peloponnesus** in Greece, the center of Mycenaean civilization, ruled by Agamemnon

Ariadne: a princess on the island of Crete who helped Theseus to make his way in and out of the **Labyrinth**

Assaracus: an ancient king of Troy and the son of Tros; the grandfather of Anchises and the great-grandfather of Aeneas

Astyanax: the son of **Andromache** and Hector, killed at Troy

Athesis: a river in northern Italy

Athos: a mountain in Macedonia

Atlas: a Titan, a mythical figure of great strength who was believed to support the world on his shoulders

Atreus: the father of Agamemnon and Menelaus, the two Greek brothers who launched the invasion of Troy

Aufidus: a river in southern Italy

Aurora: goddess of the dawn

Ausonia: an ancient name for Italy

Avernus: a lake near Cumae on the western shore of Italy, associated with entry into the Underworld

Bacchus or **Dionysus:** the god of wine

Bacchae: women followers of Bacchus, associated with wild rituals

Baiae: a town near Cumae, on the central western coast of Italy

Bellona: a Roman goddess of war

Briareus: another name for Aegaeon

Brutus: a Roman leader who drove the Tarquin kings out of Rome and felt obliged to kill his own sons for their treachery

Caieta: a nurse of Aeneas; her name was given to a port on the western coast of Italy

Calliope: Muse of Epic poetry

Capri: an island off the western coast of central Italy

Cassandra: a princess of Troy, a prophet whose words were never heeded

Catiline: a Roman who threatened the Roman republic in Virgil's century

Cato: a leader of the Roman republic who urged the total destruction of Carthage

Centaur: a mythological and combative figure who was half man and half horse

Ceres: the Roman goddess of grain and bread

Chaos: the name of a god representing the primal, confused state of the world

Chimaera: an Underworld monster, part goat, snake, and lion; also the name of a Trojan ship

Circe: an island goddess who attempted to enchant Odysseus and his men in Homer's *Odyssey*

Cnossos: the ancient capital of the island of Crete

Cocytus: an Underworld river

Cupid: the Roman god of love; a son of Venus

Cybele: a mysterious mother-goddess of Troy

Cyclades: a group of islands off the southeast coast of Greece

Cycnus: a legendary king who while mourning the loss of a friend was turned into a swan

Cyllenius: another name for the god Mercury, who was born, it was said, on Mt. Cellene in Arcadia in Greece

Cynthus: a mountain on the island of Delos

Cyprus: a large island in the eastern Mediterranean associated with a cult of Venus

Cythera: an island off the southern coast of Greece, a center of the worship of Venus

Danaan: a synonym for **Greek**; Danaus was an ancient king of Argos

Danae: the founder of Ardea in Italy, the city of Turnus and the Rutulians; she came from Argos originally where she was the daughter of King Acrisius

Dardan: a variant for **Trojan**; Dardanus was the legendary founder of Troy

Delos or **Ortygia:** an island in the Aegean Sea, once thought to be floating, later a center of the worship of Apollo

Delphi and the **Delphic Oracle:** in central Greece, the ancient and important oracle of Apollo or Phoebus

Diana: a complex Roman deity, sometimes called **Trivia,** the "three-facing one": (1) goddess of the hunt and of forests; (2) goddess of the moon; and (3) goddess, often with the name of **Hecate,** of the Underworld

Diomedes: a powerful warrior on the Greek side at Troy, who settled later in Italy

Dionysus: another name for **Bacchus**

Dis: another name for **Pluto**

Elis: a region on the western coast of Greece in the Peloponnesus

Elissa: another name for Dido, queen of Carthage

Elysian Fields or **Elysium:** a green and pleasant region of the Underworld

Enceladas: a Titan who, for revolting against Jupiter, was buried alive under Mt. Etna.

Erato: a Muse associated with love poetry

Erebus: the son of Chaos; his name is also used for the Underworld

Eridanus: a river of the Underworld

Erymanthus: a mountain in southern Greece

Eryx: a legendary king of Sicily; also, the name of a mountain on Sicily

Etna: a volcano on the southern shore of Sicily

Etruria or **Etruscan:** an ancient land or people of north central Italy

Euphrates: a river of the Near East

Fates: three goddesses, Clotho, Lachesis, and Atropos, seen as the spinners of life's threads

Furies: punishing goddesses who often attacked, physically or mentally, criminals or sacrilegious persons

Ganges: a great river in northern India

Ganymede: a beautiful young man, son of Kin Laomedon at Troy, loved by Jupiter and taken to Mt. Olympus

Geryon: a three-bodied monster killed by Hercules

Glaucus: a sea god; also the name of the father of Deiphobe, the Sibyl at Cumae; and the name of a Trojan warrior, son of Antenor, mourned by Aeneas in the Underworld

Gorgon: a female monster with snakes in her hair, capable of turning humans into stone

Hebrus: a river in Thrace; also the name of a Trojan warrior killed by Mezentius in Italy

Hecate: another name of **Diana**

Hecuba: wife of Priam and queen of Troy

Helen: the wife of Menelaus, king of Sparta in the southern Peloponnesus, before and after the Trojan War; taken by Paris to Troy, renowned for her beauty, believed to be a cause of the war

Hercules: a son of Jupiter famous for his strength and accomplishments or "labors"

Hippolyta: queen of the Amazons, near the Black Sea

Hippolytus: a son of **Hippolyta,** killed when his horses went mad, restored to life, and sheltered by **Diana** in Italy; he changed his name to **Virbius** and had a son by the same name

Hydra: the name of more than one monster with a number of heads
Hyperion: another name of **Apollo**

Ida: a mountain near Troy, sacred to **Cybele**
Idomeneus: a king of Crete who fought against the Trojans at Troy
Ilium: another name for **Troy**
Ilus: another name for Ascanius, the son of Aeneas; the name of a founding father of
    Troy; and the name of a Rutulian follower of Turnus
Iris: goddess of the rainbow, a helper of Juno
Iulus: another name for Ascanius, the son of Aeneas

Janus: a Roman god of doorways and gates, presented as looking both forward and
    backward

Labyrinth: a confusing system of caves on the island of Crete, designed by the great
    artist Daedalus, to house the Minotaur, a dangerous monster who was half man
    and half bull
Laertes: the father of Odysseus; their home was the island of Ithaka
Lapithae or **Lapiths:** a people of Thessaly, famous for their battle with the **Centaurs**
Latium: a large area surrounding the ancient site of Rome
Latona: a goddess loved by Jupiter, and mother of Diana and Apollo
Laurentians: the name of King Latinus' people in Italy
Lavinia or **Lavinian:** the Italian princess or her land, destined for Aeneas
Lethe the river of forgetfulness in the Underworld
Lydia: an area of Asia Minor; since the Etruscans may have come from there, **Lydian**
    may also suggest **Etrurian**

Manes: spirits of the Underworld
Mantua: a city in northeast Italy; Virgil was born nearby
Mars: the Roman god of war
Maximus: a member of the Fabii family at Rome, called *Cunctator*, the "Delayer," for
    his effective tactics in dealing with Hannibal during the latter's invasion of Italy
Megaera: one of the **Furies**
Metabus: father of Camilla and king of the Volscians
Metiscus: Turnus' chariot driver whose form is assumed in battle by Juturna, a
    goddess and sister of Turnus
Minos: a king on the island of Crete; in the Underworld, a judge of spirits' actions
    during their lives on earth
Muses: nine goddesses associated with various arts such as epic poetry and lyric song
Mycenae: the great "golden" city of Agamemnon, the center of Argos in the
    Peloponnesus, from which the invasion of Troy was initiated
Myrmidons: followers of Achilles during the Trojan War

Numicus: a river in Latium
Nymphs: goddesses associated with various rivers, groves, caves, and fountains

Ocean: the name of a god associated with a large and flowing body of water believed
    to surround the world's lands

Olympus: a mountain in northeast Greece, the home of Jupiter and other gods and goddesses

Orcus: another name for **Pluto**

Orestes: the son of Agamemnon; the husband of Hermione, he killed a rival, Pyrrhus, the son of Achilles

Orion: a legendary hunter whose name was given to a winter constellation often associated with storms

Orpheus: a great legendary poet of Thrace who almost succeeded in rescuing his wife, Eurydice, from the Underworld

Ortygia: another name for **Delos**

Padusa: one of the mouths of the Po River in northeast Italy

Pallas: a complex Greek goddess associated with wisdom, battle strategy, and certain domestic arts—her Roman name was Minerva; Pallas is also the name of the warrior son of Evander, king of Pallanteum, on the site of ancient Rome

Pan: a Greek god of forests and shepherds

Pandarus: a warrior who fought on the Trojan side at Troy

Panopea: a sea nymph, called a Nereid, a daughter of the sea god Nereus

Paphos: a city on the island of Cyprus in the eastern Mediterranean, a center of the cult of Venus

Paris: a prince at Troy who judged that Venus was more beautiful than Juno, thus incurring the latter's enmity during and after the Trojan War; Paris was rewarded by Venus with Helen, the Greek wife of Menelaus, who with his brother Agamemnon began the Trojan War in reprisal

Pasiphae: the wife of King Minos on the island of Crete; she became, through intercourse with a bull, the mother of the Minotaur; see also **Labyrinth**

Pelasgians: another name for the Greeks

Penthesilea: the queen of the Amazons who fought at Troy

Pentheus: a king of Thebes, a town in Boeotia, driven mad by Bacchus for opposing worship of that god

Phaedra: a daughter of King Minos on the island of Crete, she fell in love with Hippolytus, her stepson, who rejected her love; she then caused his death and took her own life

Phaethon: a son of Apollo who tried to drive the chariot of the sun god across the sky but lost control and was killed by Jupiter

Pheneus: a city in **Arcadia**

Phlegethon: a river in the Underworld

Phoebus: another name for Apollo, or Hyperion, the sun god

Phoenicia: see **Sidonian**

Phorcus: a sea god; also, the father of seven brothers aligned against Aeneas in the war with Italy

Phrygians: another name for the Trojans

Picus: a god of agriculture and the grandfather of latinus in Italy; Picus was also the first king of Latium, and the son of Saturn, an ancient god who fathered Jupiter

Pluto: the Roman god of the Underworld

Portunus: a sea god associated with protection of harbors

Praeneste: an old city in Latium in central Italy

Proserpine the "Underworld's Juno," the wife of **Pluto**

Punic another name for Carthaginian
Pyrrhus: the son of Achilles who assumed leadership in battle at Troy after his father's
     death

Quirinus: see **Romulus**

Remus: the brother of **Romulus** and killed by Romulus
Rhadamanthus: king of Crete, a brother of Minos; after his death, a judge of spirits in
     the Underworld
Rhea Silvia: a priestess of Vesta, the goddess of the domestic hearth; also known as Ilia,
     she was the daughter of Numitor, a king of Alba Longa; and the mother, by Mars, of
     Romulus and **Remus**
Romulus: the founder of Rome, according to legend, and nursed by a wolf along with
     his brother, **Remus**; Romulus gave his name to the city and was later identified with
     Quirinus, an ancient Italian god

Sabinus or the **Sabines:** the legendary ancestor or his people who lived in ancient Italy
Salamis: an island near Athens, ruled by King Telamon when Priam, king of Troy,
     visited his sister, Hesione, there
Samos: an island off the coast of Asia Minor, the focus of a cult of Juno
Saturn: the father of Jupiter; after being driven out of Olympus, according to legend,
     Saturn settled in Italy, thereby initiating a "golden age" in that country
Sidonian: like **Tyrian**, used as an epithet for Dido; Sidon and Tyre were cities in ancient
     Phoenicia, on the shore of Asia Minor
Simois: one of the rivers near ancient Troy
Sirens: beautiful female singers who lured passing sailors to their deaths
Sirius: the so-called dog star, brightest in *canis major*, the "greater dog," and often
     associated with illness
Styx: the river of crucial passage into the Underworld
Syrtes: dangerous sandbanks off the coast of north Africa

Tarquins: a line of early kings of Rome; the name is Etruscan
Tartarus: a region of the Underworld where various criminals were punished
Teucer: an ancient Trojan patriarch; also the name of an enemy of Troy who neverthe-
     less spoke very highly of the Trojans
Tibur or **Tiburtines:** an old town near Rome or its people
Theseus: a prince of Athens who killed the Minotaur on the island of Crete; later he
     attempted, with Pirithous, to take **Proserpine** away from the Underworld
Tithonus: the lover of Aurora, goddess of the dawn
Triton: a sea god, the son of Neptune, proud of his blowing a conch horn
Tuscan: see **Etruria**
Tyrian: see **Sidonian**

Umbria: a large area in north central Italy

Vesta: the Roman goddess of the domestic hearth
Virbius: see **Hippolytus**
Volscians: a people living in the southern part of Latium when Aeneas arrived in Italy
Vulcan: the Roman god of fire, the forge, and the making of weapons

Xanthus: a river near ancient Troy

The Aeneid:
Translator's Preface

"Never forget: Virgil was an *Italian*." So a colleague told me years ago (admittedly *he* was Italian) and the implications of his pronouncement were quite clear: Virgil loved his earth dearly, he relished wine and conviviality, and he urged reverence for the gods—of the sky, the middle world and the Underworld. His epic voice rises to the occasion of Italian empire, of courtly formality and splendor, while he laments the inevitability of war, the mystery of divine opposition, the loss of family and friends through age, sickness or battle, and the loss of a lover through Fate—that strange embodiment, *Fatum*, of divine pronouncements, *effata*. The dramatically and at times operatically Italian world of *The Aeneid* unfolds its sea-storms, volcanic rumblings, passionate struggles with the self and with *la forza del destino*, the full gamut of rage, grief and ecstatic wonder. My colleague's reminder often kept me in touch with Virgilian essentials.

Others have reminded us of course that *The Aeneid* is also the epic of Augustan Rome, with all the ancient honor and modern doubt associated therewith, that Virgil is a worthy imitator of Homer, and that the poem is highly representative of a golden age in Latin literature, composed as it was from 30 to 20 B.C. True, Virgil was writing at the end of a bitter civil war in Italy and he hoped to re-establish *pietas*, translatable (depending on the context) as "reverence" towards the gods, "duty" towards one's family, and "conscientiousness" towards one's friends. Aeneas exemplifies *pietas* best. He is a caring leader of exiled Trojans, he tries to stay (sometimes against his instincts) close to the gods, he loves his father Anchises, his wife Creusa, and his son Ascanius, or Iulus. Although he's been called "pious" (when *pius* is translated simplistically), although Virgil's *pater Aeneas* has been rendered simply "father Aeneas" ("the hero is a *priest,*" one wag has said), Virgil's central character is a man struggling among human and superhuman forces, sorrowing from one lost home or landfall to another, and determined to keep himself and his people together. Fatherhood is not an evil, nor is reverence an old-fashioned virtue, in this poem.

To some it has all seemed too well arranged. Jupiter, the father of gods, tells Venus in Book I (she is the goddess of love and mother of Aeneas) where things are going generally, giving much of the plot away. If Virgil is the father of Jupiter, in a sense, is the poem simply playing into the hands of the poet? And perhaps into the hands of Augustus, Emperor of Rome in Virgil's day. Wasn't he somewhat like Aeneas, having struggled and often killed to achieve his ends, a man who would welcome an epic celebrating the return of ancient order and values in himself?

Yes and no. Virgil's is a double perspective: gods and demigods generally know the direction of events; Aeneas and his people are much less sure. How often they blunder, in fact, misinterpreting signs and speeches from heaven! Aeneas, for example, told to pack up and leave a burning Troy in Book II, repeatedly throws himself into battle instead, sometimes moved by military duty, sometimes by wild rage and despair. For many others—Anchises, Creusa, Dido and Turnus—the world of *The Aeneid* is not neatly arranged at all. Distinguishing between true and false love, between helpful and spiteful Gods, between right and wrong leaders—frequently all that is impossible for them. Dido involves herself with occult or would-be religion in Book IV, half suspecting her error, hardly able to correct it. As for Turnus, Aeneas' principal opponent in the war in Italy, his best initial instincts in Book VII are snuffed quickly. When he dismisses alarms about the newly arrived Trojans he is set upon by a sudden madness, provoked by Allecto, an Underworld power. Off he rushes into battle, commanding thousands to join him. Thus, though the overriding thrust of *The Aeneid* could be called imperialistic (Aeneas and the Trojan-Latin bloodline do triumph), *inside* the poem is darkness and tension. So much is lost and mourned on the way. The final killing of Turnus himself has struck many as extreme, especially in its matter-of-factness. Virgil's Roman friends must have wondered: where is the triumphal march, why isn't the new wealth described in detail, and what about the all-important marriage of Aeneas and Lavinia, King Latinus' daughter? Virgil does not conclude or perorate. *The Aeneid* painfully stops.

The human drama of the poem matters enormously. Virgil was influenced by Homer—Books VII through XII are a kind of *Iliad*, I through VI an *Odyssey*—but he was also influenced by Greek tragedy, especially by Euripides. The passion of Dido in Book IV has its counterpart in the tragedy of Medea; the Odysseus-Circe story is also there but less insistent. Indeed Virgil is so taken by Dido (in Books I and VI as well as IV) that he allows the emotional center of the poem to drift somewhat away from Aeneas. Thousands of readers from Augustine to the present have empathized profoundly with the Carthaginian queen.

The drama of Book VI is also most compelling. The Underworld through which Aeneas is guided by the Sibyl is vast, complex and crowded with emotion, with figures like the brutally maimed Deiphobus, who recalls the treachery and sadism of the beautiful Helen on Troy's final night; Dido appears again, grimly silent towards Aeneas and accompanied only by Sychaeus, her husband in a former life at Tyre; and of course Anchises, the proud and garrulous father of Aeneas, overjoyed at reunion with his son—or *is* it reunion? Three times the son tries to embrace the shadow-like father, and fails. The epic introduction of future Romans by Anchises is not without dramatic interruptions of its own: it pauses, it actually stumbles over human error and set-back—the bitter fight between Caesar and Pompey, for example, or the funeral of the boy Marcellus—a loss Anchises begs Aeneas not to inquire about. If Virgil is determined to point up Roman virtues, the power to govern as well as the obligation towards the father—and towards the mother as well, as we see in the mysterious figure of Cybele, mother of all the gods—Virgil is just as determined to hear out, to linger over and care about troubled humans. The Sibyl, taught by a Goddess, urges us to persist along the destined road but Aeneas, taught by the exigencies of the human condition, like us, at times must stop. He'll speak for instance with Palinurus: what happened after the helmsman fell overboard? Why is he here, on the wrong side of the Styx River? Virgil's epic design carries us forward; his human drama must give us pause.

How can an English translation capture such poetry, this music so highly praised by Tennyson, a Latin style which William Arrowsmith has called mandarin? Virgil's language itself may provide clues. He works with a variety of diction (as the excellent new Oxford commentaries point up), even including phrases from Roman comedy; he builds a variety of sentences, from the most elaborately architectonic to the simplest quip (the latter usually in dialogue); and he orchestrates most carefully, often clustering musical variations, over the course of five or ten lines, around a single vowel-and-consonant theme. Though he has daunted the most ingenious of translators, his epic style is clear in (1) its momentum, an often relentless forward movement that echoes the necessity of Aeneas' going on despite his human desire to linger and delay, and (2) its melancholy, the *lacrimae rerum*, the tears shed over human affairs: for *mentem mortalia tangunt*,—the sorrows of others do touch the human heart. The momentum is often achieved by Virgil's letting the long dactylic hexameter line run on (unlike the line of predecessors like Lucretius), hurrying story and rhythm along onto the next verse. The second quality he often achieves by crowding consonants and vowels together, building assonance and alliteration, all tending to slow the rhythm, to stress the pathos.

One must also assume a certain strength and resilience in one's own tongue. The resources of modern English do come up to a translation of Virgil—though perhaps not the resources of any modern English poetry—not the deceptively relaxed and collo- quial idiom of Robert Frost, for example, or the Pound of many *Cantos*, or the Ginsberg of *Howl*. The style of Yeats in the 1920s, of Robert Lowell in the 1940s, and of Derek Walcott in the 1970s—all might have produced a fine English *Aeneid*. My version has taken inspiration and courage from their work and from others, since no one can translate Virgil without great help. I gladly credit Donald Hall, who has provided dependably trenchant advice about many a limping, banal phrase. Richard Wilbur led me back more than once to the right, highly disciplined track. The late William Arrowsmith's encouragement—comprehensive and de- tailed—has been invaluable. I owe many thanks to the late John Workman at Brown, to Ronald Knox, to many others near and far, including colleagues at Providence like Rodney Delasanta, Charles Duffy, Patrick Reid and Terrie Curran. Forrest Gander, who as poet and publisher of poets is well aware of the resources of modern English, gave his close attention to the entire work. It is Robert Bly who receives the book's dedication: his support has been the *sine qua non*.

I strived for an English *Aeneid* as varied and intense, as momentous and dramatic, as the Latin original, and of course I did not succeed. But what a hearty and heady experience to have strived! Working with a flexible five-beat line for this translation (some have six beats), usually with a dactyl-trochee combination at the line's end (as in Virgil), I often ran one line onto the next and paused after the first foot—another frequent tactic of the original. Without going into all the technicalities, I can claim to have followed Virgil line for line (as C. Day Lewis did in his very able "reading" version): students and teachers of the original will find their place here very readily. I also tried to vary the syntax considerably, as Virgil does, to pay close attention to his occasionally novel diction (well attested to by Austin and others in the Oxford commentaries), and to keep the idiom rather elevated as in the Latin—this was especially hard—without sounding pompous or stiff in the English. Perhaps presumptuously, I even tried to imitate his orchestration often, working with harsh vowels and hard consonants for example when he describes a battle scene. I came to discover and appreciate a hundred intricacies of Virgilian craftsmanship—a great benefit for the poet-translator. Hard and pleasureable as all that was, trying to create a perfect counterpart in English turned out to be far harder—impossible, truly. So I strived for the closest possible equivalent. If the results lead a few ardent souls to take on the Latin itself for the first time, I will be most content.

No doubt the translation nods at times—no doubt the original does—even as Homer nods. But how often Virgil amazes the reader with imaginative energy and passion! I've worked especially hard on those passages. The most striking epic similes, for example, I hope will read well in this translation. Elsewhere it's a little thing, a striking phrase which for a variety of reasons has lost its impact in English translations over the years. When Achaemenides, for example, a lost member of Ulysses' crew, begs Aeneas for help in Book III, he calls the gods to witness, the stars, and *hoc caeli spirabile lumen*. Three of the words are no problem—"this light of the sky"; *spirabile* is another matter. Although the Latin verb *spirare* means "to breathe," giving us the English *respiration* and *inspire,* some translators render the passage "the *air* we breathe" (*lumen,* or "light" is lost), "by the breath and light of life" (there's no "life" in the original, and *caeli* or "sky" is lost) and "the vital air" (losing both the "sky" and the "breathing"). Two others retain some of the metaphorical power but warily, diluting the adjective or introducing a relative clause: "by the light of heaven that we breathe" and "this lightsome air we breathe." In the present translation, "this breathable daylight" retain's Virgil's metaphor, strange-sounding though it be, and also retains something of the Latin line's rhythm. Clarity is a high priority in translation but I think one has to guard against making *too* much sense of this Latin, especially in elusive and highly imaginative moments.

In fact artists as well as poets following Virgil have responded to his most dramatic and imaginative exertions in extraordinary ways. The intense and ambiguous moment in the cave when Aeneas and Dido come together, the ferocious attack of the sea-serpents upon Laöcoön and his sons, the sudden burning of Lavinia's hair, the dark struggle for a doomed Troy, the crossing of the Styx River, the transformation of Aeneas' ships into sea-nymphs: these and many other moments have haunted the imaginations of painters, sculptors and translators for centuries. The present writer and illustrator are no exceptions—the hardest thing in the long run, in fact, may be resisting the tendency to linger over and labor—even indefinitely!—the great scenes. Virgil's power of fantasy may be so pronounced (not only in the Underworld of Book VI) and his capacity for dramatic confrontation so profound (not only in the bitter romance of Book IV) that one closes *The Aeneid* sensing, momentarily, that reality is behind one, not ahead. The grim vividness and variety of those battle scenes in the later books, the verve and color of the games in Sicily, the warmth and conviction of characters everywhere, down to the last no-non-sense appeal of Turnus—and the no-nonsense reply of Aeneas—all are images that cry out for new expression, in translation and in art, from generation to generation.

The last word, I suppose, should be *fidelity*. If a translation is not to be a free adaptation, what Robert Lowell called "imita-tion," neither should it turn out to be mere transliteration. Because the latter is difficult in prose and quite impossible in poetry, some have despaired of translation altogether, arguing that no attempt will be "faithful" to the original. Too much distortion of sound and sense will take place.

So goes the theoretical opposition. To get from day to day, however, I must be practical. I tried working with the idea that everything really significant in the Latin could take significant form in English; that a final version could be adequately if not absolutely faithful; that it could be readable, too, and enjoyably so. Did I blandly suppose that these two languages could live and work together? Not exactly; it all took a good deal of mediation. Thus a Latin verb might better appear as an English noun here, a specific noun might appear as a general one, and a complex phrase or clause might rearrange itself somewhat in the English— as the famous first line,

Arma virumque cano Troiae qui primus ab oris,

might read,

> My song is of war, and the first man from a Trojan
> coast . . .

Since my idiom derives from writers like Yeats and Wilbur, Lowell and Walcott, some readers may find the style of the translation rather high and solitary, stern at times. But Virgil's vision and manner are both generally somber and serious. I attempted no novel-writing, no leveling of *The Aeneid* into pop story and easy message. Every reader has to rise to the occasion of this magnificent epic as he or she can. The rewards, of course, have been known to last a lifetime.

Edward McCrorie
Providence, Rhode Island
August 1990

Principal Characters
in the Epic

AENEAS, a Trojan prince through his marriage to CREUSA, the daughter of PRIAM, king of Troy, is the son of ANCHISES, a former Trojan warrior, and VENUS, the Goddess of Love.

ASCANIUS, or IULUS, the son of Aeneas, saved as a boy by his father from the destruction of Troy, is brought by him to Italy, where he will continue the royal line.

JUNO, the Goddess-and-sister-and-wife of JUPITER, King of the Gods, opposes Aeneas and the Trojans generally because of a former judgment against her beauty by PARIS, a Trojan. She sometimes enlists the aid of IRIS, the Rainbow-Goddess, and ALLECTO, an avenging force (or FURY) from the Underworld.

DIDO, former princess of Tyre, is now queen of Carthage, a city reached by Aeneas and his people on their way to Italy.

SINON, a Greek warrior, managed to deceive the Trojans into bringing a large, apparently ritualistic horse into Troy; the horse was actually filled with Greeks like ULYSSES.

PYRRHUS, who led the Greek forces attacking the palace of Troy, was the son of ACHILLES, the great warrior of Homer's *Iliad*. He killed POLITES, one of King Priam's sons, then Priam himself. He enslaved and married ANDROMACIIE, the former wife of HECTOR, Achilles' principal opponent in the war at Troy.

14

NEPTUNE, God of the Sea, and PHOEBUS, or APOLLO, the Sun-God, are often helpful to Aeneas, but (like other Gods and Goddesses) not always predictable.

HELENUS, a son of Priam who survived the war, was enslaved by Pyrrhus. He actually comes to rule a small Greek city when Pyrrhus dies. He predicts the future for Aeneas.

NISUS and EURYALUS, two Trojan warriors, the latter a beautiful but impulsive youth, compete in the sprint in the funeral games in honor of Anchises at Sicily, and later volunteer for a dangerous mission at night in the war with the Latins.

DEIPHOBE, commonly called the SIBYL, an elderly virgin priestess and prophet of Apollo at Cumae (a small city south of Rome), guides Aeneas down through the Underworld.

LATINUS, King of Latium, rules a broad area of central Italy where the Trojans under Aeneas wish to settle. His daughter, now of marriageable age, is LAVINIA.

TURNUS, King of Rutulia, another district in central Italy, is the principal opponent of Aeneas when war breaks out. Favored by AMATA, Queen of Latium and wife of Latinus, he also seeks the hand of Lavinia.

CAMILLA, an ally of Turnus and queen of a band called the Volscians, is a favorite of DIANA, Goddess of the hunt.

EVANDER, King of Pallanteum, an ancient town he founded on the site of Rome, supports Aeneas in the war in Italy and sends his son PALLAS to fight alongside the Trojan leader.

MEZENTIUS, an Etruscan king, opposes Aeneas in Italy together with his son, LAUSUS.

VULCAN, the God of Fire and husband of Venus, helps Aeneas in the war in Italy by constructing weapons, including a supremely hard and beautiful shield.

CYBELE, a mysterious Goddess, Mother of Jupiter, brings about a transformation of the Trojan ships to prevent their being fired by Turnus at one point in the Italian war.

I

ARRIVAL AT CARTHAGE

The Epic Theme and Story

My song is of war and the first man from a Trojan
coast to arrive in Italy, forced by Fates to Lavinian
shore: the power of Gods repeatedly tossed him
on land and sea, Juno's fierce and remembering anger
caused him to suffer greatly in war while founding a city,
bringing his Gods to Latium, leading to Latin
and Alban fathers, to high walls of the Romans.

Invocation of the Muse

Muse, tell me the reasons: what slight to her power,
what grief drove the Queen of the Gods to involve him,
10 a man so known for reverence, in struggle and hardship
over and over? Can so much spite reside in a Goddess?

The Anger of Juno

An old city, held by Tyrian settlers,
Carthage faced the far-off Italian Tiber's
mouth: rich and resourceful, fierce and avid in warfare.
Juno they say loved this land more than all others,
preferred it even to Samos; keeping her weapons
and chariot here, the Goddess warmly strove from the outset
to make it a world kingdom—if only the Fates would allow it.
But now she'd heard of a family descended from Trojan
20 blood who would someday crumble her Tyrian towers:
a widely ruling people, proud of their warfare,
would come to destroy Carthage: the Fates had unrolled it.
Saturn's daughter was anxious. She thought of that former
war she'd waged at Troy, the Greeks she had cared for.
Pretexts for anger and bitter grief had not vanished

yet from her mind: stored deep in her memory
lay Paris' insulting judgment, scorning her beauty.
Troy was hateful, kidnapped Ganymede's honors
worse provocation. Trojans had scattered on every
30 sea—remnants left by the Greeks and a ruthless Achilles—
she'd kept them far from Latium, wandering many
years over the water, forced by Fates into circles.
To found Rome and her people required such exertion.

Juno's Mounting Frustration

The glad Trojans had hardly unruffled their canvas,
bronze plowing through foam, Sicily's farmland behind them,
when Juno, preserving the old wound in her bosom,
asked herself, "Have I lost? Do I stop what I started,
helpless to keep this Trojan leader from Italy?
Fates prevent me, of course! Then how could Pallas incinerate
40 Greek ships, plunge their crews under water,
because of one mad crime of Ajax, the son of Oileus?
She hurled Jupiter's lightning herself from a cloudburst,
overturned waves with a windstorm, and scattered the vessels.
When she struck Ajax he exhaled fire from the chest-wound,
she seized and threw him on sharp rock with a whirlwind.
While I, Queen of the Gods, who walk as the sister
and wife of Jupiter, wage war with a single
people for years. Will anyone reverence Juno's
name now or humbly honor my altars?"

Lord of the Winds

50 It all fired her heart as she mulled it. The Goddess
came to a land of rainclouds, a place where Southwinds were
        feuding,
called Aeolia. King Aeolus tempered and mastered
wrestling gales and highpitched gusts in a monstrous
cave here: chains and a prison restrained them.
The winds bridled; they rumbled all of the mountain,
growled and thrashed in their cages. Aeolus ruled from a
        stronghold
above: gripping a scepter, he soothed and steadied their anger.
The winds, had he not, would have quickly and surely carried the
        ocean,
land and depths of the sky away, and swept them through heaven.
60 Fearing as much, the all-powerful Father had moved them
to dark caves; he'd massed high mountain above them.

He gave them a lord who knew how to tighten or loosen
their bindings, and follow the rules of a definite compact.
Juno now modestly spoke to this ruler.
"Aeolus, the Gods' Father and monarch of mankind
gave you seas to calm or build with your windstorms.
A people I hate are now crossing the Tyrrhene,
carrying Household Gods from Troy into Italy.
Strike force in your winds: crush those vessels, capsize them,
70   drive them apart: acquaint their crewmen with sea-depths.
I have fourteen Nymphs of exceptional beauty
and none has a finer form than Deiopea.
I'll say she's yours: I'll join you in durable marriage.
She'll render all her time yours for the service
you do me. She'll help you father beautiful children."

A Storm Begins

Aeolus answered, "Your task, my Queen, is to ponder
your own will; my law is to welcome your wishes.
Whatever I rule you gave: Jupiter's friendship,
my scepter, the gift of divine couches to lie on.
80   You made me rule raincloud and violent tempest."
Soon as he finished he turned and struck at the mountain's
hollow side with a spear. Winds, like volleys of soldiers
given an opening, rushed out to blow through the countryside,
        twirling.
They fell on the sea: they roiled its bottom completely.
Eastwind joined with Southwind; Southwesterly, crowded
with squalls, ran out and rolled huge tumblers at beaches.
Cables creaked on the ships. Crewmen were yelling.
Clouds had suddenly stolen the brightness of heaven
from Trojan eyes. A black night sat on the water.
90   Poles thundered; the air, dense with lightning, ignited.
Everything threatened instant death for the crewmen.

The Prayer of Aeneas

Chills weakened the legs now of Aeneas.
He sighed, extending both hands to the heavens
and raising a cry: "You, three and four times as lucky,
who fell by chance near Troy's high walls while your fathers
watched—and you, bravest of Greeks, Diomedes:
I wish I'd fallen myself there on some Trojan
field struck by your hand and pouring my life out
where fierce Hector fell by a spear of Achilles,

100   where big Sarpedon lay, the Simois River collecting
      the shields of strong men, dispersing corpses and helmets.''

The Heavens Answer

      He'd hardly stopped when the Northwind screamed and collided
      hard with his mainsail, seas built to the star-heights
      and oars fractured. A ship was turned and presented
      to waves broadside, swamped by a torn-off seawater mountain.
      Men hung on a wave's crest; to others the gaping
      trough exposed ground, sand swarming with water.
      A Southwind seized three ships and threw them on hidden
      rocks (Italians call them "The Altars"—surrounded by water,
110   a massive ridge in the deep sea); then an Eastwind
      drove three more from the sea into shallows—the scene was
              pathetic—
      it slapped them with surf and piled up girdles of pebbles.
      The ship carrying Lycians and loyal Orantes
      Aeneas could barely see: a peaked and ponderous roller
      struck her astern, pulled out and tumbled the helmsman
      headlong: water twirled the ship in the same place
      three times, round and around, till a whirlpool devoured her.
      Scattered swimmers appeared in that desolate swirling,
      men's armor and shields, Troy's wealth in the water.
120   The storm was beating them now. The durable galley
      of Ilioneus and steadfast Achates, of Abas
      and aging Aletes—all were filling with water,
      planks loosened, seams turned into fissures.

Neptune Ends the Storm

      Neptune meanwhile sensed a mixed-up and far-flung
      commotion at sea, a storm loose: even the bottom
      currents shifted. The God, seriously troubled,
      gazed at the water. Raising a calm face on the wave-tops
      he saw Aeneas' fleet scattered completely,
      Trojans crushed by waves and the sky's inundation.
130   Juno's anger and guile: they were clear to her brother.
      He called Eastwind and Westwind to tell them in person,
      "Since when has exorbitant pride in your birthright possessed you?
      Without my will now you winds have dared to entangle
      heaven and earth, you rouse great masses of water
      which I—! First I'll calm the turbulent billows.
      Later you'll pay with some rare pain for your doings.
      Hurry back to your master for now and inform him

that rule at sea, this rugged trident, was given
to me, not him, by lot. He owns that barbarous rockpile—
140   your home, Eastwind. Let Aeolus busy himself with
ruling you winds in that locked-up jail for a palace."
He finished and quick as his word he quieted puffed-up
seas, dispersed the dense clouds and brought back the sunshine.
Triton helped Cimothoë work at and push from
sharp rocks the ships that Neptune raised with his trident.
He cleared the wastes of sandbanks and steadied the sea-swells,
his nimble chariot wheels brushing the wave-tops.
At times in a great city a riot abruptly
begins, common people turn willful and savage,
150   rocks and torches go flying, anger providing the weapons.
By chance if they spot one man of serious merit
and justice their ears perk up, they stand there in silence:
his words guide their minds and calm their emotions.
So all the noise at sea diminished when Neptune
gazed at the water. Skies cleared where he guided
his willing horses, giving them rein, the chariot flying.

Arriving at a Strange Shore

Aeneas' men were exhausted. They made for the nearest
shore, changing course for the Libyan coastline.
There in a deep lagoon was a place like a harbor,
160   formed by an island's barriers. The surf was divided,
broken here and there into ripple and eddy.
On either side were high rocks menacing heaven—
paired cliffs—the sea was quiet and harmless
under their broad crowns. The heights were a picture of trembling
leaves, darkly hanging trees and bristling shadow.
Facing a cliff was a cave with stalactites hanging
inside, a freshwater pool, and couches of living
rock where Nymphs rested. Here was no mooring
required for tired ships; no biting hook of an anchor.
170   Aeneas approached the beach with seven remaining
vessels regrouped. Their love for land overwhelming,
Trojans emerged and clutched at sand they had prayed for.
They lay on the beach. Salt dripped from their shoulders.
Achates was first to strike sparks with a flint-piece.
Fire began among leaves and circling wood-chips.
He fed it fuel; he drew out flame from the tinder.
The sea had spoiled some grain but the crewmen, though weary
of things, brought out Ceres' tools to grind down the remnant

of flour with stone. A fire was ready for baking.

The Killing of Seven Deer

180 Aeneas meanwhile climbed a bluff to examine
the whole far sea. He hoped for a glimpse of the wind-tossed
ship of Antheus there, some Phrygian galley
or Capys, the arms of Caicus high on the fantail.
No sign of a ship. He did see deer on the shoreline,
three stray stags. Large companies followed
next—a long line grazed on the lowland.
Aeneas approached and paused, holding a bow and some lively
arrows, weapons Achates had loyally carried.
He struck first at the leader himself, with his tree-like
190 antlers held high. Then he drove at and scattered
the large herd into thicket and bush with his arrows,
only resting in triumph when seven cumbersome bodies
lay on the ground—matching his number of vessels.
He made for the harbor to share with all his companions.
Wine was apportioned—a kindly Acestes had weighted
jars back in Sicily—a kingly gift when they left there.

The Trojans' Ultimate Destiny

Aeneas tried to remove their sadness by asking,
"My friends, haven't we known disaster before this?
You've suffered worse. A God will end this agony also.
200 You've come close to the raucous cliffs of a rabid
Scylla—once you even hazarded Cyclops'
boulders. Renew your spirits, abandon this mourning
and fear: remembering all this someday may cheer you.
Through every crux, each separation and setback,
we head for a home and peace in Latium shown by
the Fates: the Gods' word on Troy's kingdom reviving.
Hold on—save yourselves for a better tomorrow."
He stopped: large concerns had made him uneasy.
He'd put on hopeful looks but felt repressed disappointment.
210 His men girded themselves for the fine meat in the offing:
they tore off hides from ribs, revealing the innards,
they sliced and fixed quivering cutlets
on spits, set bronzes in sand and tended to fires.
Food recalled their strength. They lay on the dune-grass,
filling with old wine and fat-dripping game-flesh.
Feasting ended their hunger; removing the tables,
in long talks they mourned the loss of companions,

caught between faith and fear: should they hope they were living?
Or done with the worst, no longer hearing when summoned?
220 Aeneas rightly mourned the death of forceful Orontes
especially now, and Amycus, the merciless killing
of Lycus, intrepid Gyas, intrepid Cloanthus.

The Complaint of Venus

While all that ended, Jupiter gazed from the highest
heaven down on spread-out lands and the sail-winged
sea, on far-off nations. He paused on a sky-peak
and focused his eyes' light on the country of Libya.
Concern ruffled his heart. Venus approached him,
speaking sadly, her eyes filled with the shining
tears of a Goddess. "You, the Ruler forever
230 of Gods' and men's affairs with your fear-spreading lightning:
what crime has my Aeneas committed against you?
What have the Trojans done to be cut off from every
land, to suffer such loss? Did Italy cause this?
Rome would surely come, that was your promise:
leaders would help restore someday the bloodline of Teucer:
as years passed they would rule the ocean and govern
every nation. Father, what sentiments changed you?
Your word consoled me when sorry Troy was collapsing,
I hoped in fact to balance bad luck with good luck;
240 now the same bad luck, all these reversals,
pursue them. My great King, will you end their affliction?
Antenor could slip from a whole Greek force—he was able
to pass through Illyrian gulfs and penetrate safely
remote Liburnian kingdoms. He reached the Timavus,
where nine springs rumble a desolate mountain,
the water an uproar that swamps pasture and breaks for the delta.
There Antenor founded the city of Padua,
Trojan homes, he gave his name to a people,
retiring Trojan arms for the quiet of peacetime.
250 But we, your family, promised a fortress in heaven,
lose our ships. An outrage!—the spite and deception
of one person keeps us far from Italy's coastline.
That's the reward for loyalty? That's the scepter you saved us?"

The Trojan Future in Italy

The Father of Gods and men lavished on Venus
the smile he used to clear stormwind from heaven.
He kissed his daughter's lips and answered her fully:

"Cytherean Lady, don't be alarmed. Your family's future
will not be changed. You'll see the Lavinian city,
the walls I promised; you'll bear the great soul of Aeneas
260　high into starlight. No one's thinking has changed me.
I'll speak right now, in fact—anxiety gnaws you—
I'll show you the Fates' distant twists and their secrets.
First Aeneas will wage a hard war in Italy, smashing
fierce tribes. He'll set down walls and ways for his people,
three full summers will see him reigning in Latium:
three winters will pass once the Rutulians are conquered.
Then his boy Ascanius, surnamed Iulus
(Ilus at Troy as long as a kingdom survived there),
will rule through an ample cycle of thirty revolving
270　years in all. He'll move the throne from Lavinium's
base and greatly fortify Alba Longa.
There the people of Hector will rule for a total
of three centuries. Next Ilia, priestess
and pregnant queen, will bear twins to the War-God:
Romulus, proud of the tan hide, the she-wolf that nursed him,
now will assume the line: he'll settle a city
for Mars and call it Rome after his own name.
I set no time or wealth limits on Romans:
I'll give them endless rule. And what about Juno?
280　Harsh and worried, wearing the sky, water and land out?
She'll change for the better. My own counsel will help her:
she'll cherish as world rulers those men in their togas!
You've heard my will. A time will come after the lustral
years pass which will see Assaracus' people
enslave Phthia and dazzling Mycenae—the Greeks will be
　　　conquered.
A Trojan Caesar will rise from your beautiful bloodline,
only the stars will limit his fame, the ocean his empire:
Julius—a name that comes from a great one—Iulus.
Someday you'll calmly welcome the man into heaven,
290　loaded with Eastern wealth; prayers will invoke him.
War will end, then. Violent times will diminish.
Elderly Faith and Vesta, Remus and Romulus, brothers,
will draft laws. The feared gates of war, with their iron
hinges grinding, will shut. Inside on its cruel
weapons mad Rage will sit, tied by a hundred
bronze knots, its bloody mouth savagely howling."

The Messenger of the Gods

He finished and sent down Maia's son from Olympus
to open the young fields and fortress of Carthage,
to welcome Trojans and not let Dido, not knowing her future,
300 block the borders. Quickly plashing the air-waves—
broad wings were his oars—Mercury came to the Libyan
shore and obeyed the command: people discarded uncivil
acts as the God wished. The queen was especially gentle
in spirit, well disposed to receiving the Trojans.

Venus Confronts Aeneas

Aeneas all that night had dutifully pondered
many matters. With Dawn's kindly glow he determined
to set out, explore the strange land where the sea-winds had
        brought him,
to seek and learn what men or animals lived there
(he'd seen no farmland) and bring back word to his people.
310 Hiding the fleet in a cove closely surrounded
by trees, hollow rock and chilly obscurity,
Aeneas himself set out, joined by only Achates.
Each hand gripped a spear with its broad spearpoint of iron.
His mother confronted the man there in the forest.
She'd put on a girl's dress, the appearance and weapons
of young Spartans, or those like Harpalyce's, tiring
a Thracian horse or winning a sprint with the fast-flowing
        Hebrus.
A supple, stylish bow hung from her shoulder.
The huntress had let her hair ruffle in breezes,
320 her knees were bare and knots collected her flowing
dress. "Hello, you men," she spoke up first, "can you tell me
whether you've seen by chance one of my sisters?
She sported a lynx's spotted hide and a quiver.
She followed a sweating boar, chasing and shouting."
The son of Venus answered when Venus had finished.
"I haven't seen or heard one of your sisters,
young lady. But you, what shall I call you? Your features
and voice aren't human merely. Of course you're a Goddess—
from one of the Nymphs' families? A sister of Phoebus?
330 Be kind, whoever you are, lighten our burden:
tell us what sky we're under, what world and shore we've
        been thrown on,
please—we wander around, not knowing the country

or people, driven by winds here and a desert of water.
My hand will bring down scores of beasts at your altar."

The Tragic Story of Dido

Venus told him, "I hardly deserve such distinction!
Tyrian girls customarily carry a quiver
and lace their calves high with violet bootstraps.
The kingdom you see is Punic; the Tyrian town, of Agenor.
Libyans live next door—intractable fighters.
340 Dido rules this land. She left a Tyrian city,
she ran from a brother—a long story of outrage
with many twists. I'll trace the matter in outline.
Her husband Sychaeus, one of the richest Phoenician
farmers, was loved by the wretched woman intensely:
her father gave his virgin daughter in marriage
first to Sychaeus. But Tyre's king was her brother
Pygmalion, far more criminally vicious than any.
Anger came between them: Pygmalion, blinded
by greed for Sychaeus' gold, attacked him in secret:
350 he stabbed him before an altar profanely—the love of his sister
irrelevant. For days he hid the facts from the sickened
woman, played with her love, falsely hoped and deceived her.
But then a vision came in a nightmare to Dido,
her husband himself: unburied, fearfully lifting
his drained face, he showed her the cruel altar, the chest-wounds
where metal had pierced—the whole secret family murder.
Then he urged her to hurry and run from the country.
To help her leave he showed her underground treasure,
old and secret silver and gold in abundance.
360 Deeply shaken, Dido planned to escape with companions:
others who hated the despot's crimes or intensely
feared him joined her. By chance vessels were ready,
they boarded, loading the gold, and carried the greedy
Pygmalion's wealth to sea. And the action's leader a woman!
At length they arrived here, and soon you'll see the enormous
walls of her young Carthage, a citadel rising.
They bought up land and called it Byrsa, 'The Bull's-Hide':
all they could circle with hair-thin strips of a steer-skin.

An Omen of Twelve Swans

"But tell me, who are you men? What coast have you come from?
370 Where are you bound?" Deeply sighing, Aeneas
tried to answer her questions, dragging the words out:

"Goddess, if I could trace it, repeat it all from the outset,
if you had time to hear our annals of struggle,
Evening would sooner close down Day and lock up Olympus.
Old Troy was our home—if the word Trojan has happened
to reach your ears. We were driven on various sea-lanes;
a storm drove us by chance to the Libyan coastline.
I, who revere the Gods, am Aeneas. I salvaged my House-Gods
from Greeks; they're borne on my ships. My name is known on
    Olympus.
380 I look to a home in Italy, high Jupiter's nation.
With twenty ships I scaled the Phrygian sea-peaks,
a Goddess-Mother my guide, I followed the Fates I was given;
hardly seven are left, convulsed by Eastwind and water.
I am unknown here, destitute, wandering Libyan wasteland,
forced out of Asia and Europe—" Venus could suffer
no more distressful complaint and so interrupted,
"Whoever you are, I hardly believe you're hateful to heaven:
you breathe, you're alive, close to a Tyrian city.
Only persist—continue from here to the threshold of Dido.
390 As for your friends and ships, I tell you they're rescued,
nudged into safe harbor by gathering Northwinds—
unless my parents explained omens for nothing.
Look at those twelve glad swans in formation.
Jupiter's raptor just plunged from the sky and dispersed them
in open air. They now can be seen to be looking
to land in their long line, or landing already.
Just as they're saved, their wings whistling and playing,
just as they circled the sky, regrouping and singing,
I'm sure your ships and crews are either approaching
400 a harbor in full sail or actually mooring.
Just keep on—walk this path where it leads you."

Revelation of a Goddess

She finished and turned, her neck rose-colored, glowing.
The Goddess' hair exhaled a scent of ambrosia,
her clothing loosened and flowed down to her ankles:
her walk revealed her truly a Goddess. Aeneas
knew his mother now, he followed and spoke as she left him:
"Even you, cruel to your son—why do you always
play with tricks and disguises? Why are we stopped from
joining hand in hand, and hearing our actual voices?"

Enveloped in Mist

410 He stopped accusing. He took the path to the city.
Venus enclosed their walk in an air of opaqueness:
she spread a mantle of thick vapor around them
so no one could see, no one could touch them
or cause delay, or ask their reasons for coming.
The Goddess returned to Paphos. She went to a pleasant
mountainside home where a hundred shrines in her temple
breathed of fresh flowers and smoldering incense from Saba.

The Labor of Bees

The men, meanwhile, hurried along the path she had shown
     them.
Already they'd climbed a long ridge overlooking
420 the city and gazed down at the fortress that faced them.
Aeneas admired the large buildings, formerly hovels,
he admired the gates and noisy paving of roadways.
The Tyrians worked hard, some men rearing a stronghold
or raising a wall, manually rolling the stones up.
Others picked out homesites and framed them with trenches.
They chose magistrates, laws, and a venerable senate.
Here they dredged a harbor; there they were laying
a theater's deep foundation or sculpting its massive
rock columns—high decor for scenes that were coming.
430 Just as their work wearies bees in the sunlight
of young summer on blossoming farms where the old ones
lead out the hive's young or pack syrupy honey
in cells, filling the hive with nectar-like sweetness:
they either take on loads from arrivals or form up
ranks to keep the lazy group of drones from the storage:
the work teems amid fragrant, thyme-scented honey.
"How lucky you are—your walls are rising already,"
Aeneas remarked. He gazed at the skyline of Carthage
and entered the city. Enclosed in the mist—a wonder to speak of—
440 he mixed right in, surrounded by men, and no one took notice.

Paintings of the Trojan War

A grove in the central city was pleasantly shaded.
Here the Tyrians, after water and whirlwind had struck them,
first broke ground where Queen Juno commanded,
unearthing a wild stallion's head—a sign of their future
greatness in war, and the lasting natural wealth of their nation.

Here the Sidonian, Dido, planned a magnificent temple
to Juno, endowed with gifts and the Goddess's power.
A stairway rose to a bronze threshold and cross-beams
of linked bronze, and bronze portals rang on their hinges.
450   Now in this grove for the first time an unlikely
thing lessened Aeneas' fear. He hoped to be safe here,
despite losses, he dared trust in change for the better,
for while he stared at the huge and intricate temple,
expecting the queen, amazed at the luck of the city—
at craftsmen's hands competing among themselves in their
      art-work—
he saw *Troy*. A long sequence of battles—
word had spread that war worldwide already—
the sons of Atreus; Priam; and menacing both men, Achilles.
The tears came to Aeneas. "What place," he asked of Achates,
460   "what part of the world is not yet full of our struggle?
Look at that Priam! Even here they value your honor,
they weep for things, their hearts are touched by the dying.
Dismiss your fear: you're saved by your own reputation."
While speaking he fed his heart with empty depictions,
he often sighed, the big tears wetting a cheekbone
whenever he saw Greeks, in a roundabout skirmish
at Troy, routed by young Trojans and run off;
or Trojans chased by the team of crested Achilles.
Aeneas recognized, weeping, the bivouac of Rhesus
470   nearby like sails of snow—till Diomedes exposed them
in deep sleep, wrecked the camp, bloodied and killed them.
He turned the sweating horses back to their campsite before they
could taste Trojan fodder or drink from the Xanthus.
Another scene: Troilus dropped his weapons and ran off:
the sorry youngster had faced a full-grown Achilles
and slipped backwards while holding the empty
chariot's reins, the horses had pulled, dragging his neck-bone
and hair on the ground. His reversed spear scrawled on the gravel.
Meanwhile, Trojan women filed to the temple
480   of unfair Pallas. Wildhaired, bringing her vestments,
palms beating their breasts, they prostrated, wailing.
The Goddess kept her looks on the ground to avoid them.
And Hector: Achilles had hauled the spiritless body
around the walls three times, then sold it for money.
Truly Aeneas felt deep hurt, painfully moaning
to see that armor and chariot, even his comrade's
corpse, and the hands of Priam, weaponless, pleading.

Aeneas found himself as well in a tangle with Grecian
chiefs; brigades from the East; dark Memnon's equipment;
490 and crazed Penthesilea, the Amazon leader,
blazing among crescent shields, surrounded by thousands.
One breast bared, a gold girdle beneath it,
the war-queen dared to charge into men though a virgin.

The Arrival of Dido

Now as Aeneas, a Dardan, stared in amazement
at all those wondrous art-works, fixed in that single direction,
the queen entered the temple. Most beautiful, Dido
was thronged by circling young groups of her people,
the way Diana works a circle of dancers
across a Cynthus slope or a bank of the River Eurotas,
500 Oreads gathering here and there by the thousand to follow:
she shoulders a quiver, outstrides all of the Sky-Gods
and stuns with joy the quiet heart of Latona.
Dido carried herself as proudly and gladly,
surrounded; she urged forward the work of her kingdom.
Soon at the temple's arched center, the portals of Juno,
she sat on a raised throne, cordoned by weapons.
She spelled out people's legal rights, distributed labor
in equal parts, or drew lots for each duty.

Lost Trojans are Found

Another large crowd was approaching. Aeneas
510 suddenly spotted Antheus, brave Cloanthus, Sergestus
and other Trojans—people scattered completely
by dark waves and squalls to different beaches.
It all stunned Aeneas; Achates was also
struck by joy and fear. Anxious, eager for handshakes,
still they faced the unknown, their spirits were troubled;
they hid in the mist's cave-like covering, watching
these men describe their luck, what shore the ships had been left
    on,
why they'd come here, chosen to march from the galleys,
to make for this temple's commotion, to ask for Dido's indulgence.
520 They entered, received permission to speak in her presence
and Ilioneus, the eldest, began with quiet emotion.
"My queen, Jupiter gave you power to settle
a new city and check the pride of people with justice.
We are miserable Trojans, driven by all of the sea-winds.

We beg you: stop your men from burning our ships: it's
    unspeakable.
Spare a decent people. Look on our cause with some kindness.
We haven't approached you with swords to plunder the House-
    Gods
of Libya, to drag stolen goods to the beaches.
Swagger and brute force are not for us losers.
530 There *is* a place, the Greeks called it Hesperia,
an ancient land with rich soil and powerful armies:
Oenotrians lived there once but now they say that a younger
people have named it Italy, after their leader.
We set that course
but Orion suddenly surged and stormed on the water,
heaved us at blind shoals and drove us completely
apart with blustering southwinds and massed waves, impassable
sea-cliffs. Some of us reached your beaches by swimming.
Who are these men, your people? What barbarous country
540 allows them to act so? To keep us from welcoming beachsand,
to goad us to fight or stop us from standing our ground here—
if human kind and dying weapons are sneered at,
remember the Gods remember the law and the outlaw.
Our prince was Aeneas. No one's justice was higher,
no one was more conscientious or stronger with weapons in
    wartime.
If Fates rescued the man, if he still savors this higher
air, not lying yet with Underworld shadow,
we fear nothing. And first competing in kindness
won't harm you. There's also Sicilian land to return to,
550 Trojan farms and towns of well-known Acestes.
Let us haul our wind-rattled ships from the water,
shape new oars and refit our hulls with your timber.
If Gods restore our king, our friends and a heading
for Italy, gladly we'll make for Latium's country.
If not—if you're not safe, you best father of Trojans,
if Libyan water holds you, the hope of Iulus demolished—
at least we'll head for Sicilian straits where we came from.
Homes are ready there. We'll look for kingly Acestes."
When Ileoneus finished, all of the Trojans
560 voiced their approval.

Dido's Warm Welcome

With downcast looks Dido spoke to them briefly.

"Release fear from your hearts, Trojans. Banish anxiety.
Our life is hard here. The kingdom's youth has compelled me
to mass defenses and post watches at outlying borders.
The house of Aeneas! Who's not heard of the city
of Troy, your brave men in that great war and its firestorms?
Our own Phoenician hearts have not been so blunted:
your Sun-God's horse-team is not that far from our Tyrian city.
Whether you choose broad Hesperia, the farmland of Saturn,
570   or sail for the country of King Acestes and Eryx,
I will help. I'll send you in safety; our wealth will assist you.
And what if you wish to remain as our equals in Carthage?
The city I'm building is yours. Draw out your vessels.
I'll treat you without bias, Trojan and Tyrian.
If only Aeneas himself, your leader, were present,
nudged by the same Southwind! In fact I'll order reliable
troops to search the shore and Libyan outposts,
to see if he's thrown by surf into bush, or lost in some village."

Aeneas Appears from the Mist

Her words inspirited both lordly Aeneas
580   and steady Achates. Both for a long time had been eager
to break from the mist. Achates first encouraged Aeneas:
"You, the son of a Goddess, what are your thoughts now?
You see they are all safe: our friends and ships have been rescued.
Except for one—we saw him ourselves in the maelstrom,
sucked down—the rest confirms the word of your mother."
He'd hardly spoken when suddenly all the surrounding
mist parted itself and cleared away in a crosswind.
Aeneas stood there, a clear glow on his godlike
shoulder and face. Venus herself had exhaled on
590   her son's hair a splendor, a youthfully ruddy
light on his face, on his eyes a luster and gladness,
the way a craftsman's hand might add splendor to ivory
or set in yellow gold Parian marble or silver.
Abruptly he spoke to the queen and everyone present,
saying openly, "Here I am, the person you're seeking,
Aeneas of Troy, snatched from Libyan water.
And you, the only person to pity our struggle,
the curse on Troy, to share your home and your city
with us, remnants exhausted by Greeks on land and by every
600   mischance at sea, utterly beggared! To properly thank you,
Dido, is not in our power: all that's left of the Trojan
people throughout the world is everywhere scattered.

Gods must bring the reward you deserve, if a Power
regards reverence, if justice continues to matter,
and men's knowledge of right. What glad generation
gave you birth, what great parents conceived you?
While rivers flow to the sea, while shadows in mountain
coombs wander and skies nourish the starlight,
your name, honor and praise will continue to live on,
610   whatever land calls me." He finished and held out
hands to his friends Ileoneus, Serestus,
then to the others, rugged Gyan and rugged Cloanthus.

Invitation to the Palace

Dido of Sidon was struck first by the face of Aeneas,
then by the man's hard losses. She answered,
"The son of a Goddess! What great danger and downfall
have chased you? What Power leads you to primitive coast-lines?
You're truly Aeneas? The one whom kindly Venus delivered
to Troy's Anchises close to the flowing Phrygian Simois?
And yes, I recall a Teucer coming to Sidon,
620   expelled from his fathers' land. He looked for a younger
kingdom with help from Belus, my Father, when Belus
exploited the wealth of Cyprus and held it under his power.
From that time on I knew of the fall of your Trojan
city, the names of Pelasgian rulers, and your name.
Your enemy Teucer gave you Trojans exceptional credit
and claimed he branched himself from an old family of Trojans.
Come, then, all you men—enter our household.
A similar luck drove me as well through a number
of hardships, picking this land at last for our settling.
630   I know of pain. I've learned to alleviate sadness."

Preparation for a Banquet

She stopped and led Aeneas at once to the royal
palace, commanding thanks be to God in each temple
and sending no fewer than twenty bulls to the seashore,
a hundred huge swine with bristling backs for the crews there.
She added a hundred plump ewes with their young ones
and glad gifts of the Wine-God.
The palace built up soon to a queenly resplendence.
Inside the central hall a banquet was readied
in proud purple, tapestries' intricate patterns,
640   silver massed on tables, and golden engravings
of strong ancestors' work: a long sequence of actions

traced through men from the ancient birth of their people.

Presents for a Queen

Aeneas, whose fatherly love truly prevented
his mind from resting, sent Achates fast to the moorage
to bring Ascanius news and guide him back to the city.
All his care and parental concern stood in Ascanius.
He ordered gifts brought back as well that were saved from
Troy's rubble: a stiff cloak with its stitching
of gold; the veil bordered in saffron acanthus
650 worn by the Greek, Helen—brought from Mycenae
to Troy when she sought that perverse marriage with Paris,
and Helen's marvellous gift from Leda, her mother;
the scepter, too, which Priam's eldest daughter
Ilione once carried; a pearl necklace and double
crown with gold plaiting and jewels. Achates
hurried away to do all this at the moorage.

Plans of Venus and Cupid

But Venus was mulling a different maneuver, a novel
scheme in her heart: how Cupid might change his appearance
and walk as her dear Ascanius, warming the manic
660 queen with gifts and winding fire through her marrow.
Venus deeply feared Tyre was evasive and two-tongued,
Juno cruel and seething. At night when anxiety rushed back
Venus hurriedly spoke to the quick-flying Love-God:
"My son, my supreme strength and power—the only
son who shrugs at our highest Father's Typhoeus-destroying
bolts—I come to you humbly. I ask for that power.
Your brother Aeneas is thrown by seas onto every
shore, Juno's caustic hatred has caused it,
you know all that: you've often shared his grief, and your
          mother's.
670 Now a Phoenician, Dido, detains him with lovely
talk, and I'm worried. How will a welcome of Juno
turn out? At such a crux she's hardly relaxing.
Therefore I plan to capture Dido beforehand,
to trick her, ring her with fire which no one can alter:
to keep her by me, through a deep love for Aeneas.
Listen: adopt my plan on how we might do this.
The boy, my prince and greatest worry, is ready
to leave for the Tyrian city, his loving father insisting.
He'll bring on gifts that survived Troy's fire and the sea-storm.

680 I'll hide him in dreamy sleep on the heights of Cythera,
and lay him down in my sacred shrine at Idalium:
he won't be aware of our tricks or be able to stop them.
For just one night you fake the prince's appearance,
put on—you're a boy—a boy's familiar expressions.
Then, when Dido takes you in pure joy to her bosom,
surrounded by royal tables and wines of Lyaeus,
soon as she hugs and kisses you firmly and sweetly,
breathe in your flame: unnerve her with dark aphrodisiac."

Cupid Becomes Ascanius

The Love-God liked the loving request of his mother.
690 He doffed his wings and gladly skipped like Iulus
while Venus diffused a gentle sleep through Ascanius'
body. The Goddess took him, warmed in her lap, to the Cyprus
high country where soft marjoram blossoms
embraced him with fragrance. He lingered in amiable shadow.
Cupid moved along, complying with orders. He carried
princely gifts into Carthage gladly led by Achates.
The queen, when he came, already reclined on a golden
sofa placed in the midst of exquisite drapery.
Aeneas, the father, had joined her already with Trojan
700 youths who lay on spreads emblazoned in purple.
Servants washed their hands, wiped them with shaggy
towels, and offered the bread of Ceres in baskets.
Fifty girls in back were concerned with arranging
long lines of food and with fires that honored the Hearth-Gods.
Two hundred others, girls and boys of the same age,
helped by loading tables with food and setting the cups out.
Tyrians too were gathering, crossing the joyful
threshold in groups, shown to embroidered couches to lie on.
Admiring the gifts from Aeneas, admiring Iulus—
710 the Love-God's flagrant cheek and play-acting chatter—
they gazed at the cloak, at the veil of painted yellow acanthus.
Dido especially (sadly doomed to a sickness
soon) could not get her fill of feverish gazing:
the queen was moved both by the gifts and the boy-God.
And he, after he'd hung on the neck of Aeneas
and satisfied the deep love of his make-believe father,
sought out the queen. Her eyes and bosom completely
cherished him now on her lap, Dido sadly unknowing
how great a God sat there. But Cupid remembered
720 his Acidalian mother: he slowly started erasing

Sychaeus: he tried to distract the queen with a living
desire. Her feelings had long stagnated, unused.

Dido's Prayer

After the banquet's first lull and the tables' removal
wines were set out in large garlanded wine-bowls.
They caused an ovation—shouts rolled through the building's
ample halls. Lamps were lit: hanging from golden
paneled ceilings their torch-fires mastered the darkness.
Shortly the queen called for a vessel of heavy
gold and gems. By custom she poured the vintage of Belus
730 and all his descendents. She made the hallways be silent.
"Jupiter, known to provide justice for strangers:
let this day be a glad one for Tyrian and Trojan
refugees. Let our children remember this moment.
Let Bacchus bring us joy; let kindly Juno be present.
Celebrate, all you Tyrians—welcome these people!"
Finished, she poured wine first on the table
to honor the Gods. She touched her lips to the vessel,
then daringly gave it to Bitias. He drained it aggressively,
face deep in the gold, splashed by the wine-foam.

Themes of the Poet

740 As other leaders followed, shag-haired Iopas,
taught by Atlas the great, strummed on a golden
lyre and sang of the moon's wandering, solar eclipses,
where man and beast came from, downpour and lightning,
the rains of Arcturus, the twin Bears and the Hyades.
He told why winter sunsets dye the Ocean so quickly
and what prevents the slow nights from advancing.
Tyrians doubled their cheers, followed by Trojans.

A Royal Request

And luckless Dido kept drawing the night out.
Changing topics, drinking the depths of desire,
750 she asked all about Priam, all about Hector,
then of the arms that came with the son of Aurora,
then of Diomedes' horse, and the girth of Achilles.
"But no, tell us, my guest, from the very beginning,"
she said, "of Greek deceit, the fall of your people,
your whole journey. For seven summers already
have borne you on every land and sea in your travels."

II

THE LOSS OF TROY

Aeneas Complies with Dido's Request

They all hushed, their looks fixed and attentive.
High on his couch like a father Aeneas responded,
"The grief you want revived, my queen, is unbearable.
Greeks uprooted Troy's pitiful kingdom
and wealth, and I myself witnessed the misery:
I shared it in large part. Who could describe it—
Dolopians, Myrmidons, hard troops of Ulysses—
and hold back tears? Late-night dew has already
dropped from the sky: declining stars are making us drowsy.
10   Still if you greatly desire to hear of our downfall,
to learn briefly of Troy's ultimate struggle,
I'll speak, though it hurts and chills my heart to remember.

The Appearance of the Trojan Horse

"War had broken the Greeks: Fates had rejected
their leaders and many years were lost in their efforts.
They built a horse high as a hill with the cunning
of Pallas the Goddess, fitting sections of pine in the rib-cage.
It seemed a prayer for safe return—that was the rumor—
in fact they'd secretly drawn lots for the bodies
of men and shut them blindly inside, deep in its cavern:
20   they'd filled the huge belly with weapons and soldiers.

Rejoicing in Troy

"From Troy you can see the well-known Tenedos Island,

resourceful and rich while Priam's kingdom was standing—
now there's only a bay with dangerous mooring.
The Greeks left for that empty shore and they hid there.
We thought they'd gone, followed a wind to Mycenae.
All of Troy felt a release from long lamentation.
We opened gates and took delight in visiting empty
Greek camps. We stared at desolate beaches:
here Dolopians camped, there a savage Achilles.
30 Here was a place for ships. There, a front they had fought for.

What to Do with the Horse?

"We stared at the deadly gift of husbandless Pallas,
amazed at the horse's mass. Thymoetes advised us
first to haul it inside our walls to the fortress.
Was he a traitor? Or Troy's fate was already
tilted . . . but Capys and some with superior judgment
ordered the Greeks' design dumped in the water.
'Light it,' somebody shouted, 'burn the treacherous offering!'
'Probe its hiding-places, puncture the belly.'
The crowd split into groups, opposed or uncertain.

Laöcoön Condemns the Horse

40 "Before all else, with a large crowd of attendants,
Laöcoön ran from the high citadel, hotly
calling from far off, 'Are my wretched countrymen crazy?
You think the enemy's gone? You believe that a single
Greek gift is guileless? Is that what Ulysses is known for?
Either the Greeks hide in that wooden interior
or someone's crafted a weapon to spy on your city,
to get inside your walls and leer in your houses.
Don't trust the horse, you people of Troy. Some trick is concealed
    here.
Whatever it is, I fear Greeks even with presents.'
50 He finished and threw an immense spear at the horse's
flank with all his strength. It struck at the rounded
belly—the thing stood there quivering. Noises
came from the cave-like womb that sounded like groaning.
If Gods' word or our own thoughts were more lucky,
that steel's thrust would have bloodied the Greeks who were
    hidden,
Troy would be standing, Priam's high towers remaining.

The Capture of Sinon

"But look: Trojan shepherds meanwhile were dragging
a man to the king, hands tied at his back, and an uproar
around him. Sinon had known what was coming beforehand:
60   he'd rigged this capture himself to open a Trojan
gate for Greeks. A brash character, ready
either for twirling lies or falling and dying.
Young Trojans were running from everywhere, wanting
to see him, crowds jostled and poked fun at the captive.
Listen to fraud now: learn from a single
Greek how all of them lie.

Pity for Sinon

"There he stood in our sight, surrounded and trembling,
unarmed, rolling his eyes at our Phrygian armor,
'What world now,' he cried, 'what waters are able
70   to take me? What end remains for someone so wretched?
I lost my place for good among Greeks, and the Trojans
too will hate me and call for punishment, bloodshed.'
His moans changed our minds. All of our harshness
dwindled. We urged him to say what bloodline he'd come from,
what he could say, or hope to achieve as a captive.

The Enmity of Ulysses

"After his fear finally settled he answered,
'Whatever happens, King of Troy, all that I tell you
is true. First, my people—I cannot deny it—
are Greek. If Luck painted Sinon a wretched
80   person she'll never paint me a joker or liar.
Has Palamedes' name come to your hearing
by chance, Nauplius' son? His fine reputation
was widespread. But Greeks charged his innocent person
falsely just for opposing the war: they viciously framed   him
and sent him to die—and soon as he lost daylight they mourned
        him!
The man was my close blood relation and comrade.
My Father, poor in my early years, sent me to soldier
with Palamedes. So long as he ruled safely and prospered
in royal councils, we shared some of that honor
90   and pride. But after slander from vicious Ulysses—
you know who I mean—my friend withdrew from the shoreline
of life. Stunned, I dragged out sorrow and darkness,

raging inside at the death of an innocent comrade.
I spoke out madly, swearing vengeance if any
chance came, if I ever re-entered in triumph
my Greek homeland. My words provoked the bitterest hatred.
That was my first slip: from there it was always Ulysses
threatening new charges, scattering tricky
tales among people, or openly looking for face-downs.
100 He hardly rested until the collusion of Calchas . . .
but why unroll all that? It's thankless and futile.
Why stall it? If all Greeks are considered
alike you've heard enough. Impose your overdue torture.
Atreus' sons would pay you plenty! Ulysses would love it.'

The Need for Sacrifice

"No: we yearned to hear and study the motives,
blind to his deep malice, to Greek machinations.
He faltered; then he went on with spurious feeling.
'Exhausted Greeks had often hoped to abandon
Troy, to quit and run from a war that was endless.
110 If only they had! But just as often a bitter
sea-storm scared them. Southwinds kept them from going.
Especially after this maple planking was fitted,
the horse stood there—but all the sky was an uproar.
Confused, we sent Eurypylus back to the shrine of Apollo
to learn more. He brought back dismal word from the temple:

> *Blood pleased the Winds in the death of a virgin*
> *before, when Greeks sailed to the shore of the Trojans;*
> *blood is required for return now, through a single*
> *Greek's death.*

Soon as that word came to the people's
120 ears their thoughts scrambled, cold tremors assaulted
their bone marrow: who'd be claimed by the Fates and Apollo?
Here Ulysses dragged out Calchas the seer,
raised an uproar there in our midst and called for the heavens'
will. Many had warned me already of cruel
plots of this schemer. They quietly watched what was coming.
For ten long days the tent of Calchas was silent.
His voice named no man to be sent to the slaughter.
Finally, goaded by fierce yells from Ulysses,
he broke silence and fixed on me—as agreed—for the altar.
130 They all approved. What everyone dreaded beforehand,
changed into one man's miserable death, they accepted.

Sinon's Apparent Escape

" 'Soon the unspeakable day arrived. They were ready
with salt meal for the rite. They wreathed my temples with fillets.
Somehow I fled from death. I admit it: I broke from my bindings
and hid in a lake's marshy sedge through the night hours
until the Greeks sailed—if only they would sail!
Now I can never hope to gaze on my ancient
homeland, children I love, a Father I long for:
Greeks will probably punish my family, make them
140   pay for my guilty escape and wretchedly kill them.
That's why I beg you: through Powers above who are conscious
of truth, if anything's left to us humans, a remnant
of pure trust: have pity on someone who suffered
greatly. Pity a man not deserving such sorrow.'

Priam Himself Pardons Sinon

"We gave him life for those tears, and even compassion:
Priam himself first commanded the captive's
tight chains to be loosened and spoke as a friend would:
'Whoever you are, the Greeks are gone now and forgotten.
You are ours. And tell the truth when I ask you:
150   why did they build a massive horse? Who designed it?
What God does it pray to? Or is it a battle contraption?'

The Greeks' Quarrel with Pallas

"He stopped and Sinon, trained in the art of deception
by Greeks, lifted a chainless hand to the heavens.
'You Fires that last forever, undamageable Powers,
I call you to witness,' he said, 'by the altar and horrible dagger
I fled from, the Gods' fillets I wore as a victim:
allow me to end my sacred Greek obligations,
allow me to hate my countrymen, tell every secret
pertinent now, and not be bound by the laws of my homeland.
160   You Trojans, only keep your trust and a promise:
save me if I save you: if truth has worth then reward it.
All the Greeks' hopes and trust in the war from the outset
rested in constant help from Pallas. But after the reckless
Diomedes aided that crime-monger, Ulysses,
to raid her revered shrine, stealing the fateful
Palladium, killing guards on the citadel's rooftop,
grabbing her sacred statue, daring to bloody
and manhandle garlands reserved for the virginal Goddess:

from that time on the Greeks' hopes were a backward
170 gliding flow, their strength broken, the Goddess against them.
Pallas gave them signs, nothing was doubtful:
her image had hardly arrived in camp when the upraised
eyes flashed and flamed, the torso exuded
salt sweat and it leaped from the ground—amazing to say it—
three times by itself, shaking the shield and the javelin!
Calchas immediately chanted, "Try for escape on the water.
Greek force cannot demolish the city
unless you return home for signs of the Goddess's power.
She carried your rounded keels to sea in the first place."
180 So now with a wind they head for their native Mycenae.
Armed and ready with Gods on their side, they will recross
the sea and arrive suddenly. Calchas will sort out the omens.
They stood this figure here to atone for the insult
to Pallas' statue and power, a crime they've regretted.
And Calchas commanded the huge mass to be raised up,
oakwood-plaited, left right out in the sunlight,
to stop your people from guiding it past the gates of the city
and earning help—our ancient religious protection.
For if your hands profane our gift to the Goddess,
190 Troy and Priam's rule will meet with total destruction—
I wish the Gods could turn that curse on its speaker!—
but if your hands help it to climb to the city,
Asia will march in a great war on Peloponnesian
walls: that doom waits for all of our children.'

Sinon's Trickery Works

"Because of Sinon's deceit and treacherous tactics
the thing was believed. Captured by gushing tears and by lying—
not by Diomedes or Larissaean Achilles—
ten years of war and a thousand ships had not beat us.

Laöcoön and his Sons are Killed

"But then a monstrous, far more frightening omen
200 crossed our path, disordered our feeling and shocked us.
The priest of Neptune chosen by lot was Laöcoön:
just as he killed a large bull at a ritual altar,
imagine: two sea-snakes came from Tenedos' quiet
water—how cold to remember!—their coils were enormous,
they leaned onto waves and drove at our beaches together,
breasting the seas. Their raised crests were a bloody
red high on the swells, and trailing behind them

were long backs and slithering tails in the current.
Making a stir in the frothy surf they already
210 reached our land, eyes burning bloody and fiery,
flickering tongues and mouths licking and hissing.
We scattered, pale at the vision. The serpents were heading
straight for Laöcoön: first their windings entangled
his two small sons' bodies, and each snake
bit off pieces of hapless muscle and chewed them.
Laöcoön ran to help, carrying weapons:
they seized him, tied him in huge rounds that already
circled his chest and neck twice, down to the scaly
tails, their tall necks rising above him.
220 The man pulled at the knots, he struggled to free them.
His garlands a slaver of dark bloodstain and poison,
he sent a horrible scream to the sky at that moment,
just as a bull bellows after it's wounded,
runs from the altar and shakes a clumsy ax from its neckbone.
Slowly the two big serpents left for the temple
heights. They made for truculent Pallas's fortress
to hide at her feet, by the round shield of the Goddess.
A new and sinuous terror certainly troubled
every heart now. A few claimed he deserved it:
230 'Laöcoön paid for the sin of damaging sacred
wood with a spear.' 'The weapon he threw up was evil,'
they shouted, 'Lead the horse to the Goddess's temple,
invoke her will!'

The Trojans Lead the Horse into Troy

"So. We spread our walls and bared the homes of our city.
Everyone worked: wheels went under the horse's
hooves for rolling; we stretched towlines of oakum
tight at the neck. A death-machine rose to our wall-tops,
crammed with weapons. Boys went hymning around it,
unmarried girls kept touching the towlines and laughing.
240 The horse moved closer. It menaced the heart of the city.
Ah, my country! The Gods' home, famous in battle,
you walls of Troy! The horse got stalled at the gateway
itself four times, four times weapons clanked in that belly
and still we pushed, mindless or blind from some madness.
We brought the beast, our curse, to a stop at the temple.
Cassandra too opened her mouth about coming
death. At a God's word we Trojans never believed her.
Cursed, we adorned the shrine of each God on that final

day and strung festival greens through the city.

The Attack Begins

250 "Meanwhile the sky changed. Dusk ran to the Ocean,
wrapping in deep shadow the earth and the heavens—
and Greek lies. People were wearily scattered
throughout the city in silence. Sleep gathered their bodies.
The Greek fleet sailed from Tenedos Island,
squadroned ships in the quiet companionable moonlight.
Heading for well-known shore, the flagship discreetly
signaled by flare; Sinon, saved by some unfair
God or Fate, secretly loosened the pinewood
doors for Greeks shut in that belly: the opened
260 horse returned men to the night-air, glad to emerge from
their hardwood cave. Thessandrus and Sthenelus, leaders.
Cruel Ulysses slid down a rope. Acamas, Thoas
and Pyrrhus, Achilles' son. Machaon, a chieftain.
Menelaus. Epeus himself, the hoax's designer.
Wine and sleep had buried the town. They attacked it,
cut down the guard, opened a gate for an army
of welcome friends, joined and plotted their forces.

A Vision of Hector

"The hour had come when the first relaxation has started
to seep through sickly men, thanks to the Sky-Gods,
270 when look—a vision appeared: Hector was grieving
right there before my eyes, heavily weeping,
dirtied by blood, dust, the chariot's dragging,
feet pierced and swollen by thongs at the ankles.
My God, what man was this? How changed from the Hector
who'd galloped to Troy sporting the gear of Achilles
and hurled Phrygian fire at the ships of Danaans!
Mucked beard, his hair stiffened with bloodshed,
he carried so many wounds he'd taken defending
Troy's walls. Now I seemed to be weeping
280 myself, I called to the man and questioned him sadly,
'Light of Troy, surest hope of our people,
what kept you so far so long? What shore do you come from?
How we've missed you, Hector, after so many
deaths of friends, the jumbled work of our people
for worn-out Troy. What criminal dirt has disfigured
your clear face? Why do I see lacerations?'
But no, he'd waste no time responding to trifles.

Chest heaving, he moaned deeply and told me:
'Son of the Goddess, run, escape from the firestorm!
290 Greeks hold your walls. Troy will drop from its summit.
Enough's been done for Priam's nation. If Trojan
defense were possible, here was the hand to defend it!
You will be trusted with Troy's House-Gods, our relics:
take them as Fates' friends and look to the massive
walls you'll found at last, after you've wandered the sea-lanes.'
He stopped and his hand held out powerful Vesta's
fillets and permanent fire from the heart of the temple.

Aeneas Longs to Do Battle

"A mingled wail meanwhile came from the city.
More and more, although my Father Anchises'
300 house was far removed and shrouded by foliage,
I heard noise, a mounting terror of warfare.
Shaken from sleep I climbed upstairs to the building's
roof and stood there, my ears excited and tingling.
Fire appeared like the fire in a cornfield when Southwinds
rage, or rapids that rush from a hillside to flatten
farmland, proud crops flattened, the labor of oxen,
trees dragged down headlong: the farmer, astounded,
stands on a tall rock resigned to the bedlam.
Surely the truth was clear now, the deception
310 of Greeks plain. Already Deiphobus' stately
house crumbled, the Fire-God above it; his neighbor's,
Ucalegon's, burned, and the broad Straits of Sigea mirrored
the flames. Men cried out, trumpet's blaring had mounted,
I grabbed for a sword madly—arming was mindless,
yet my spirits burned to fight, to muster a column
of friends and rush to the palace. Anger and frenzy
drove me headlong. It seemed splendid to die in my armor.
But look: a priest named Panthus, eluding the weapons
of Greeks: Othrys' son, from the temple of Phoebus.
320 Holding relics himself, he carried some conquered
Gods, and a small grandson. He ran to my doorstep distracted.
'Panthus, how is the palace? What place do we fight from?'
I'd hardly spoken when Panthus moaned and responded,
'The last day's come, the unavoidable ending
of Troy. Trojans belong to the past with their signal
Trojan glory. Jupiter's angrily shifted
all to Argos: Greeks have burned and mastered the city.
That tall horse we stood in the midst of our buildings

poured out troops. Sinon's won—scattering arson,
330 cavorting. Thousands of men marched through the open
gates, just as they once marched from splendid Mycenae.
Others have blocked winding alleys with weapons:
tight steel lines confront you, they glimmer and stand there,
ready to kill. The first watchmen hardly attempted
to hold the gates. When Mars is blind who can resist him?'
The words of Othrys' son and the will of some Sky-God
moved me to arm and burn. A grief-spreading Fury
yelled in my ear to hurl death-cries to heaven.
Ripheus joined me, a friend. An excellent fighter,
340 Epytus. Dymas and Hypanis came through the moonlight,
swelling our ranks. Coroebus followed, a younger
son of Mygdon. Just that week he'd happened to enter
Troy fired by a mad love for Cassandra,
bringing a son-in-law's help to the Trojans and Priam—
vainly. He'd paid no heed to that Fury-lashed woman's
warning.
Seeing men gather, anxious for battle,
I started to say, 'Your hearts are strong but it's futile,
men. If you really desire to back me by daring
350 the worst and last, admit what luck's in the matter:
every altar and shrine empty, abandoned by every
God the empire stood on. You're helping a city
in flames. Die, then: rush in the middle of battle:
the only help for a loser is hoping for nothing to help him.'

Clashes with Greeks

"That's how frenzy addled men's minds. Like a wolfpack
hunting in dark fog when desperate hunger
blindly compels them to leave pups in the wolf-den
waiting with dry mouths, we maneuvered by hostile
weapons, hardly in doubt about death. We made for the city
360 center. The night was black, hovering, hollow.
Who can describe that night's death and destruction?
What speech or tears are ever right for such struggle?
An old city fell, a ruler for decades.
Hundreds of listless corpses casually littered
yards, streets, and Gods' venerable doorways.
And Trojans were not alone paying with bloodshed:
strength often came back to the guts of the losers
and Greek conquerors fell. Everywhere bitter

mourning, everywhere fright, and death with a hundred
    expressions.
370 The first Greek to confront us, followed by several
friends, was Androgeos. Guessing naively our column
was Greek, he spoke up blithely and harried us outright:
'Move it, you men! Why are you stalling and dragging
behind while others burn, plunder and haul off
Troy? You came just now from our tall-masted vessels?'
He stopped and guessed shortly—no answer we gave him
hit the mark—he'd slipped into enemy circles.
Stepping back dumbfounded, he ended the parley
just like a man whose weight comes down on a serpent
380 abruptly in rough bush, he hurriedly backs off,
scared by the angry swell of that purple and rising
neck: Androgeos feared what he saw and retreated.
We rushed them. Keeping our ranks close we out-flanked them,
they hardly knew the locale, terror constrained them:
we killed them. Fortune favored the first of our efforts.

Disguised as Greeks

"And here Coroebus, buoyed with success and with spirit,
called out, 'My friends, Fortune's pointed the way to our safety
first: let's follow the right path she has shown us,
swap shields with the Greeks and wear their equipment
390 ourselves. Who needs courage to fight them? Be cunning!
They'll give us their own arms.' While speaking he put on
Androgeos' crested helmet and shield with its graceful
design. He strapped a Greek sword near his hipbone.
Ripheus gladly followed, together with Dymas,
the whole group—each man armed with booty just taken.
We moved and mixed among Greeks, hardly by Power
of our own in the groping dark, skirmishing often.
We grappled and sent down scores of men to the Hell-God.
Some of them fled to the ships to look for protecting
400 beachhead while shame or fear forced others to climb in
the horse again to hide in a big familiar belly.

Reversals

"It's right to believe in nothing if Gods countermand you.
Witness the virgin daughter of Priam, Cassandra,
dragged by her strung-out hair from the temple altar of Pallas,
her eyes yearning, reaching in vain to the heavens,

her eyes—for her soft hands were manacled tightly.
Coroebus could not stand the maddening picture.
He threw himself, a certain death, at the midst of the column.
We all followed in close ranks to attack them.
410 But first a bombardment: from high roofs of the temple
friends overwhelmed us—a pitiful slaughter—
the look of our Greek armor and helmets had fooled them.
Then the Greeks howled in rage at our stealing the virgin,
they gathered and struck us from all sides. Ajax was fiercest,
Atreus' sons and a whole Dolopian cohort
drove like a whirlwind splitting at times into warring
gusts, Westwind and Northwind, the Eastwind that glories
in Dawn's horses, when trees groan and a foam-flecked
Nereus rattles his trident, churning the sea-depths.
420 Troops we'd scattered that blurred night through the shadows,
men we'd tricked and chased through all of the city,
showed up now. First they recognized every deceitful
sword and shield. They noted the wrong sound of our voices.
The mob swiftly crushed us, Penelus toppling
Coroebus first by hand close to the war-strong
Pallas' altar. Ripheus fell, one of the justest
men at Troy, preserving the best of the law-courts—
Gods may see things otherwise—Hypanis, Dymas,
killed by friends. None of your reverence, Panthus,
430 no Sun-God's headband could hide you or keep you from
        falling.

Aeneas Escapes to the Palace

"You ashes of Troy! My friends in that final cremation,
witness how when you fell I never avoided
a Greek spear or defeat. If the Fates had been willing,
this hand would have earned my death.
But then we were pulled off—
Iphitus, Pelias and I, Iphitus heavier
now with age and Pelias slowed by a wound from Ulysses.
Shouts called us straight to the palace of Priam.
Fighting here was most intense, as if there were fighting
nowhere else, no one dying in all of the city.
440 The War-God raged, Greeks rushed at the palace,
we saw them ram doors in shielded formation,
they hooked ladders on walls, and close to the entry
itself men struggled to climb—left hands upraising
shields to ward off arrows, right hands grasping at ledges.

Trojans who faced them wrenched roofing from towers,
palace battlements—ready, now that the final
hour of death had appeared, to defend with such weapons.
Old gold-leafed oakbeams, the pride of our Fathers,
tumbled down. Trojans below at the doorway
450 closed up ranks and blocked it, swords in a cluster.

Aeneas Helps the Rooftop Defenders

"My spirits revived: I'd run to the roof of the building,
add my strength to the men there, help out the losers.
I knew of a door in back, an invisible entrance
used by Priam's family, an old way in the building.
So long as the kingdom lasted, Andromache often
had come this way sadly, unattended, to visit
her in-laws or lead Astyanax, her boy, to his grandsire.
I slipped upstairs, emerged on the rooftop and looked out:
sorry Trojans hurled down impotent weapons.
460 A tower stood at the edge, raised to the highest
stars from the roof. All of Troy could be sighted
once from here, Greek ships and camps of Achaians.
Now we chopped around it wherever a higher
level exposed weak joints. We ripped out and toppled
the tower from its high base—a sudden destruction
fell roaring, dragging down as it slashed through
Greek ranks. But others ran up. None of our boulders,
no weapon now could stop them.

Pyrrhus at Priam's Doors

"Right at the entrance's very threshold was Pyrrhus.
470 He leaped in that light, weapons flashy and brazen,
just like a snake in sunlight after it's fattened
on bitter plants in cold ground covered by winter:
now with its skin sloughed, new and sleek as an infant,
chest lifted, it twirls unctuous hind-parts,
flicking a three-forked tongue high in the sunlight.
Hulking Peripas joined him; Achilles' chariot driver
and armor bearer, Automedon; whole Scyrian cohorts:
they all bore down on the doors or flung torches at rooftops.
Pyrrhus led on. He gripped a two-edged ax and he broke through
480 the hard doors, he sheared sockets from door-rails
of bronze: already he'd gouged a panel of solid
oak, making a hole large as a window.
The palace interior showed, long corridors opened.

Rooms of ancient kings were revealed, and of Priam.
Armed men showed themselves in the foyer.
Inside however the house was a tangle of tumult
and misery. Women yelled and wailed to the concave
ceilings above them—noise carried to gold constellations.
Trembling mothers wandered the length of their bedrooms
490 or clung to doors, embracing and giving them kisses.
Pyrrhus drove with his father's force: nothing could stop him,
bolts, guards, nothing. His battering weakened
door-rails, dislodged them from sockets, and crumbled them
        forward.
Force made its way. Greeks broke through the entrance,
cut down sentries, and filled a broad space with their soldiers.
Rapids are not so wild when they ravage a levee,
masses of water breaching and wrecking the barrier,
raging across a meadow, whole fields in a body,
dragging off cattle and stalls. I witnessed the rabid,
500 murderous Pyrrhus and Atreus' sons at our threshold.
I saw Hecuba's hundred daughters by marriage, and Priam—
an altar he'd blessed with fire he'd soon smear with his own blood.
Fifty bridal rooms, our great hope for descendants,
doorframes proud of Eastern gilding and prizes,
fell forward. Greeks took them. Our hearth-fires were failing.

Priam and Hecuba Seek Refuge

"Perhaps you'll also ask what happened to Priam.
Soon as he saw Troy falling and taken,
palace doors destroyed, Greeks in the building's interior,
he foolishly cupped his quavering shoulders in rusty
510 armor. Old as he was he belted a futile
sword on, determined to die in the midst of invaders.
Under the bare axis of sky in the central
court was a large altar next to an aging laurel
that leaned on the altar and thickly shaded the House-Gods.
Hecuba huddled around the altar in vain with her daughters,
doves in a dark storm diving and swerving.
Often they crouched and embraced a Goddess's image.
Hecuba, seeing Priam himself decked in a young man's
armor, asked, 'What madness forced you, my pitiful husband,
520 to bear such arms now? Where will you rush to?
The hour is dire not for help or defenses
like yours—no, not even if Hector were present.
Come here, please. Either the altar will guard us

or we'll all die.' She stopped speaking, embraced him
and sat the aging king on a seat by the altar.

Pyrrhus Kills Polites

"But look: one of the sons of Priam, Polites,
running from Pyrrhus' killing, eluding the spear-throws
of Greeks through a long arcade, circled the empty
courtyard, wounded. Pyrrhus threatened and sweated
530 behind him. Now he's gripped him: *now* he pushes the spear in.
Just when the son had escaped in the eyes of his parents,
he fell in thick blood and emptied his life out.
Priam, although surrounded now by the dying,
could not hold back or keep from screaming in outrage:
'For such a crime, for all your daring,' he shouted,
'may God grant you the prize and credit you rightly
deserve, if goodness and care exist in the heavens!
To make me witness my son's killing in person,
smearing a father's face with family murder––
540 not even Achilles, hardly your father, related
to hostile Priam that way. The rights and trust of a lowly
petitioner shamed him. He gave me the bloodless body
of Hector to bury, and sent me back to my kingdom.'
Finished, the old man threw an impotent weapon
without much force. It clunked on the shield that quickly repelled
     it,
only scratching the boss high on the circle.

Pyrrhus Kills Priam

" 'Well, then,' Pyrrhus answered, 'carry a message.
Go to Achilles, my Father: remember to tell him
how vile were all the acts of Pyrrhus, his bastard.
550 But first you'll die.' While speaking he dragged the king to the
     altar
itself as he doddered and slipped on the thick blood of Polites.
He twisted the king's hair with a left hand and brandished
a sword with the right, then sank it deep in the ribcage.
So Priam's luck ended. That was the finish
that took him by chance. He'd watched Troy in flames and
     collapsing,
Troy with so many once-proud peoples and homelands,
the ruler of Asia! He'd lay there, a big trunk on the beachsand,
head swiped from the shoulders. The body was nameless.

Aeneas is Tempted to Kill Helen

"Then for the first time brute terror surrounded
560 and stunned me. My dear Father rose in a vision,
he looked like the old king breathing his life out,
viciously wounded. Lonely Creusa was rising,
my wrecked house, a dying little Iulus.
I looked behind, searching for forces around me.
They'd all left, thrown themselves in exhaustion
downward, madly flung themselves in the firestorm.
So I was alone, still living. I recognized Helen:
keeping quiet, she hid in a dark place by the doorway
of Vesta the Virgin—fires gave off a glare when I wandered
570 past, my vision carried around and about here.
Dreading Troy's wrath now that Troy was demolished,
dreading the Greeks' angry reprisals, having deserted
her husband—a curse on both Troy and her homeland—
she tried to hide herself and sat by the altar.
What heat burned in my mind, what anger and vengeance,
to make her pay for the criminal fall of my country:
'Should Helen actually gaze on her native Mycenae,
march through Sparta safely, a queen in some triumph,
look on her husband, parents, her home and her children,
580 with Trojan women—Trojan slaves—in attendance?
With Priam put to the sword and Troy an inferno?
With every Trojan beach sweating and bloody?
It must not be. Although no name is remembered
for punishing women—the work merits no honor—
I'd still be praised for quashing a curse, for inflicting
deserved pain. I'd fill my heart with a joyful
flame of revenge and assuage relatives' ashes.'

Venus Rebukes and Enlightens Aeneas

"I threw out those words, my mind in the grip of some madness,
when there before my eyes, never so brilliant,
590 my dear Mother appeared, a clear radiance glowing
through all that darkness, her godhead displayed in a vision
accustomed to dazzling Sky-Gods. Her right hand restrained me;
after a pause her rose mouth gave me a warning:
'My son, what lawless anger and great sorrow compel you?
Why this fury? Where's your concern for your mother?
Look first where you left your father Anchises,

worn with age. Is your wife Creusa surviving,
your boy Ascanius? Greeks were around them completely
in close ranks: unless my love had withstood them,
600 fire would have seized your family, Greek swords would have
     drained them.
It's not for you to damn the face of Tyndareus' daughter
or guilty Paris. No, the rancor of Sky-God and Goddess
rips out Trojan wealth and levels your city.
Look: I remove all the cloud which is blurring
your human vision now, that mist which is dulling
your eyes, so you won't fear commands of your mother
at all, and not neglect to follow my orders.
There in that mass of rubble where stone has been broken
from stone you see dust and smoke mixing and curling,
610 and Neptune: he heaves with a huge trident that rumbles
foundation and wall: he tears the city completely
loose from its base. And there: Juno, armored in iron,
first at the Scaean gate, fiercely tenacious and madly
calling for men from the ships.
Look behind you now: Tritonian Pallas, presiding
high on that fortress, a stormcloud flashing, wild as a Gorgon.
Jupiter strengthens Greek spirit himself and in person,
building strife and abetting the Gods' war upon Trojans.
Escape, my son. Put an end to your struggle.
620 I won't leave you: I'll bring you safe to the home of your father.'

Aeneas Returns Home

"She stopped and disappeared in the dense, shadowy darkness.
Terrifying forms had appeared, hostile to Trojans,
great and powerful Gods.
Then I saw the whole city actually settle
in cinders, the Troy of Neptune pried from its bases
just like an old ash-tree high in a mountain,
repeatedly struck by two-edged axes of farmers
trying to fell it: it still threatens to topple
when each blow rustles its hair, jolting its forehead.
630 Slowly the wounds win: finally sighing,
torn from that ridge, it drags down clutter behind it.
Down from the roof, led by a Goddess, I managed among them:
Greeks and fire gave way, armor retreated.

Anchises Refuses to Leave

"Soon as I reached the house and door of my Father,
our ancient home, I wanted to carry my Father
first into high mountains: I looked for him foremost.
The man refused, with Troy cut down, to continue
living or suffer exile. 'You, with your youthful
blood intact,' he said, 'your strength hard as a standing
640 oak—you should escape.
Had Gods of the sky wanted my life to continue,
they'd save my house. I saw my fill of disaster
before when I lived through Troy's earlier capture.
So here is my laid-out body: greet it and leave it.
My hand will find some death; or Greeks will have mercy,
finding my wealth. The toss in the grave will be easy.
I've stalled death for years now, useless and hated
by God from the time when mankind's king and the Father
of heaven exhaled fiery wind of lightning and scorched me.'
650 So he went on, fixed in memory, rigid.
We all wept—my wife Creusa was crying,
Ascanius, all our household—afraid my Father would bring us
all down with himself, pile one death on another.
Still he refused: he clung to one purpose, to sit there.
Moved to fight once more, I longed for some wretched
death. What else had luck or talking provided?
'You really expect I could run off and leave you,
Father? What sin falls from the lips of my Father!
If Gods are glad nothing is left of our Trojan
660 grandeur, if adding Troy's death to your own and your
            children's
will bring you joy, the door to such killing is open.
Pyrrhus will stand here shortly, blood-spattered from Priam:
he butchered a son while the father watched by a shrine—then
            the father.
Dear Mother,' I shouted, 'is this the reason you saved me
from fire and spear? To see Greeks enter my household,
Ascanius close to my Father, close to Creusa,
all in each other's blood like beasts at a slaughter?
Bring arms, you men! A last light calls to the losers.
Back at the Greeks: let me re-enter the battle
670 and fight again. We won't go down today completely revengeless.'

Fire Over Ascanius

"Once more belted in armor, passing my left arm
fast through a shield, I turned and made for an exit,
when look—my wife clasped my knees at the doorway.
She held our little Iulus up to his father.
'You're going to die? We're yours in everything: take us.
Still, if you place trust in the armor you're wearing,
guard our house first. To whom will little Iulus
be left, your father and me? They called me your wife once.'
Her speech and moaning filled each room of the building.
680   Suddenly a sign appeared—astounding to tell of—
there between the hands and tearful looks of his parents
we saw a gentle flame at the top of Iulus'
head that lit and licked at the soft hair with a harmless
tongue and seemed to feed on the forehead and temples.
We trembled in fear. We tried to shake out the burning
hair, to extinguish the sacred fire with water.

Anchises is Moved to Leave

"But now my Father Anchises looked to the heavens
in joy, held both hands to the sky while he pleaded,
'All-powerful Jupiter, watch us if any
690   prayer inclines you: if faith is deserving I only
ask you to give one sign and confirm everything, Father.'
The older man had hardly spoken when thunder
suddenly cracked on our left and a star plummeted downward,
leading a brilliant trail of fire through the darkness.
We watched it fall past the roof of the building
and bury itself with a flash in forested Ida,
showing the way. For a time the luminous furrow
gave off light, and sulfurous fumes covered the region.
Now my Father was truly convinced. Rising to heaven
700   he thanked Gods and called that meteor sacred.
'No further delay! I'll follow now where you lead me,
Gods of my Fathers. Save my house, save my descendants!
The omen was yours: Troy lies in your power.
My son, I yield truly. I want to go as your comrade.'

Aeneas Leads his Family Out of Troy

"Fire could now be heard more clearly through walls when he
      finished
speaking: waves of seething heat had come nearer.

'Come then, kindly Father, climb on my shoulders,
my own back will support you. The task is no trouble.
Whatever happens we'll face danger together
710 or reach safety together. Little Iulus,
walk as my friend. My wife, follow our steps at a distance.
You servants, give my instructions all your attention:
leave the town where you see that mound by the aging
temple of lonely Ceres. An old cypress is nearby,
kept for many years by the faith of our Fathers.
From different routes we'll reach that one destination.
Father, hold our sacred family House-Gods:
for me, coming from bloody recent fighting and bloodshed,
it's wrong to touch them—not till I've washed in a living
720 river.'
After speaking I lowered my neck to be covered
with hide across the shoulders—the tan skin of a lion.
I lifted my Father. Little Ascanius threaded
fingers in mine and pursued me, walking and skipping.
My wife followed behind. We moved through shadowy places
where I, not bothered before by any projectiles,
not even by Greek lines in massed opposition,
trembled now at every nightwind. I tensed up
at each sound, fearing for both my son and my Father.

Creusa is Lost

730 "In time we approached a gate. I seemed to have covered
the whole distance when suddenly footsteps were thudding
nearby, crowding my ears, my Father peered through the shadows
and told me, 'Son, hurry, my son, they are closing!
I see their burning shields and shimmering breast-plates.'
I still don't know what hostile Power alarmed me
there or stole my focus. For while I was running
swiftly away, leaving the byways I knew of,
some Fate stole Creusa, my wife. How wretched it made me!
Where did she lose her way? Or stop in exhaustion?
740 No one knows. She never returned to my vision.
I gave no thought nor searched for anyone missing—
not till we came to the ancient hill and the sacred
temple of Ceres. We all assembled finally. With only
one missing. Slipped from her friends, her son and her
          husband.
What God or man did I not blame in my madness?
What crueler thing had I seen in Troy's devastation?

I left our Trojan House-Gods, my Father Anchises
and son safely with friends, hiding in thicketed hollows.

The Search for Creusa

"I made for the city again belted in glittering armor.
750 Bent on renewing every risk in returning,
through all of Troy I'd offer my neck again to the danger.
First I looked for the entrance, the gate I had slipped through
along the dark wall. I picked up and followed
my trail back through the night, my eyes probing and circling.
Everywhere cold, even the quiet alarmed me.
I went to my house—by chance she had gone there, if only
by chance—but Greeks had rushed the whole building and
        seized it.
Now a starving fire rolled to the rooftop:
wind-blown flame and heat surged, rampaging skyward.
760 I went on. Again I saw the house and fortress of Priam.
Hand-picked guards were already in Juno's deserted
shrine near a pillar. Phoenix and vengeful Ulysses
watched booty. Treasure from all through the city
pulled from burning altars, crater-like drinking
bowls of gold, vestments and stolen ritual tables,
were piled high. Boys in a long line with their mothers
stood around, shivering.
I even dared at times to hurl shouts at the darkness.
I filled streets with sorry calls for Creusa.
770 Sighing, I called again and again. It was futile.
Then as I madly, endlessly searched through the city,
a joyless image appeared: the shade of Creusa
herself before my eyes, her form familiar but taller.
My hair stood up, my tongue stuck in my throat and I stood there,
dumb. She said some words that eased my anxiety:
'Why do you take such pleasure in madness and mourning,
my sweet husband? Things happen according
to God's will. The high King of Olympus won't let you
take Creusa from here as a friend on your travels.
780 Look to a long exile. You'll plow deserts of water,
arriving in Western Land where the Lydian Tiber
gently meanders through rich Tuscany farmland.
A time of joy will come in that realm, and a queenly
wife to be claimed. Resist tears for Creusa, your loved one:
I won't see Mrymidon thrones or Dolopian
swagger: I won't slave for Greeks and their mothers:

I am of Troy—Venus' daughter in marriage!
I'm kept on our shore by the great Mother of Sky-Gods.
For now, good-by. Love your son and mine, and protect him.'
790 Finished speaking, she left me weeping and wanting
to say so much. She vanished, thin as the night-air.
Three times my hands reached for her neck to embrace her;
three times her form eluded my grasp—reaching was futile.
She moved like a dream with wings or a stirring of breezes.

Final Departure

"At length I rejoined my friends. Nighttime was ending.
And there I found a huge number collected,
new and striking groups of men, adolescents
and mothers gathered for exile. A sorry assortment.
They'd come from everywhere, ready with savings and spirit
800 for sea or land, wherever I wanted to lead them.
The morning star, high over the ridges of Ida,
signaled dawn. Greeks held and blockaded
the gates of Troy: no hope for help was allowed there.
Resigned, I lifted my Father and made for the mountains."

III

THE JOURNEY WEST

Setting Sail

"After the Gods had seen to the wrecking of Priam's
nation, the undeserved fall of our Asian
city, all of Neptune's proud Troy in a smoke-cloud,
Gods drove us far and wide into exile.
Signs pointed to empty lands. In the Phrygian
mountains near Ida we built a fleet, close to Antandros,
in doubt where the Fates would lead or allow us to settle.
We gathered men and our first summer had hardly
begun when my Father Anchises ordered sail to be trusted
10   to Fates. In tears I left the shore of my native
land, the harbor and fields where Troy had stood. As an exile
I went to sea with friends, a son, our Household Gods and the
    Nation's.

An Outcry from Plants at Thrace

"Far to the north were large fields of the War-God,
planted and tilled by Thracians, ruled by a bitter Lycurgus
once, an old friend of Troy, with sociable House-Gods,
when we had Luck. Borne to that sinuous coastline
I founded my first city, led on by some hostile
Fate. I named it Aenos, after my own name.
I carried sacred gifts to my Mother, Dione's daughter,
20   to all the Gods who'd helped us make this beginning.
I killed a glistening bull for the Sky-Gods' King on the beachsand.
By chance a nearby hilltop was covered with copses,

59

ₒornel trees and myrtle, bristling densely
with spikes. I approached, tried uprooting some saplings
to cover the altar with green branches and leaflets,
and saw an omen. I shudder and wonder to tell you:
the first sapling's roots that I tore from the humus
began to bleed—black-red drops had already
stained and clotted the soil. A shuddering, chilling
30 dread ran through my body—my own blood was congealing.
Yet I tried once more. I tore up a second
tough shoot, probing deep for the cause of the omen.
Black-red blood flowed from the bark of the second.
Profoundly stirred I prayed to the Nymphs of that woodland,
to Lord Grandivus, presiding in Thracian farmland,
to make the omen auspicious, to lighten our vision.
But after I came to a third shoot and engaged it
with greater effort, my knees in soil that resisted—
how can I say this? or stay silent?—I heard a pathetic
40 moan deep in the ground, a voice restored to my hearing:
'Why do you tear my wretched body, Aeneas?
Spare my burial! Keep your sacred hands from pollution.
Troy bore me: no foreign blood runs from your sapling.
Leave this cruel shore, run from the greed of this country!
I'm Polydorus. Here an iron harvest of weapons
covered and pierced me. Now they sprout into thorn-points.'

The Trojans Leave Thrace

"My mind teetered. Awe completely possessed me,
my hair stood up, my tongue stuck in my throat, I was speechless.
Luckless Priam once had secretly trusted
50 Polydorus with huge weights of gold to be kept by
Thrace's king, who soon lost faith in the Trojan
cause, hearing Troy was besieged and surrounded.
When Luck abandoned Troy, our resources demolished,
the king joined Agamemnon's force—a conquering army.
He broke all faith and law, he killed Polydorus
and took the gold by force. A cursed hunger for money—
where will it drive a man's mind? After the trembling
left my bones I brought the Gods' word to my Father
first, and picked heads of our people. I asked their opinion.
60 All agreed to leave land which had cursed and polluted
hospitality, to trust our fleet to the Southwind.
First we began rites again. We mourned Polydorus:
a large earth-mound was built and altars erected for Manes

in sad sky-blue fillets and darkling cypress.
Trojan women, hair loosened, moved in a circle.
We brought out warmed milk, frothing in vessels,
and dishes of ritual blood. We lowered the spirit
in burial, loudly calling his name for the last time.
Soon as the sea could be trusted and breezes provided
70 a gentle swell—the Southwind's rustling call on the water—
friends crowded the shore and dragged down our vessels.
We left the harbor. Land and buildings receded.

The Oracle of Apollo

"We came on sacred ground tilled in the central Aegean,
dear to the Nereids' mother and Neptune.
This island had wandered from shore to shore till Apollo
moored it to hilly Gyaros again, and to Myconos,
making its farms stable. Now it can shrug at a wind-storm.
I sailed in here. Safe, quiet anchorage welcomed
our tired people. We emerged and revered the town of Apollo.
80 Anius, king of that people and priest of the Sun-God,
his head wreathed in sacred fillets of laurel,
met us and recognized an old friend in Anchises.
Host and guests joined hands and entered the household.
I prayed to the God in an old temple of granite.
'Lord of Thymbra, grant us a permanent city,
our own home, walls of a second Troy for exhausted
Trojans, left by the Greeks and a ruthless Achilles.
Command us: whom do we follow? Where do we travel and settle?
Give us a sign, Father—descend on our spirits.'
90 I'd scarcely spoken when all the doors of the temple
suddenly rattled and opened: the God's laurels and hillside
moved around me, the Delphic cauldron droned on its tripod.
I fell to the ground, prostrate. A voice came through to my
        hearing:
'Hard sons of Dardanus, the Earth which delivered
your parents first will take you back to her joyful
breast. Return: find your primordial Mother!
Sons of Aeneas, men born of your children,
sons of your sons, will rule everyone's country.'

Anchises Urges Return to Crete

"What high joy leaped at the voice of the Sun-God!
100 Everyone shouted. Where is that city, they wondered,
calling to wanderers? Where did Phoebus want a return to?

Then my Father remembered a story of elders.
He said, 'Listen, you leaders, learn and be hopeful.
Jupiter's great island of Crete lies in the middle
sea with Mount Ida. There's the crib of our people:
rich kingdoms, a hundred fine cities to live in!
Teucer, our grandest Father, sailed from there to Rhoetean
land first—if memory serves me correctly—
he chose that shore for a kingdom. Troy and the towers
110 of Trojans were not yet standing. We lived in that lowland.
Our Mother Cybele cares for Crete, for Corybants' cymbals
and groves on Ida, for mute faith in her mysteries.
Lions yield and are yoked to the Goddess's chariot!
Come, then. Follow the Gods' command where it's pointing.
Placate the Winds, make for the kingdom of Cnossus.
It's not a long run. If only Jupiter joins us,
the third dawn will rest our fleet on the coastline
of Crete.' He stopped and sacrificed duly at altars:
a bull for Neptune, a bull for you, brilliant Apollo,
120 a dark ram for the Storm-God, a light one for following
            Westwinds.
Rumors flitted: Idomeneus, the king, had been driven
from Crete, he'd left the land of his father abandoned,
every home cleared of Greeks and deserted.
We left the Ortygian harbor and flew on the sea-swell,
past the Wine-God's heights at Naxos, verdant Donysa,
Olearos, snow-peaked Paros and Cyclades scattered
at sea. We saw bubbling straits where islands had crowded.
The shouts of sailors mingled, loudly competing,
encouraging friends: 'Head for Crete, the land of our fathers!'
130 A wind came up astern and held our momentum.
We finally glided ashore at ancient Curetes.

Plague Strikes

"Anxious, I picked a site for raising walls of a city.
I gladly called it Pergamea, after my people.
I urged them to love our hearths and raise our citadel roof-beams.
In time the fleet lay high and dry on the beachsand.
The young were involved with new farmland and marriage.
I set down laws and arranged for homesites. But sudden
disease from a tainted tract of sky wasted our bodies.
Crops and wretched trees were blighted, a death-burdened season:
140 people ended their precious lives or they dragged on,
sick. Fields turned sterile, burned by the Dogstar.

Plants dried up and pale shoots took no nutrition.
My Father urged us back to the Ortygian oracle,
back to sea, to ask for help from Apollo:
the God would bring an end to exhaustion or tell us
who might help in our crisis, what course we might follow.

A Vision of Troy's Household Gods

"Then it was night. Land and livestock were sleeping.
I saw the sacred forms of the Phrygian House-Gods,
figures I'd brought from Troy when the heart of the city
150   flamed: standing close to my eyes while I lay there
sleeping, they shone with a glow clearer than moonlight
pouring through glass placed in its way at the full moon.
Then they spoke—their speech reduced my anxiety:
'All that Apollo would say if you sail to Ortygia,
look!—he sends us freely to sing in your household.
Since Troy was burned down we have followed your army.
With you commanding the fleet we've measured the sea-swells.
We'll also extol your future descendants in starlight,
and make your city an empire. And you: prepare for that city,
160   greatness for greatness! Take on the long labor and travel.
Move from this home. Apollo advised you at Delos
but never asked the coast of Crete to be settled.
There is a place, the Greeks called it Hesperia,
an ancient land with rich soil and powerful armies.
Oenotrians lived there; but now they say that a younger
nation named it Italy, after their leader.
That's our proper home. Dardanus grew up
there and Iasius, first father and leader of Trojans.
Rise quickly and bring to your long-lived father the joyful
170   word. There is no doubt: look for Etruscan
land in Italy. Cretan soil is forbidden by Jupiter.'

Departure from Crete

"Gods' voice and vision stunned me like thunder.
And that was no dream: I seemed to recognize faces
in person, mouths up close, wreaths on their foreheads.
Cool sweat soon flowed the length of my body.
I leaped from the bed and prayed, directed my upturned
hands to the sky and then I offered inviolate
gifts at the hearth. Rites finished, I gladly
spoke to Anchises, describing the whole situation.
180   He nodded: the double parentage of Troy was confusing:

a new mistake about old places had tricked him.
He said, 'My son—how Troy's fate can fatigue you!—
only Cassandra spoke of that chance in our future,
now I recall. She often prophesied Western
Land owed to our people, she sang of Italian kingdoms.
Who could believe Troy would venture to Western
Land? No one heeded Cassandra's vision at that time.
Yield to Apollo now. Better to follow this warning.'
All concurred and cheered when Anchises had finished.

A Storm at Sea

190 "We left that home as well. A few would remain there;
most set sail to run deserts of sea in our galleys.
After we reached deep water, with nothing of shoreline
left—sky everywhere, everywhere water—
blue-black stormclouds rose upright before us,
freighted with noise and night. Waves shivered in darkness,
quickly the wind came up amd tumbled enormous
rollers, in monstrous troughs we were jumbled and scattered.
Cloud concealed daylight, a squall-ridden darkness
removed the sky and at cloud-breaks lightning re-doubled.
200 Pushed off course by seas and wandering blindly,
Palinurus himself, our helmsman, could not distinguish
day from night or plot a course through the water.
We wandered at sea three whole days of obscuring,
dark mist, three whole nights without starlight.

The Island of the Harpies

"At last we sighted land at dawn of the fourth day.
Rising mountains appeared; smoke curled in the distance.
Our sail drooped and we bent to immediate rowing.
Oarsmen worked and the foam curled where they swept through
        the water.
Saved from the sea! The shore of a Strophades Island
210 received us first. Greeks had called them the Strophades
Islands: they stood in the wide Ionian, home for Celaeno
and other fearsome Harpies. After Phineius
had closed their former house they left that table in terror:
monsters grimmer than any, the worst epidemic
hauled up by angry Gods from Stygian water,
Harpies have girls' faces but guts of the foulest
droppings, hands with claws, and permanently whitened
mouths from hunger.

Led in here, we entered the harbor. We spotted
220   a fine herd afield. Imagine: cattle were scattered
across the grass and a flock of goats with no herdsman.
We rushed them. Calling on Gods, Jupiter mainly,
to share the prize, we speared some. Soon on the winding
shore we built up mats for a feast, an excellent banquet.

The Trojans Are Attacked

"Suddenly now in a fearsome dive from the mountains
Harpies arrived, their wings a loud clatter of flapping.
The tore at the meat with grimy talons and dirtied
the whole feast, badly stinking and frightfully screeching.
We moved to a deep hollow. Under a concave
230   cliff densely circled by trees and bristling shadow
we set out tables again and restored fire on the altars.
But noise pealed in the sky again from a hidden,
different quarter, talons hooked on the prime beef,
mouths defiled our food. Now I told my companions
to take up arms: we'd wage war on the horrible creatures.
They followed orders precisely, covering weapons
with grass and shrub, keeping shields in concealment.
Then, when Harpies made their racket and dove on the winding
shore, Misenus sent a signal from high in a lookout,
240   using a horn. My friends attacked. The fight was a strange one—
swords trying to bloody nauseous sea-birds.
They took no wounds, however, no swipe at a feather
or back, but flew up fast to the sky when their eating
was half done, leaving rancid claw-marks behind them.

Celaeno Lays her Curse

"One bird perched on a tall boulder—Celaeno.
A voice broke from her chest predicting disaster:
'War as well, you sons of Laomedon? Ready
to wage war for the bulls you killed, the heifers you slaughtered?
And drive innocent Harpies away from the realm of their fathers?
250   Well, then. Take my words to heart and remember:
what all-powerful Jupiter told to Phoebus, and Phoebus
to me, I'll show you—I'm the greatest of Furies—
set your course for Italy, Winds will be summoned,
reach your Italian port with permission to enter.
But no wall will surround the town you were promised
before desperate hunger and criminal killing
compel you to gnaw your own tables and eat them.'

She stopped and rose on the lift of her wings into forest.

The Trojans Leave Hurriedly

"Fear abruptly chilled and slowed my companions'
260 blood. Spirits dropped. They told me to battle
no more; to seek peace through prayer and promise,
whether the birds were foul, revolting, or godly.
My Father Anchises, palms upturned on the shoreline,
called on great Powers, named gifts that were due them
and prayed, 'Void that curse, you Gods, avert a disaster,
be pleased and save your devoted people.' He ordered
cables cut on the beach, sail loosened and shaken.
Southwind tensed our canvas, we fled on the foaming
water, our course directed by wind and by helmsman.
270 Already the woods of Zachynthos appeared on the water,
Dulichium, steep cliffs of Neritos, Samos.
We ran on past Laertes' kingdom, Ithaca's boulders,
cursing the land that nursed a savage, Ulysses.

Aeneas' Boast

"Mount Leucata soon appeared with its misty
ridgeline—Apollo's coast, dreaded by seamen.
We put in here, exhausted. We entered the little
city, anchors thrown from prows, our fleet on the beachsand.
We'd finally taken land which no one had hoped for.
We worshipped Jupiter, burning gifts at an altar.
280 Trojans gathered for games on Actium's beaches.
Bare, in slippery oil, my friends were engaging
in wrestling bouts, glad to have skirted a number
of Greek cities by keeping up speed past enemy centers.
The grand wheel of the sun meanwhile was turning.
Frozen winter chafed the water with Northwind.
I fastened a curved shield of bronze that was carried
by Abas, a great one, to fronting pillars, and wrote an inscription:

   AENEAS DEPRIVED CONQUERING GREEKS OF THESE WEAPONS.

Then I ordered men to their thwarts, to depart from the harbor.
290 Strokes competing, crewmen swept through the water.
Soon we were hidden from airy Phaeacian towers.
We followed Epirus' coast; we entered Chaonia's
port and climbed to the high town of Buthrotum.

Andromache and Helenus Are Alive

"Here an incredible story seized our attention:
Helenus, Priam's son, ruled Greeks in that city!
Through marriage he'd gained the scepter of Pyrrhus, son of
    Achilles,
Andromache passing again to a man of her homeland.
Stunned and moved, I burned with wonder and longing
to see the man and learn of this great transformation.
300 Leaving ships and shore, as I walked from the harbor,
by chance Andromache now was offering mourning
gifts of meal in a grove by a would-be Simois River
before the city. She called on spirits, the ashes
of Hector—they caused her tears—at a grassy but empty
tomb, a mound she'd sanctified along with two altars.
Now she saw me coming: Trojan weapons around me:
she lost her senses. Afraid we were terrible omens,
she stiffened, lost in some vision, the warmth of her marrow
left her: she fainted. In time she spoke to us weakly:
310 'Your form is real? You bring me word, is it truthful?
Son of the Goddess—alive! Or if nourishing light has been taken,
where is my Hector?' Tears flowed when she finished—
her crying filled the entire region. Alarmed by her anguish
I hardly spoke at all, just muttered some phrases.
'Yes, I'm alive—alive through every disaster.
You need not doubt it: you see what is real.
And you, who fell from a great marriage, God, what misfortune
claims you now? What Luck was right to revisit
Hector's Andromache? You serve as the wife of Pyrrhus?'
320 She lowered her glance and voice when she answered.
'The luckiest one of all was the virgin daughter of Priam,
ordered to die at the high wall of Troy, by her enemy's
death-mound. No casting of Greek lots would oppress her:
she'd never touch some lord-and-master's bed as a slave-girl.
But we, driven to different seas when our houses were burned
    down,
put up with a proud son of Achilles, an insolent offspring.
I bore him slaves. In time he went chasing Hermione,
Leda's grandchild: he wanted a wedding in Sparta.
He turned me over to Helenus, slave to be had by
330 slave. But Orestes, fired by intense love for a stolen
bride, driven by Furies for old crimes, overtaking
Pyrrhus, hacked him down from behind at the shrine of his
    father.

Pyrrhus' death restored and yielded part of the kingdom
to Helenus then, who called the meadows Chaonian,
called it all Chaonia, after Chaon, the Trojan.
He added a citadel high as Troy's on the hilltop.
But you—what wind, course and Fates were you given?
What God landed you here, unaware, on our coastline?
What of your boy, Ascanius? Living, breathing the fresh air?
340 In Troy already . . .
still, does the boy love and feel the loss of his mother,
and some of the old male spirit and courage
stirred by his father Aeneas and Hector, his uncle?'
She kept on weeping while speaking, uselessly crying.
She mourned and mourned.

A New and Lesser Troy

                                  Helenus came from the city
wall, the son of Priam, a leader with many companions.
Seeing his own people he gladly conducted
us back to his home, often speaking and weeping together.
I went along and saw a little Troy that resembled
350 the great one, a near-dry brook they'd labeled the Xanthus,
the threshold and frame of a Scaean gate. I embraced it.
My Trojan friends were also enjoying the city.
The king welcomed us all on a portico grandly.
We raised cups in the central hall to the Wine-God.
He served us a feast on gold. We lifted our vessels.

Aeneas Asks for a Prophecy

"So there a day passed, and another. A sea-breeze
called to our sail, Southwind swelling the canvas.
I sought out Helenus, asking king to be prophet.
'Son of Troy, seer for Gods, you studied Apollo's
360 tripod, the laurels at Claros, you sense the stars' intimations,
birds' language, the fleeting omens of feathers:
speak to me now. Gods favored and told me
of all this travel. Every Sky-God powerfully urged me
to seek out Italy, aim for faraway country.
Only a Harpy, Celaeno, sang of a startling
portent, revolting to speak of, and blamed our regrettable anger
and sinful hunger. What risks can I skirt at the outset?
To get by great hardships what course can I follow?'

Apollo Speaks Through Helenus

"First Helenus killed steers according to custom.
370 Praying for Gods' peace he loosened the garlands
around his priestly head, took my hand in his own hand
and led me, awed by your strong will, to your threshold,
        Apollo.
Finally, priest and voice of the Sun-God, he chanted:
'Son of the Goddess: great signs have established
clearly your path at sea: heaven's King has allotted
your Fates, rolling the wheel: your cycle is turning.
I'll show you some things—there are many—to help you
watch and wander strange sea-lanes in safety,
reaching Ausonian moorage. Fates prevent me from knowing
380 more: Juno, Saturn's daughter, stops me from speaking.
First the Italian soil you think you are close to—
thinking to reach, unaware, a neighboring harbor—
it's far. Uncharted seas keep you away from that country.
Your oars must bend in Trinacrian water beforehand,
your fleet wander the salt swells of Ausonia,
Underworld lakes, and the island of Circe, Aeaea,
before you can safely set out land for your city.
I'll teach you signs: keep them stored in your memory.
You'll find a huge sow by the flow of a secret
390 river to ease your concern. Near oaks at the seashore
her womb will bear thirty strenuous young ones:
she'll lie on the ground, white as the young at her nipples.
There's the place for your city, and sure rest from your labor.
Don't be afraid of distant prospects of eating your tables.
Fates will find an escape: Phoebus will come when you call him.
Avoid land on the near Italian coastline,
the closer shore, bathed by the flow of our own sea:
vicious Greeks have settled all of the cities,
there Locrians mass the walls of Narycium,
400 Idomeneus of Crete fills Salentinian clearings
with Greek soldiers. There little Petelia
trusts walls of a Meliboean prince, Philoctetes.
Now, when your ships have crossed our sea and stand on your
        shoreline,
set down altars directly, offer your pledges,
wearing a purple robe. Your hair should be covered,
stopping every hostile form from opposing your holy
fire in the Gods' honor or troubling your omens.

Your friends and you indeed should keep to this custom.
Faith and rite should stay pure in your children.
410 Then, when the Winds move you away to Sicilian coastline,
as close headlands appear to diverge at Pelorus,
hold to port! The water and land on the port side
are long and roundabout; still, run from the waves on the
    starboard.
Those land masses once tore from each other—
aeons of time can cause change that's titanic—
a vast rupture, they say, where both had been sharing
the same stretch. Violent water thrust in between them,
cut the Sicilian side from Hesperia, leaving
town and field divided by beach and turbulent narrows.
420 Scylla blocks the right side. Hungry Charybdis
blocks the left—three times each day she sucks a tremendous
wave down to her Underworld depths and uplifts it
again to the sky, lashing stars with her water!
Scylla stays in a blind cave, unobtrusive—
only her mouth snaps out to drag ships onto boulders.
Human down to the waist, her form has a virgin's
lovely breasts; below, her shape is gross as a sea-beast's,
tails of dolphins tangling with wolves in her belly.
Better to wander slowly Sicily's coastline,
430 gaze at Pachynus—a long, circuitous journey—
than see just once the vast cave of that monster,
Scylla, her sea-blue dogs and re-echoing rockpiles.
Moreover if Helenus knows the future and merits
faith as a prophet—his mind filled with truth by Apollo—
more than all else, son of the Goddess, I warn you
of one thing, I'll tell you one thing over and over:
pray and honor the will first of powerful Juno.
Intone your vows gladly to Juno and conquer
the high Lady with humble gifts: you'll finally win her.
440 Sent from Sicily next, you'll leave for Italy's coastline.
Borne there you'll reach the city of Cumae,
lakes of Gods and rustling woods of Avernus.
You'll find a Sibyl chanting the future in trances,
committing to leaves in a deep cave her names and predictions.
Whatever song the virgin inscribes on leaves she arranges
in sequence and sets them back in the cavern.
They stay right there in place, remaining in order,
unless a door opens: even a slender
breeze can move and ruffle the delicate foliage.

450 She never cares to catch them in flight through the rocky
    cave or connect and recall oracles later.
    Unhelped people leave with contempt for the seer in her cavern.
    You should stay. Don't think much of loss or delay here
    though friends chide you and deep-sea powerful currents
    call to your sail, favorable Winds filling your canvas.
    No: linger and pray for the Sibyl's predictions.
    Ask her to open her mouth herself and willingly speak out.
    She'll tell you of coming war, people in Italy,
    how to escape from some force, or carry some burden.
460 Revere that woman. She'll give you plans to rely on.
    That is all the warning my voice may deliver.
    Go and act. Carry Troy's greatness to heaven.'

The Trojans Leave Buthrotum

    "After the prophet spoke in such an encouraging manner
    he ordered gifts of heavy gold and ivory sections
    brought to the fleet. He crammed our holds with enormous
    weights of silver, bronze bowls from Dodona,
    a breastplate with triple gold stitching and linking,
    an excellent helmet, the apex tufted with feathers,
    and armor of Pyrrhus himself. He added gifts for my Father,
470 added guides and horses,
    re-supplied crewmen, and armed my men with his weapons.
    Anchises meanwhile had ordered the fleet to be fitted
    with sail to avoid delay when the wind should be stirring.
    Phoebus' prophet, with great deference, told him,
    'Anchises, deemed the worthy and proud consort of Venus,
    cared for by God, taken twice from Troy's devastation:
    look, now: Ausonian land is yours, sail there and seize it!
    Only move with care through the water on this side:
    the far Ausonian shore Apollo has opened.
480 Go,' he said, 'take joy in your son's devotion. Beyond that
    why talk? Words will stall the surge of the Southwind.'
    Andromache, too, though sad at our final departure,
    brought us clothing designed in golden embroidery.
    Still not failing to honor, she weighted Ascanius
    down with a Phrygian chlamys, her loom's gift, and she told him,
    'Take it all as a sign, my child, and remember
    the handiwork and long love of Andromache,
    Hector's wife. My last gifts are yours for the asking—
    you only surviving sign of my own Astyanax!
490 The same eyes, hand and mouth . . . and your ages

too would be close now if my son were still growing.'
I spoke myself, tears welled as we left there,
'Live in joy. The course of your luck is already
finished; we're still moved by one Fate or another.
Your rest has begun: no fields of sea to be plowed up,
no need to search for land of an ever-retreating
Italy. Look—a stream like the Xanthus, a type of our city
built with your own hands! Your omens are better,
I trust. You're less exposed to the Greeks and their army.
500 If I ever reach the Tiber, the land in the Tiber's
demesne, if city walls are bestowed on my people,
we'll make our states acquainted someday like neighbors:
we'll make one Troy in spirit then, your Epirus
and our Hesperia, both descended from Dardanus,
both with the same setbacks: the union will last in our children.'

The First Sighting of Italy

"Driven along at sea we came close to Ceraunian
cliffs—the shortest distance by sea to Ausonia.
In time the sun dropped. We saw mountains in shadow.
Oars were assigned, we soon dotted a shoreline,
510 we lay in a welcome lap of sand by the water,
anxious and weary. Sleep spread through our bodies.
Night had not yet passed through half of her cycle,
drawn by the Hours, when Palinurus rose in a hurry
from bed to check the wind. He listened for breezes,
noting every star gliding through peaceful
skies—Arcturus, the twin Bears and the Hyades,
rain-signs—he scanned the golden-armored Orion.
Soon as he saw the whole sky quiet and steady
he signaled loudly astern. Our course re-established,
520 we broke camp and spread out feather-like canvas.
Stars were fleeing, Dawn was blushing already
just as we saw dim, far-off hills: the Italian
coast. Achates called out first, 'Italy!' loudly:
quickly our crewmen called out, 'Italy!' cheering.
My Father Anchises crowned a large bowl with a garland,
filled it with wine and called to the Sky-Gods while standing
high on the stern:
'Lords of the land and sea, Masters of stormwinds,
bring us an easy course with following breezes.'
530 The winds he prayed for gathered: a harbor had opened
now and closer, a temple of Pallas appeared and a fortress.

Crewmen furled sail; we swung our prows to the shoreline.
Eastwind and surf had shaped the port like an archer's
bow. A reef protruded, bubbling the water.
The port lay hidden—high cliffs were a double
wall, or hanging arms—the temple removed from the shore-line.

The Wrong Shore

"I saw the first omen here in a meadow:
four white horses, grazing apart on the fieldgrass.
My Father Anchises: 'The land is unfriendly and warlike.
540 The mounts are armed for war, threatening battle.
Yet the same horse trained for a chariot
once can bear the agreeable yoke of a farmer:
hope for peace,' he said. We prayed for the holy
force of Pallas, the shield-clasher, and first to receive us:
we cheered, our heads in Phrygian veils by her altar.
Helenus clearly had told us which rites were most urgent:
we offered the vows and victims he'd ordered for Juno.
Wasting no time, the sequence of ritual finished,
we turned the ends of our sail-weighed yard-arms to seaward.
550 We ran from those Greek homes, a land we distrusted.

Avoiding Charybdis

"Soon we saw Tarentum, Hercules' Bay—if the story
is true—and rising to face it, Lacinian Juno's
temple. We spied a wrecker of ships, Sylaceum;
the fortress at Caulon; and rising from far-off water, Mount Etna.
We heard a loud roaring of sea and a pounding
of rocks in the distance, broken sound on the beaches
where surf leaped and sands were seething and swirling.
My Father Anchises: 'Surely that sound is Charybdis.
Helenus warned of her cliff and perilous rockpile.
560 Men—together—lean to your rowing, deflect us.'
Following orders precisely first Palinurus
swung the creaking bow to port through the water,
all the squadron heeled to port, rowing and sailing:
we rose to the sky on an arching crest and we sank in
the same wave's trough to the Underworld level.
We heard calls from the cliff three times, from a belly-like cavern;
three times we saw the stars dripping with sea-spray.
We tired meanwhile. Wind and sunlight were leaving.

The Land of the Cyclops

"Unsure of our course we glided ashore near the Cyclops.
570 The cove itself was large and safe from the sea-wind
but close to the fearsome thunder and wreckage of Etna,
which coughed up black cloud often to heaven,
pitchy, twisting smoke and flickering ashes.
Throwing up globes of fire that lapped at the starlight
it often heaved up high some fragment or boulder
torn from the mountain's gut, or exposed to the open
air rumbling lava boiled in the deepest interior.
They say Enceledas, half consumed by a lightning,
was weighed down by that mass—Etna's entirety
580 pressed his body—he exhaled flame like a ruptured
forge when he changed position wearily, smoke-cloud
often wreathing the sky. All of Sicily trembled.
Hiding in woods that night we lived through outrageous
portents, unable to see a cause of the uproar.
Every star's fire went out, the clear constellations
and high zenith gone. Mist darkened the upper
air, unhealthy night cloud obstructed the moonlight.

Achaemenides' Tale

"Later, when first light appeared and Aurora
parted the sky's dewy grey for some sunlight,
590 a man suddenly stepped from the woods—or an unknown
species of man—in extreme hunger and weakness,
the pitiful shape humbly extended a hand to our beach-camp.
We stared back. Dirty and grim, with a scraggly
beard and clothes linked by thorns, he was otherwise clearly
Greek. He'd once been sent to Troy in arms from that country.
Now, seeing Trojan weapons and Trojan
garb so close, he stopped for a while at the vision,
frightened. He took a step, then threw himself on the beachsand
headlong, weeping and praying: "I swear by the starlight,
600 by every God and the sky's breatheable daylight:
take me, you Trojans, do whatever your destined
nation will do. You know I sailed with the Grecian
fleet that warred on Troy, I admit it, we wanted your House-Gods.
For which, if the crime or insult was monstrous,
scatter my flesh in the sea, some desert of water—
I'll die but gladly die at the hand of a human.'
He stopped to embrace my leg. He clung to an ankle,

groveling. Asking his name, I urged him to tell us
what luck had forced him here, what bloodline he'd sprung from.
610 My Father Anchises himself, with the least hesitation,
gave him his hand, a pledge on the spot. It strengthened his spirits.
Shortly the man set aside terror and told us,
'I'm from Ithacan country, a friend of sorry Ulysses.
My name's Achaemenides. My father was poor, Adamastus;
his changed luck compelled me to sail for your Trojan
shore. Later, leaving a cruel household in horror,
thoughtless friends abandoned me here by the Cyclops'
huge cave—a house of blood and scraps decomposing,
obscure inside, immense—and a monster so tall he could knock at
620 the high stars. You Gods, clear such plagues from the country!
No one watched or spoke to that creature in comfort.
He fed on the dark blood and innards of wretches,
I saw it myself: the grotesque hand apprehended
two of our number, and lying back in the cavern
he broke their bodies on rock, spattering even
the entrance with blood. I watched him gnaw on their members,
flowing in dark red, his teeth shaking their still-warm
joints. But not with impunity. Unable to bear it,
Ulysses recalled himself in our horrible crisis.
630 Soon as the Cyclops, filled with flesh, in a wine-doze,
let fall his drooping neck and sprawled through the cavern
immensely, sleeping and belching pieces of clotted
blood mixed with wine, we prayed to the strongest
Powers and cast lots. Together we rushed him,
surrounded the one huge eye with our pointed
stakes and stabbed where it lay under the brutal
forehead, big as a Greek shield or a lamp of the Sun-God.
At last we took revenge for the loss of our comrades.

The Trojans Must Leave Quickly

" 'Run now, escape from this beach, you miserable people—
640 slash your cables!
Huge and fierce as Polyphemus stood in that cavern,
corraling wooly lambs or milking their udders,
a hundred more unspeakable Cyclops inhabit
the winding shore and wander high in the mountains.
Three times the horns of the moon have filled up with moonlight
since I first dragged my life through their forest,
by empty bog and den of beast. I saw the enormous

monsters on cliffs. I shook when they called, when their footsteps
    came thudding.
Cornel branches doled out pebbles of berries,
650 torn-up plant-roots fed me: a barren existence.
I surveyed the whole shore and finally spotted
your fleet coming. Now, whatever the outcome,
I offer myself. It's enough to run from a blood-clan of terror—
better that Trojans take my life however you kill me.'

The Giants Come Closer

"He'd scarcely finished when there, high on a ridgeline,
we saw Polyphemus himself, a cumbersome herdsman
moving sheep. He made for a beach he remembered:
a hulking, dreaded, deformed creature, blind in his only
eye. One hand propped his gait with a pine-trunk.
660 Thick-wooled sheep joined him—the criminal's little
joy and comfort.
After he reached the shallows he moved into deeper
water and flushed the stabbed eye of a trickle
of blood, grinding teeth and grumbling. He waded
through open sea—and still no wave had wetted his middle!
We hurried to leave. Nervous, we took the deserving
beggar aboard, quietly severed our cables,
leaned on the oars and swept hard through the water.
He heard us. He turned and walked to the sound of our voices.
670 Then, knowing he lacked power to reach us—
he could not match our speed in Ionian water—
he raised a gigantic cry, causing the surface
and depths of the sea to shudder. Sicily's heartland
shook; Etna boomed from its crooked interior.
Every Cyclops, the whole tribe, was alerted.
Running from forest and mountain heights, they filled up the
    shoreline.
We watched them stand there frustrated, each with a savage
eye, holding heads in the sky—brothers of Etna.
Their feared council looked like a stand of oaks in the open
680 air with high crowns or cypresses lofting
their cones, like Jupiter's tall trees or a grove of Diana.

Escape Eastward Then Westward

"Pointed fear drove us headlong, wherever—
we shook out canvas, wind stretched it and followed—
to where Helenus warned us away: to Charybdis and Scylla!

Death lay on either side by the slightest misjudgment:
we must steady our course. We struggled to turn back
canvas and look: a Northwind arrived, sent from the narrow
straits of Pelorus. I rode past the Pantagias' delta
(where rocks are alive) and the Bay of Megara where Thapsus
690 lay. Achaemenides pointed them out while he wandered
again coastline passed by his wretched leader, Ulysses.
A stretch of island lay in Sicilian water,
facing surf-dashed Plemyrium. Elders had called it
Ortygia, saying that Alph, the God-River of Elis,
found a secret path under the sea-bed and later
mingled with Sicily's waves—your mouth, Arethusa!
We worshipped supreme Lords of the place as commanded.
From there I passed the rich soil and marsh of Helorus,
then the high cliffs and jutting rock of Pachynus—
700 we scraped some. Soon Camerinus loomed in the distance,
a place never allowed by the Fates to be troubled.
Plains and the town of Gela—named from a barbarous river.
Steep and distant walls of a great city, Acragas,
appeared, once the breeder of spirited horses.
Wind permitting I skirted the palm-flecked Selinus.
I dodged rugged surf and blind rock—Lilybaeum's.

The Death of Anchises

"Now Drepanum's coast and harbor received me,
joyless: for here I lost the man who had suffered
through every sea-storm, lightened every disaster
710 and worry: Anchises. Best of fathers, you left me,
worn down. I'd pulled you from great danger for nothing.
The prophet Helenus warned of many anxieties
but not this grief—nor did that scare-bird, Celaeno.
My worst burden came at the far end of my journey.
Then some God drove me away to your coastline."

The Story is Finished

So Aeneas, our ancestor, told of his journey
alone to the anxious crowd, reliving commandments
of Gods. He'd come to the end at last and was quiet.

IV

THE PASSION OF DIDO

Advice from a Sister

Ah, but the queen had hurt for a long time from a grievous
wound that took her blood. Blind flame had consumed her:
Aeneas' Trojan pride and vigor came back to her over
and over, the man's looks and speech had embedded,
clung to her breast. This love brought no peace to her body.
When Phoebus' lamp brightened and gazed on the country,
Dawn parting the dewy shadows of heaven,
she felt quite ill. She told her affable sister,
"Anna, my sister, what dreams have scared and confused me!
10 How strange this man, the guest who's advanced on our throne-
        room,
what bearing and looks, what a strong chest in that armor!
Yes—my faith's not empty—I know he's born of a Goddess:
fear would reveal low birth. My God, what a Fate-tossed
life he described, what war and exhaustion he told of!
If I were not so set, so firmly decided
never to join in marriage again with a person,
after my first love died and deprived me,
if every suitor's torch and bed were not tedious . . .
I might be able to yield to a single involvement.
20 Anna, to tell you the truth, since poor Sychaeus, my husband,
died, since an evil brother scattered our House-Gods,
only Aeneas has moved me, bending conviction,
stirring feeling. In old fire I know there are cinders.
Yet I'd hope the depths of the earth would be opened

first and strongest Jupiter's lightning drive me to darkness,
deep into Erebus' night and colorless shadow,
before I'd break a law of Shame or relax it.
The man who married me first took all of my passion.
I pray he'll keep and protect my love when I'm buried."
30   She stopped—tears had welled and dropped to her bosom.
Anna told her, "Dearer than Light to your sister!
Why waste youth on constant grief and aloneness,
never knowing sweetness and joy, those children of Venus?
You think love concerns much the ashes of dead men?
Perhaps. But no one suitor has moved you from mourning,
no Libyan, no one from Tyre before. You scoffed at Iarbas
and other chiefs nurtured on African triumph,
land and wealth; if love delights you now will you fight it?
Consider too the men whose land you have settled:
40   here, Gaetulian villagers, warlike invincible people,
wild Numidians close by, the perilous Syrtes;
there, dry stretches of desert and widely
marauding Barcaeans. Need I mention your brother,
the rising threat of war from Tyre?
I truly believe some God favored the Trojan
fleet's course. The wind had Juno's approval.
Sister! Imagine the city and towering kingdom
from such a marriage: with Trojans joining our army,
what great affairs and glory Carthage will climb to!
50   Only ask for divine favor: with ritual victims
welcome the Trojans. Knit some pretext to keep them—
winter weather at sea, rains from Orion,
damage to all their ships, the sky in disorder."

Love Sacrifices

So a sister's words fed the fire of her passion.
Doubt yielded to hope. Modesty weakened.
They went to a shrine first and prayed at the altar
for peace: the right sheep were chosen and slaughtered
for Ceres, the law-bearer, for lordly Bacchus, Apollo,
and mainly for Juno, who cared for marital union.
60   Dido, herself radiant, carried a vessel
and poured wine between the horns of a white-coated heifer
while Gods looked on. Each day she renewed with procession
or gift at a fat-rich altar. She peered in the opened
breast of a dying beast and studied the entrails.
Ignorant ways of augury! What joy can a temple

or vow bring to a love-craze? Soft flame was devouring
her marrow still. Her breast's wound was quiet but spreading.

Love Moods

Feverish, cursed, Dido restlessly wandered
the whole town like a doe struck by an arrow
70 in Crete's forest, hit off-guard by a distant
herdsman trying a shot and unknowingly leaving
metal lodged: the deer dodges through undergrowth, wanders
Dicta's ravine, but the point clings to the ribcage and kills her.
Dido soon conducted Aeneas through Carthage,
displaying Sidonian wealth, a ready-made city.
Starting to speak she'd break off right in the middle.
Then with daylight lapsing she'd call for a banquet
again and wildly plead for a hearing of Trojan
hardship. Again she'd dote on the mouth of the speaker.
80 After they left, the dim moonlight declining
in turn, when setting stars inclined her to drop off,
she pined alone in the empty hall and reclined on
an empty couch. He'd gone but she heard him and saw him.
She often hugged Ascanius, thrilled by the father's
image, as if to escape an unwordable passion.
A tower she'd started stopped rising. Her young men
worked no weapons. Port and fortifications
were unprepared for war. Work was unfinished.
Projecting walls and sky-tall cranes were inactive.

Juno and Venus Confer

90 Now, when the dear wife of Jupiter noticed
sickness gripping Dido, her name no match for the madness,
Saturn's daughter approached Venus and told her,
"You've certainly won a rich prize, exceptional honor
for you and your Boy. What grand, memorable power:
two great Gods deceive and conquer a woman!
Yes, I've known how very suspicious of Carthage
you are. You fear our high rampart and buildings.
Where will it end? What's next in this bitter contention?
Why not work instead for lasting peace, for a marriage
100 contract? You've gained what your whole spirit had aimed for—
Dido burning in love, her marrow a trail of madness—
so now let's rule this people together with equal
omens. Let Dido serve a Phrygian husband,
placing people of Tyre in your hand as a dowry."

Venus felt deceived. Juno was lying,
turning the rule of Italian shores into Punic.
Still she started to answer, "Who could refuse you,
madly choosing to wage war with your godhead?
If only Luck would approve the action you speak of!
110 Unsure Fates concern me. If Jupiter wants it—
one city standing for both Tyrian and Trojan
people, refugees mixed or joined in a compact—
you're his wife: by law you probe his will with your prayer:
you lead, I'll follow." Juno regally answered,
"I'll do that work. Now, for what is impending,
listen. I'll briefly describe a way it can happen.
Love-sad Dido is ready, joined with Aeneas,
to go hunting in woods tomorrow when daybreak
leads out beams of the Sun, revealing the landscape.
120 I will darken clouds, pack them with hailstones:
while trembling beaters lash nets in a hollow
I'll send down squalls and thunder: I'll rattle the cosmos.
Groups will scatter in night-like darkness for cover.
Dido will rush to the same cave as the Trojan
leader. I'll be there. Assure me you're willing:
I'll join and pronounce them surely and properly married.
There's our wedding." Not opposed to the offer,
Venus agreed. But she saw and smiled at the cunning.

Preparations for a Hunt

Dawn arose in due time, leaving the Ocean
130 behind. Handpicked men moved through the gateways
at sunrise with loose-strung nets and wide-pointed lances,
snares and scenting dogs, and a rush of Massylian horsemen.
The queen stayed in her room. Below at the threshold
Carthaginian chiefs waited. Her mount was a dazzling
purple and gold, frothing his bit, aggressively stamping.
Finally she emerged with a huge party around her.
She wore a Sidonian chlamys, hemmed and embroidered,
her quiver was made of gold, her hair in a golden
knot, her purple robe held by a golden
140 clasp. Trojan friends, too, with a happy Iulus,
marched along, Aeneas himself the most graceful
of all when he rode up, linking their columns together:
just like Apollo leaving the Xanthus in winter,
his Lycian home, to see his motherly Delos,
renewing the dance when Dryopians honor and circle

altars with Crete's people and daubed Agathyrsians:
the Sun-God himself striding a ridgeline of Cynthus,
the flow of his hair checked by a delicate gold-twined
wreath, and shouldering jumbling arrows: Aeneas
150   rode that lightly, his face exceptionally handsome.
After they reached a high plateau, impassable wetland,
look—wild goats flushed from escarpments
ran downhill and deer bolted from other
parts, crossing an open field in a column,
massing a dustcloud running down from the mountain.
The boy Ascanius, proud of his vigorous charger,
already had raced past various groups in the central
lowland: he vowed and prayed for spirited quarry,
a sweating boar from the heights or a sand-colored lion.

Juno Sends a Storm

160   The sky meanwhile began to rumble profoundly.
Rain followed and changed to a mixture of hailstones.
Young Trojan and Tyrian company scattered
at random through fields. The Trojan grandson of Venus,
alarmed, looked for cover. Streams rushed from the hillsides.

A Love Cave

Dido came to the same cave as the Trojan
leader. Primal Earth and Juno, Goddess of Marriage,
gave a sign to the knowing Air, and the lightning
flashed at this rite. Nymphs called from a hilltop.
That was the first evil day, the first of her dying,
170   for Dido. No longer concerned with appearance or rumor,
dwelling no longer now on a secret liaison,
she called it "marriage." The word covered her weakness.

No Evil is Faster

Rumor instantly moved through large Libyan cities.
No other evil we know is faster than Rumor,
thriving on speed and becoming stronger by running.
Small and timid at first, then borne on a light air,
she flits over ground while hiding her head in a cloud-top.
Mother Earth, they say, deeply provoked by the Sky-Gods,
bore this daughter last: Enceladus' sister
180   and Coeus', light on her feet and agile at flying,
but broad and fearful: a monster whose bodily plumage
matches her numerous leering eyes (amazing to hear of),

her many mouths, upraised ears and jabbering accents.
At night she flaps between earth and sky in the shadows,
buzzing—her eyes won't yield to the pleasure of sleeping.
By day she squats on a house roof like a watchman
high in his tower, scaring eminent townsmen,
telling some truth but clinging to lies and distortion.
Now she filled people with various gossip,
190   gladly singing both her fact and her fiction:
Aeneas had sprung from a Trojan bloodline and come here,
lovely Dido accepted the man as her husband,
now they passsed a long winter together in pleasure,
thralls of a shameless desire, forgetting their kingship.
The Goddess spread her dirt on the lips of the people.

Love Frustration

Swiftly she veered in flight to a ruler, Iarbas,
scorching his mind with chatter and building up anger.
Son of a ravished African Nymph and of Hammon,
Iarbas had built in his broad kingdom a hundred
200   shrines and altars to Jupiter, blessing the watchful,
long-lived flames for his God. Fat-dripping victims
bloodied the ground; portals flowered with various garlands.
Bitterly smarting now where Rumor had burned him
he prayed at a shrine with the God's power around him,
palms upturned, humbly begging of Jupiter often:
"All-powerful Father, for whom my Maurusian people
feast on embroidered couches and offer up wine-gifts,
you see all this? You hurl thunderbolts, Father:
it's foolish to dread them? Your blind flashes in cloudbanks
210   cowing the mind, rumbling heaven: they're empty?
A woman wandered our land, paid to establish
a skimpy town, we gave her shore-land for plowing,
laws for the place: this woman, who spurned our proposal
of marriage, takes as lord of her kingdom Aeneas.
Now even a Paris attended by eunuchs,
hair oiled, his chin wound in a Lydian headdress,
can take and own her. Surely we carried our presents
to all your shrines and cherished your glory for nothing."
He spoke and prayed like that, holding an altar.

Jupiter Sends Down Mercury

220   The strongest God heard him. He turned and looked on the royal
halls where the lovers now had forgotten their better

name. He summoned Mercury next and advised him,
"Hurry, my son: call for the Westwind and glide on
your wings to the Trojan prince who dallies in Punic
Carthage, neglecting walls our Fates will provide him.
Carry my word through the air quickly and tell him:
you're not the man promised to God by your lovely
Mother who saved you twice from Greeks and their weapons:
he was to rule Italy, fully an empire,
230 a people who'd clamor for war, descended from Teucer's
high bloodline, submitting the whole world to their treaties.
If all that glory in great affairs will not fire you,
if honor itself won't make you carry your burden,
think of your fatherhood: don't keep Rome from Iulus.
What do you plan and hope for dawdling with hostile
people, ignoring Lavinian land and Ausonian children?
Sail: that's the point. Give him that message."
The God Mercury prepared to obey his majestic
Father's command by strapping his feet in the golden
240 shoes first which would carry him high over water
and land, each wing on the footwear faster than gale-wind.
He took the caduceus next which could summon the pallid
spirits from Orcus or send them down to Underworld sorrow,
give or remove sleep, and sign the lids of a dead man.
Its force could drive a wind or help him in swimming
through stormcloud. Already he noted the steeps of a mountain,
the hard peak of Atlas, supporting the ecliptic—
Atlas, whom dark clouds constantly circle,
the pine-carrying top pelted by Northwind and downpour,
250 shoulders covered in snow, waterfalls plunging
from the old chin, his beard bristling with glacier.
Mercury stopped here first, maintaining his balance
with wingbeats. Then his whole body dove in a headlong
descent like a bird circling a shoreline and diving
fast into water close to rocks where the fish are:
that's how the God flew from a midpoint in heaven
to Libyan shore and sand, cutting through crosswind—
truly his mother's father's grandson, raised on Cyllene.

The God Rebukes Aeneas

Soon as he touched with winged feet by a cottage,
260 he saw Aeneas founding defenses and building
new homes—the sword he wore a starring of yellow
jasper, the cape that hung from one shoulder a burning

Tyrian purple, a lavish present that Dido
had made, weaving gold thread in the webwork.
Mercury stopped him fast. "Laying foundations
for high Carthage now? Building a beautiful woman's
town, sadly forgetting your own realm and resources?
The Gods' Ruler himself dispatched me from brilliant
Olympus: his will rotates the land and the heavens:
270   he told me himself to carry this word on the fast-moving air-waves.
What do you plan or hope for, idling in Libyan country?
If taking glory in great affairs will not move you,
if honor itself won't make you carry your burden,
look to Ascanius: growing, in hope of inheriting
Roman land. An Italian kingdom is owed to
Iulus." Cyllenius broke off speech and he left him
there in the midst of that warning, he vanished from human
sight in the distance, buoyed on a tenuous updraft.

Love Confusion

Aeneas was truly amazed, struck dumb by the vision.
280   Words stuck in his throat; his hair bristled in terror.
He yearned to escape, to leave that pleasureable country,
stunned by the great warning and power of heaven.
But how should he act? The queen would surely be outraged:
how could he dare approach or begin to address her?
He thought it out quickly, distinguishing this way and that way,
taking different views, considering all sides.
One option seemed, among the alternatives, worthwhile.
He told Sergestus, Mnestheus and daring Serestus
to ready the fleet quietly, gather the crewmen,
290   break out arms on the beach, and improvise reasons
for any strange move. With excellent Dido
doubting, meanwhile, her great love could be injured,
Aeneas would try at the gentlest time to approach her
and speak: he'd look for the right way. Everyone quickly
and gladly prepared to obey the commands of their leader.

Love Awareness and Outrage

Ah, but the queen suspected deceit. Can a lover
be fooled by anyone? First she heard of their movements.
Fearing it all, though safe, she fumed. Maliciously Rumor
told her the fleet was armed and ready to travel.
300   She felt angry, helpless. She heatedly wandered
the city the way Bacchae react to their brandished

icons when shouts to the Wine-God startle and call them
at night to Mount Cithaeron's biennial revels.
At length confronting Aeneas she willfully told him,
"You actually hoped to hide the extent of this malice?
To break faith and sneak from my country in silence?
Our love won't keep you, the hand that you gave me
once? Or hard death coming to Dido?
No. You even load your ships under a winter
310 sky, rush off to sea surrounded by Northwind.
Ruthless man! What if the home and land you are seeking
were known and friendly—if ancient Troy were surviving—
would ships go looking for Troy in billowing water?
You run from *me?* My tears and the hand that you gave me
implore you—I'm left with nothing else in my folly—
our marriage rite, the wedding we started together,
if I've deserved well of you, think of the pleasure
I gave you, if any, pity a house that is shaken:
change your mind. If prayer has a place then I pray you.
320 You're the reason Numidian chiefs and Libyan people
hate me, my Tyrians hate me—*you* are the reason
my shame went out, my former name—and my only
approach to the stars. My guest, what death do you leave me?
Is 'guest' all that I have? Once you were 'husband' . . .
Why live on? Either my brother Pygmalion
wrecks my walls, or Iarbas, the African, makes me a captive.
At least if I'd borne your child before we had parted,
if only an infant were here, a little Aeneas
to play in my hall and go on recalling your features,
330 I shouldn't seem so utterly seized and abandoned."

Demands of God and Family

She stopped there. Aeneas, warned by Jupiter, struggled
to keep his vision steady. He deeply repressed his emotion.
He answered soon, briefly: "My queen, I'll never deny them—
all the claims you have power to list, and deserve to.
For me there'll never be shame to remember Elissa
while spirit and memory themselves last in my body.
I'll speak of my cause in brief. I never hoped to dissemble
and run off—don't think that. And I never extended
a husband's torch or entered a marital contract.
340 If God's word had allowed me to live out my life there,
freely arranging my own concerns and my omens,
I'd live in the city of Troy first and care for a precious

remnant of people. Priam's high roof would be standing,
I'd try to restore Troy myself for the losers.
No: Grynaean Apollo commands me to Italy.
Wrest Italian greatness, the lots of Lycia tell me:
there's my love and homeland. If towers of Carthage,
the sight of an African city, engage you Phoenicians,
why should you hate Trojans for settling Ausonian
350 land? It's right for us too to seek out a kingdom.
My Father Anchises warned me often when midnight
covered fields in damp shadow: whenever the burning
stars appeared his form troubled and frightened my dreaming.
My boy Ascanius, too: should I injure the person
I love, defraud him of Western Land he's destined to govern?
Even the Gods' herald—Jupiter sent him
himself, I swear on our heads—carried the order
down on a speeding wind. I saw him myself in the clearest
daylight: he walked through a wall, I heard his voice and
          absorbed it.
360 Stop, then: don't burn yourself and me with resentment.
I don't pursue Italy freely."

Love Fury

She'd eyed him askance all the time he addressed her,
turning her glance this way and that, silently taking
him all in. Now in a fever she told him,
"No God was your parent, no Dardanus founded your people,
traitor: hard rock and frost of the Caucasus mountains
gave you birth. Tigresses' teats in Hyrcania nursed you.
Why should I hold back? To save myself for a greater
pain? Did you sigh at my tears, lower your vision
370 or weep at all, feel lost or pity a lover?
What can I say first? That neither powerful Juno
nor fatherly Jupiter looks on now with some fairness?
Trust is safe nowhere. Thrown on the beach you came begging,
I madly took you, offered you half of my kingdom,
saved your whole lost fleet from disaster.
What pain, what Furies drive and scald me! Apollo's your prophet
now, some Lycian oracle? Heaven's messenger hurried
through air from Jupiter here with your scary instructions?
Hard work for your Gods. I'm sure anxiety troubles
380 their rest! I won't detain you or counter your speeches.
Go: search through Italian winds and waves for your kingdom.
If honest Gods provide, I hope you will drink in

pain, surrounded by rock and calling on Dido's
name often. I'll be a black fire though I'm absent:
when death's cold severs the flesh from the spirit,
I'll be in shadow everywhere. Crime will be punished,
traitor. I'll hear your tale below among dead men."
Though half done she broke off and ran as if sickened,
turned from his looks, the air he breathed, and she left him
390 deeply worried, cautious but ready to tell her
more. Servants helped her, supporting her slumping
body back to her marble room. She lay on her bed there.

The Labor of Ants

Aeneas had done his duty, although he was longing
to calm her fears by talking, to soothe and soften her anguish.
He sighed deeply, unnerved by his great love for this woman.
Still he obeyed the God's order and left for the shipyard.
There on the whole shore Trojans had labored,
hauled down tall ships and caulked up the bottoms—
carrying shoots and untrimmed boughs from the woods, they had
    launched some.
400 They really longed to escape.
Imagine their rushing to quit the city completely
just like ants who have plundered ponderous caches
of corn and hauled them back to their hill to anticipate winter:
the black column works through a field on a narrow
mossy track moving their loot, some of them pushing
huge grains, their backs struggling, others corraling,
poking at stragglers: the whole path seethes with their labor.

A Sister's Help

What did you feel then, Dido, watching that bustle?
How did you sigh, observing the whole feverish coastline
410 high in your tower, seeing the breadth of that water
aswirl before your eyes with all-out hurry and uproar?
What end will extreme desire pressure a human
heart to? Again driven to tears, again to the effort
of humbly begging, her spirit yielded to passion:
she'd leave nothing untried, nor die for no reason.
"Scurrying around the whole beach—look at them, Anna,
massed everywhere. Winds call to their canvas,
crewmen already are gladly sporting their garlands.
Since I myself was able to see the agony coming,
420 I'm able to bear it, sister. It's wretched; but do me

one favor, Anna. That liar made you a signal
friend at times, he told you some innermost feelings.
Only you may know the gentlest time to approach him.
Go to him, sister. Humbly remind our imperious
guest I never swore with Greeks at Aulis to wipe out
Troy's people. I sent no fleet to the city,
nor ripped up dead spirits, the dust of his father Anchises.
Why are my words denied, his hearing so hardened?
Where does he rush to? Tell him my last wish as a wretched
430   lover: wait for a better wind and easier sailing.
I want no marriage now. He disavowed it, it's over.
Let him not lose or neglect Latium's beautiful kingdom.
I do want empty time, space to rest from this madness,
while Luck teaches me how to lose and be sorry.
That's the last favor I ask, Anna, for pity.
I'll pay him back, if he gives it, in full when I'm dying."
That was the tearful plea which her miserable sister
brought—and re-brought—to Aeneas. But nothing could move
      him.
He heard no word or weeping: the man was unbending.
440   The Fates forbade it: a God stopped up his hearing.
Just like an old strong oaktree which Alpine
winds buffet this way and that, in a struggle
among themselves to uproot it: creaking, the highest
leaves thrown to the ground when the treetrunk is jostled,
it still holds to its cliff: as high as it reaches
for air and sky, roots go down to the Death-world:
so with this leader. Words continually struck him
here, now there, he felt the anxiety deeply.
Yet he remained unmoved. Tears trickled for nothing.

Love Visions

450   Now Dido truly feared for her future.
Cursed, tired of seeing the arched sky, she went begging
for death. To help her leave the light, to end what she'd started
sooner, she saw while placing incense and gifts on an altar
the ritual water blacken—to tell it is frightful—
the wine she poured turned into blood and repulsed her.
She shared this vision with no one, not even her sister.
And more. A marble shrine stood in the palace,
tended by Dido with great devotion to honor her former
husband. White wool and sacred foliage clasped it.
460   There she seemed to hear a man as if calling,

the sound of his voice at night when the land was in darkness.
A lonely owl often complained from a rooftop
in drawn-out hoots—sad, funereal bird-calls.
Old-time prophets, too, many predictions
terrified and warned her. A savage Aeneas
himself drove her mad in a dream: always abandoned,
left to herself, always friendless, she seemed to be walking
a long road through bare country looking for Trojans.
Just like crazed Pentheus watching a column of Furies,
470 paired suns, Thebes revealed as if doubled,
or Agamemnon's son Orestes when driven
across the stage in flight from his mother, armed with her torches
and black snakes, while Furies linger in doorways.

A Massylian Priestess

Wrecked by grief therefore and caught in a madness,
she fixed on death. She picked the moment and method
herself. She approached her distraught sister and told her—
a hopeful face and calm brow concealed her decision—
"I've found a way, Anna. Be glad for your sister!
I'll bring him back or free myself from this passion.
480 Close to the setting sun, bordering Ocean,
in far-off Ethiopian land powerful Atlas
turns the world on his back while it's burning with inlaid
stars. From there I've met a Massylian priestess
who cares for Evening's temple and offers her serpent
its meals, guarding the sacred boughs of an old tree,
sprinkling poppy seeds and honey at sleep-time.
The woman claims she can free minds with her music
if so inclined, weigh someone with ponderous worry,
stop a river's flow, alter the movement
490 of stars and stir ghosts at night. The ground that you stand on
will low, you'll see: ash-trees will move from the mountains!
My dear sister, I swear by the Gods and your precious
life I do not willingly dress in magical power.
So raise a pyre under the open sky of the courtyard
quietly. Heap it with all my remnants, the armor
that evil man left, fixed on my wall—and the marriage
bed that killed me. Erasing every remembrance
of hateful men gives us joy. The priestess demands it."
She stopped speaking—pallor had covered her featur
500 Anna could not believe her sister was hiding
death in some odd rites, or conceive of a monstrous

rage: was all this worse than the death of Sychaeus?
She followed orders accordingly.
Soon as the pyre stood in the open air of the central
palace, a huge mound of pine branches and oak-logs,
the queen strung garland and crowned the assortment
with death-leaves. Now clearly aware of her future,
she placed on a couch the sword he'd left, a picture, some clothing.
Altars arranged in a circle, her hair streaming, the priestess
510 pealed out three hundred Gods—Erebus, Chaos,
three-formed Hecate, three-faced Diana, the virgin.
She sprinkled water alleged to have sprung from Avernus.
She looked for mature plants and cut them with copper
shears by moonlight, their milk poisonous, blackish.
She looked for a love-charm too—the membrane torn from a
      new-born
foal's brow, yanked by its mare.
Dido, close to the altar, dutifully carried
grain, one foot unstrapped. Her robe was unbelted.
Soon to die, she prayed and called to a Sky-God
520 conscious of destiny, just and remembering Powers,
if any, who cared for lovers contracted unfairly.

Love Wakefulness

Then it was night. Weary bodies were reaching
for sleep or rest on the earth. Forest and savage
sea had quieted; stars rolled halfway through heaven
and every field lay still. Cattle and painted
birds, roosting in rough woodland or brambles
near large lakes, were settled in sleep in the silent
dark, less anxious now, their hearts unconscious of labor.
But not that sad Phoenician heart: it was never
530 relaxed in sleep, she never accepted night in her bosom
or eyes, her concerns multiplied, passion and anger
surged again in a long, moiling surf of resentment.
She said to herself, her heart tumbling inside her,
"Look at me: what should I do? Try some earlier suitor
again, be laughed at, humbly beg for a Nomad in marriage?
By now I've scoffed too often myself at such husbands.
What then? Follow the Trojan fleet and a Trojan
command to the end? Because they're glad that I help them,
or thanks for my former help will stay in their memory?
540 Suppose I want that: which proud ship will receive me,
a person they hate? Lost, ignorant Dido—

still not seeing the lies of Laomedon's people.
What, then? Run off with a party of clamoring crewmen,
crowd my own Tyrians around me and set out
with people I pulled just now from Sidonian cities?
Drive them again into sea-wind, tell them to spread out our
    canvas?
No. Die: you deserve to. A sword gets rid of your sorrow.
Tears prevailed on Anna to start with—my sister
peaked a sickness that made me insane, exposed to a stranger.
550 I'm not allowed to pass through life as a widow
free from fault, untouched by care like some wild thing.
I failed my trust, my pledge to the dust of Sychaeus."
Breaking her own heart, she went on bitterly grieving.

Again the Gods' Messenger

High on the stern now, determined to set out,
Aeneas rested. Things were prepared and in order.
Abruptly the same God's form, with his features
close to the man while dreaming, appeared to admonish—
in every respect like Mercury's voice and complexion—
hair like gold, torso youthful and graceful:
560 "Son of the Goddess! You linger and sleep in such danger?
Can't you see right now the threat that surrounds you?
Insane or deaf to the favoring breath of the Westwind?
The queen's breast churns with deceit and desperate evil:
fixed on death, she's a moiling surf of resentment.
Fly headlong from here while flight's in your power!
Soon you'll find this water a jumble of timber,
fiercely glaring torches, the beach glowing with firelight,
unless you break from the shore. Stop waiting for daylight,
no more delays, wake up! The woman's a constant
570 swing of change." He melded in dark night when he finished.

Terror and Departure

Doubly alarmed by the sudden vision, Aeneas
yanked his body from sleep and scolded companions,
"Quickly, you men, take to the thwarts and your watches,
loosen the sail fast—a God's been sent from the highest
air to rush our escape—look, he goads us again there,
to cut our twisted cables. Holy Lord, we will follow,
whoever you are. We accept your rule once more and applaud it.
Stay close and calmly help: bring from your heaven
the right stars." He stopped to pull a sword from its scabbard

580 and slash a cable—the sharp blade was like lightning.
Similar heat possessed them all. Grabbing and running,
they cleared the whole beach, their ships covered the road-
        stead,
they strained, churned up blue-grey foam and swept through
        the water.

Love Savagery

Dawn left the saffron bed of Tithonus
shortly and scattered first light on the country.
The queen, soon as she saw whitening daylight
high in her tower, then sail and ship in formation,
seeing shore and harbor emptied of rowers,
struck her lovely breast with a fist a third and a fourth time,
590 tore out blond hair, "Jupiter, look at
the upstart go," she cried, "making fun of our power!
Won't all of Carthage take out weapons and chase them?
Tyrians wreck their cables and fleet? Hurry and bring me
torches, go! Drive at your oars, hand out the armor!
What did I say? Where am I? What madness muddles my
        thinking?
Hapless Dido: now do godless actions impress you?
They suited you *then*—when you gave him your scepter. Look at
        the faithful
man's hand: he carried a fatherland's House-Gods,
they say, shouldered an aged, weakening father.
600 Couldn't I clutch him, dismember and scatter the body
at sea? Put to the sword his men and Iulus
himself, set a feast on board for the father?
War's outcome is doubtful, yes. But what of it?
What should I fear when dying? If only I'd carried
fire to his camp, burned each gangway, murdered the father,
son and the lot—and tossed myself on the ash-heap!

The Future of Rome Cursed

"Sun-God: your fire sees and lightens all of our labor.
Juno: you know our every anxiety's meaning.
Hecate: you wail nightly at crossroads in cities.
610 Vengeful Furies, all you Gods of a dying Elissa:
hear and accept my prayer, attend with your power:
my pain has earned it. If sailing and reaching a harbor
must happen now to the man, that unspeakable person,
if Jupiter's word demands that goal be accomplished,

still let war convulse him, swords of presumptuous people:
let him be torn from his own land and the face of Iulus.
Let him beg for help and witness the shameful
deaths of friends. Let him yield to unfair terms in a peace-pact
and never enjoy the rule or sunlight he longed for,
620 but topple before his time in bare gravel, unburied.
There's my plea—the last word to be poured with my life- blood.
And all you Tyrians, hunt those men in the future,
hate them and send word of this favor down to my ashes:
give no love, make no pact with that people.
Rise from my bones, whatever revenger will follow,
pursue with fire and sword Dardanus' nation
now or whatever time gives you strength in the future.
Let sea be against sea, and seacoast at seacoast!
I call for arms fighting with arms—their own and their children's.''

Love Ending

630 While speaking she turned in every mental direction,
longing to break soon from the daylight she hated.
She spoke briefly to Barce, nurse of Sychaeus
(her own nurse's bleak remains were still in her former
land): "My dear nurse, go bring Anna, my sister.
Tell her to hurry: wash her body in river
water and lead out calves, the proper atonement.
Both of you come. Cover your temples with ritual garland.
I want to conclude rites duly begun for
the Underworld's Jupiter, put an end to my trouble,
640 and send Troy's leader in flame from the death-pyre.''
She stopped; the old one bustled away with intentness.
Dido trembled wildly now that the dreadful
thing had begun, her eyes bloody and rolling, her nervous
cheeks flecked with red. Pale at the death which approached her
she dashed to the building's inner court, she ascended
the tall pyre distractedly, pulled out the Trojan
sword—a gift she had wanted—not for this purpose.
Here, seeing the bed and familiar Trojan
clothes, she brooded, moved to weeping a little.
650 She lay on the bed and spoke—the words were her last ones:
"Sweet spoils—while you Gods and Fates were indulgent.
Take my spirit. Free my heart from its caring.
I lived: I finished the course Fortune provided.
Now my exalted form goes down to the Death-world.
I've seen my walls: I've raised an illustrious city.

I made a hostile brother pay in revenge for my husband.
Happy—yes, too happy—if only a Trojan
keel had never touched the coastline of Carthage."
Pausing, pressing her face on the bed: "We'll die unavenged here,
660 but die," she said. "So. It helps to go down into darkness.
The eyes of a cruel Trojan will spot this cremation
at sea and find an evil sign in my death-fire."

The City in Consternation

Words broke off—a servant noticed her falling,
the froth of blood at the sword, a forearm of Dido
all stained. Cries went up to the courtyard
roof, the story ran through the city and stunned it.
Buildings echoed the sighs and wailing of women
in grief, the whole sky re-echoed the uproar
as though all of Carthage had suddenly fallen
670 to hostile attack, or ancient Tyre in a frenzy
of rolling flame from Gods' and citizens' rooftops.

The Grief of a Sister

Anna rushed back terrified, shaking and breathless.
She beat her breast, her nails disfigured her features,
she ran through the crowd calling the dying
woman by name. "Dido, what's this? You wanted to trick me?
For *this* I prepared the pyre, altar and firelight?
I'm lost. How can I scold you first, for scorning a sister
and friend by dying? The same death should have called me:
your sword's pain should have taken us both in this hour.
680 My voice invoked our Fathers' Gods and my fingers
worked to place you here, so cruel—and me missing.
You've killed yourself and me, sister, your people,
the city, Sidonian fathers . . . Give me some water:
I'll wash the wounds. A last wandering breath here?
My mouth will catch it." Climbing the steep ladder while
          speaking,
she'd held her near-dead sister, embraced her and warmed her.
She cried and sopped up dark blood with her mantel.

Help from Heaven in Dying

The queen tried once more to lift up her heavy
eyes but failed, her chest deeply wounded and gasping.
690 She struggled three times to lift herself on an elbow
but rolled back on the bed three times. Her wandering vision

searched the deep sky for sun: she sighed when she found it.
At length powerful Juno pitied her wretched,
long death. She sent Iris from heaven
to free the wrestling spirit from knots of the body.
For Dido neither deserved to die nor was destined:
sudden grief and madness before her time had consumed her.
Proserpine still had not yet taken a golden
curl from her head or sent the spirit to Orcus.
700 So Iris flew from the sky, trailing a thousand
moist colors reflecting the sun, gliding on saffron
wings. She stopped by Dido: "I'm taking an offering
now at the Death-God's command. Your life is freed from its
        body."
Her hand clipped hair while she spoke. Quickly and wholly
the warmth diminished. A life was gone on the breezes.

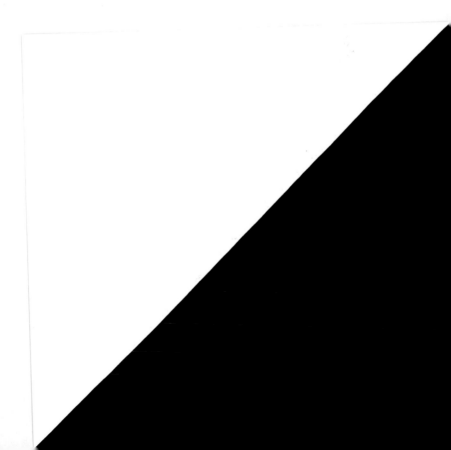

V

FUNERAL GAMES AT SICILY

New Winds, New Darkness

Aeneas meanwhile held course through the water.
The fleet steadily cut through seas darkened by Northwind.
He gazed back at Carthage, glowing with Dido's
tragic burning. Whatever began or extended
that large fire was unknown. But all the grief of dishonored
love was known, and woman's power when outraged.
Trojan hearts were moved by a somber foreboding.
Now the ships were at sea, land was no longer
in sight, everywhere sky, everywhere water:
10 a blue-black stormcloud rose and confronted Aeneas,
fraught with winter and night. Water shivered in darkness.
High on the stern even Palinurus the helmsman
called, "My God, what clouds are circling in heaven?
Our Father Neptune, what are you up to?" He promptly
ordered tackle secured, oars pulled on robustly,
canvas turned to the wind. He said to Aeneas,
"Your spirit is strong, but even if Jupiter pledged it
I'd never hope to reach Italy's coast in this weather.
Winds keep shifting abeam and muttering, rising
20 out of the west. The air is a dark, thickening stormcloud.
We lack strength to fight such power and maintain
headway. Where Luck is good or strong we should follow:
change course where she calls us. Not far is the loyal,
brotherly coast of Eryx, I think—a Sicilian harbor—
if only the stars are clear in my mind that I sailed by."

Return to Sicily

Aeneas wisely answered, "True, the winds are insistent.
I've watched you fight them hard for a long time without progress.
Alter your course and canvas. What land is more welcome,
where could I beach tired ships with more pleasure
30   than there on that coast? It harbors our Trojan Acestes
and holds in its lap the bones of my Father Anchises."
He stopped, they headed for port, a following Westwind
tensed sail and hurried the fleet through the water.
They gladly returned at length to a beach they remembered.
Watching amazed from the high ridge of a mountain,
Acestes descended to meet old friends when the ships were
        arriving.
Bristling with arrows, wearing a Libyan bearskin,
born of a mother at Troy to the God of the River
Crinisus, he still recalled the old generation,
40   welcoming Trojans back with laughter and country
comfort. The worn-out men were cheered by his welcome.

In Memory of Anchises

When Dawn and the next day's brightness had routed
the stars, Aeneas called his friends from the lengthy
shore to a meeting. He stood on high ground to address them.
"You fine sons of Dardanus, Gods' bloodline from heaven!
The months have passed, an annual cycle is finished
since Trojans buried remains, the bones of my godlike
Father, in ground nearby and blessed the altar in mourning.
The day is here, if I'm not wrong, which will always be bitter,
50   always held in respect, since the Sky-Gods desired it.
If I were an exile today on Gaetulian Sandbanks
or caught by Greeks at sea and kept at Mycenae,
I'd still complete the annual prayer and solemn
rite: I'd pile the correct gifts on an altar.
Instead we're here, by the ashes and bones of my Father
himself—hardly I think without some consenting
God's will—borne right to the port of our kinsmen.

Aeneas Announces the Games

"Come, then. Everyone join in a happy observance.
Pray to the Winds, let them grant that Anchises be honored
60   with annual rites in holy shrines when my city is founded.
Acestes, born at Troy, is contributing oxen,

two head for every ship. Bring to the banquet
both our native House-Gods and those revered by Acestes,
our host. Then, when Dawn gives us her caring
light, when her glow reveals the world for the ninth time,
I'll hold games. First for four of our Trojan
ships. Then for the best sprinters. For those who are daring
and strong with spears. For the best at a challenge with arrows.
For boxers—those who trust to leather and gauntlets.
70   Everyone come, examine the prizes and palms for each winner.
But first a silence. Everyone tie leaves to your temples."

The Snake at the Tomb

He stopped and circled his forehead with myrtle of Venus.
Helymus followed, together with aging Acestes
and young Ascanius. All the young men did likewise.
Aeneas moved from the meeting. Hundreds of people
walked to the death-mound, large numbers jostling around him.
He duly poured on the ground libations of unmixed
wine, two cups, with two of fresh milk and of sacred
blood. He scattered purple flowers. "I greet you,"
80   he said, "I greet you again, revered ashes, the Father
I saved in vain. Dark soul of Anchises,
I wasn't allowed to search for Italian country
with you, for the Fate-picked Ausonian field or the Tiber,
wherever—" he stopped: an oily snake at the death-mound's
base had coiled into seven large rounds to embrace it
gently. The seven rings trailed by an altar,
its back a mottled dark blue and its scaly
skin a burning gold, the snake like a rainbow
throwing a thousand colors back at the sun through a cloud-burst.
90   The vision stunned Aeneas. Shortly the serpent's
long column slithered among bowls and resplendent
cups where it tasted the meal. Soon it abandoned
food on the altar and crept to the tomb's base. It was harmless.
With more zeal Aeneas renewed the rites for his father
just begun, unsure if the snake were a local
God or Anchises' familiar. He slaughtered the full-grown
sheep required, two swine, two heifers with night-black
backs. He poured wine from a bowl and called on Anchises'
great soul, on the Dead freed from the Acheron River.
100 His men, as their means allowed, were also presenting
gifts gladly. They killed bulls and loaded an altar.
Some set cauldrons in place; others were searing

cutlets or feeding coal to spits while spread on the beachgrass.

The Games Begin

The longed-for day arrived. Phaethon's horses
carried the glow of the ninth dawn through the peaceful
sky. Acestes' famous name had excited
neighbors: a cheerful crowd filled up the shoreline
to see these Trojans. Some were prepared to compete there.
Awards were placed in view first in the center
110 of action: green garlands, ritual tripods,
armor and palm leaf, rewarding the winners;
robes imbued in purple, gold and silver in talents.
A trumpet called from a hill—the games were beginning.

A Ship Race

Four big ships had entered the first competition,
closely matched and loaded with oars: the best in the squadron.
Mnestheus drove *Leviathan's* quick and vigorous oarsmen
(soon *Italian* Mnestheus, naming the Memmian household).
Gyas commanded the huge bulk of the massive *Chimaera*—
raised like a town, rowed by three stories of Trojans,
120 three full teams ready to drive her together.
Sergestus (a name now held by the Sergian household)
rode in the great *Centaur*. Cloanthus (who'd father
Cluentians of Rome) sailed the indigo *Scylla*.
Well out to sea a rockpile confronted the foamy
beach. Submerged at times by a pounding of heavy
surf when Northwesterly storms blocked out the starlight,
the rock re-emerged when the sea lay calm as a level
field; sun-loving gulls welcomed the refuge.
Lordly Aeneas had placed leaves from an oaktree
130 here as a green marker, helping each captain
to know when to heel in the long race, when to circle.

Tension at the Start

They cast lots for position. Captains were climbing
aft, a glitter of purple and gold trim in the distance.
Crewmen wreathed their temples in poplar,
smeared oil on their bare, glistening shoulders
and sat on benches, arms tensed for the rowing.
Waiting, intent on the signal, hearts drained by a pulsing
fear or leaping with hope, they were peaked for this honor.
There—the trumpet loudly blared and abruptly

140 every ship jumped from its place while an uproar
from crewmen struck at the sky. Arms pulled and the water
frothed where furrows were plowed, rowers together
splashing and three-pronged bows utterly crushing
the waves. Paired chariot horse-teams will break from
their stalls and reach a field in a race-course less quickly,
charioteers waving and flurrying reins of a bolting
team while leaning forward and whipping the horses.
Cheers and shouts of sailors with cries of supporters
rang through the whole forest, the shoreline re-echoed
150 their shouts, and hills struck by the clamor re-sounded.

Turning Point

Gyas flew out to sea first, slipping by others
in all the noise and confusion. Cloanthus pursued him
closely, his rowers were better, but all of that pinewood
slowed him down. An equal distance behind them
Leviathan struggled with *Centaur* for better position:
now *Leviathan* held it, then the ponderous *Centaur*
passed and led. Soon both were together,
prow and beam side by side as they cut through the water.
In time they neared the rockpile. Reaching the marker,
160 the leading captain, Gyas, seawater swirling
around him, called to the ship's helmsman, Menoetes:
"Why so far to starboard? Alter your course there,
hug that rock. Our port-side oar-blades can scratch it!
Others can have deep water." Menoetes however
feared some blind reef and swung the bow to the open
sea. "Where are you off to?" Gyas was yelling
now: "Close to that rock, Menoetes!" And picture
Cloanthus, close astern, taking the inside
track: he scraped past the vessel of Gyas!
170 With noisy surf and rock to port, suddenly passing
the leader, he cleared the mark and headed for risk-free
waves. What intense bitterness burned in the marrow
of Gyas! Tears on his cheeks, he grabbed a fretful Menoetes,
forgot good grace and the safety of crewmen,
and threw him headlong down from the high stern in the water.
He manned the tiller himself—the skipper the helmsman,
haranguing crewmen, turning his wheel to the marker.
A heavy Menoetes bobbed up shortly from under,
older now, his clothes drenched by the water.
180 He headed for high ground, some dry rock, and he sat there.

Trojans who'd laughed at the man's falling and swimming
laughed when he spat up salt sea from his stomach.

The Men of Mnestheus

Joy and hope flared in Mnestheus now and Sergestus,
the last two men, to catch the dawdling Gyas.
Sergestus held a lead approaching the rockpile
but not by much—only part of a boat-length—
part of *Leviathan's* bow pressed him amidship.
And there amidship Mnestheus paced and encouraged
crewmen himself: "Now, *now* to your rowing,
190 you friends of Hector! I picked you all as companions
when Troy fell: it's time to show me your muscle,
show that spirit you showed on Gaetulian Sandbanks,
Ionian seas, the Malean waves that pursued us.
I cannot hope for first: Mnestheus won't be the winner—
but oh, you Neptune, let them win whom you wish to!—
only avoid the shame and loathing of last place:
do that at least, my friends." Strained to the utmost
they leaned and stroked hard, the bronze afterdeck shuddered,
sea-floor dragged by, breath labored, their bodies
200 trembled, mouths dried out, everyone sweated in trickles.
Chance itself brought them the honor they longed for.
Sergestus, frantically wedging his bow through the inside
close to the rocks, entered a teacherous passage
and sadly ran aground on a rocky projection.
The rockpile shook. Oars, forced onto jagged
ledge, splintered. The bow cracked and was dangling.
Sailors jumped up and called out: they were stuck there.
They pushed with sharp poles pointed with iron.
They gathered broken pieces of oar from the water.
210 Mnestheus, pleased and stirred at how this had happened,
headed for open water, each column of rowers
racing. He prayed to the Winds while running a downhill
swell, just like a frightened dove that abruptly
breaks from her cavelike home where the dear nestlings are
       hidden:
she flits over fields, a loud and terrified flapping
at first by the nest, and in time she glides on a current
of quiet air: her wings go fast without beating.
Mnestheus flew that way on *Leviathan,* cutting
through final waves. Momentum carried him forward.
220 First he left Sergestus behind as he struggled

high on that rock, vainly calling for help in the shallow
water, trying to race with oars that were shattered.
Next he approached Gyas himself in the massive
bulk of *Chimaera*: she yielded, deprived of her helmsman.
Only Cloanthus remained now at the finish.
Mnestheus chased him, pushing his crew to the limit,
noise actually doubled, everyone cheered the pursuer
fiercely, the whole sky split from the uproar.
One crew, resenting the loss of a prize they considered
230 their own, were willing to trade their lives for the honor;
the other, fed by success, felt strong so they *were* strong.

The Prayer of Cloanthus

The latter threatened to win—the bows were abreast now.
Hands held high over the water, Cloanthus
poured out prayer, he called on Gods and he promised:
"You Powers who rule the sea, this water we race on,
I'll gladly stand a white bull on that beachsand
before your altars, I'm bound to that promise: I'll offer
its flesh to the surf and pour wine on your water."
He stopped speaking: a whole chorus of Nereids heard him
240 deep undersea, with Phorcus and chaste Panopea:
the huge hand itself of Portunus, that Father,
moved the ship, and it flew to the land like a feathered
arrow or whizzing Southwind. It stopped in the depths of the
        harbor.

Ganymede's Flight

The son of Anchises, when all were properly summoned,
called Cloanthus the winner. Heralds proclaimed him
loudly and green laurel circled his temples.
The ships' crews were allowed to choose among prizes:
three young bulls, wine and a large talent of silver.
Aeneas offered special awards to the captains.
250 A chlamys of gold-stitched cloth for the winner: a winding
double border of Meliboean purple around it,
a young prince in the cloth's design, and forested Ida:
Ganymede, chasing spirited deer, tired them and speared them,
looking winded and wild—the one whom Jupiter's eagle,
stooping from Ida, carried high in its talons
while hands of old guardians reached for the sky-heights
in vain and savage dogs barked at the heavens.
The man who came in second now, and a strong one,

received a triply mailed golden lorica
260 with polished clasps. Aeneas himself had removed it
near Troy's heights from Demoleos, close to the fast-flowing
     Simois—
Mnestheus' gift, a prize and protection in battle.
The servants Phegeus and Sagaris hardly could lift it,
they struggled to move the layered piece; but Demoleos
once had worn it while running and scattering Trojans.
A pair of bronze cauldrons were given to third place,
and bowls in rough relief, finished in silver.

A Lost Ship Saved

With each man proud of some valuable honor
now, walking with purple fillets crowning his forehead,
270 Sergestus pushed a prizeless boat from the ragged
ledge. People laughed at all the prying and tearing,
the lost oars and disabled tier on the port side.
The way a snake, caught at times on a roadway
mound and crossed by a brass wheel at an angle,
or struck hard by a traveler's rock, left there and dying,
will twist its long form: escape may be futile
but fiercely the burning eyes look up and a hissing
tongue darts out—though elsewhere seriously wounded
and slowed, the coils of that body double and struggle:
280 rowers moved the boat of Sergestus that slowly.
Still he set more sail, it filled, and he entered the harbor.
Aeneas gave Sergestus the award he had promised,
glad that his friends were safe and the ship had been salvaged.
He gave him a female slave who knew the work of Minerva:
Pholoe, her family in Crete, twin boys at her nipples.

Sprinters

The ship-race over, Aeneas dutifully headed
for grassy field circled completely by wooded
and winding hills that formed a natural stadium
there in the valley. Thousands of people surrounded
290 and walked with their leader. He sat on a dais,
encouraging those who just might want competition
in sprinting now by offering prizes to stimulate spirit.
They came from everywhere—Trojans mixed with Sicilians.
Nisus was first, with Euryalus:
Euryalus boyish and green, exceptionally handsome,
Nisus loving the boy devotedly. Next was Diores,

of royal roots, the notable household of Priam.
Then came Salius and Patron: the one Arcananian,
the other from Arcady, a Tegean family bloodline.
300 Helymus came with Panopes, two Trinacrian youngsters—
skilled woodsmen and friends of aging Acestes.
Many others approached, their fame obscure or forgotten.
Aeneas addressed them now as he stood in the center.
"Take my word—give me your cheerful attention—
none of your number will leave my sight unrewarded!
I'll give you Gnosian arrows of brilliantly polished
steel, two-edged axes with silver engraving—
the same reward for all. Those who are winners
will take more, and fasten olive green to their temples.
310 The first will receive a horse with exceptional trappings.
The second, an Amazon quiver loaded with Thracian
arrows, the wide golden baldric that circles
around and the buckle with polished jewels that ties it.
The third, a Greek helmet—you'll go with it gladly."

Nisus Leads At First

After his talk they took their positions. On hearing
a signal they broke out fast from their marks and maneuvered
for space, flying like stormclouds, keeping their eyes on the finish.
The first to break from the others and lengthen the lead-time
was Nisus—faster then winged lightning or windstorm.
320 Salius followed next, but next by a goodly
distance. Holding third, after an open
gap, was Euryalus.
Helymus followed Euryalus, trailed by Diores—
look at him pressing, nicking that foot with his own foot,
right on the shoulder! If only the race had been longer
he might have caught them and won, or made it uncertain.

The Blood Puddle

Soon they were almost done, tiring and nearing
a last finishing stretch—when a woebegone Nisus
slipped in a puddle of blood! Bulls had been slaughtered
330 here by chance, ground and grass soaked by the out-flow.
Nisus already had cheered for his win when he staggered,
lost his footing and went to the ground in a headlong
dive into slime, soil and ritual bloodstain.
Yet he remembered the one he cared for, Euryalus:
lifting himself though slipping, he moved into Salius'

path, who also tumbled and sprawled in the sand-clots.
Euryalus leaped on past with help from his comrade,
the first-place winner, applauded and cheered when he flew by.
Helymus followed. The third-place palm was Diores'.

Fairness and Foul

340   Salius filled the whole arena with protest,
loudly shouting right in the faces of elders,
claiming the stolen prize for himself: he'd been *fouled* out.
People favored Euryalus, though—his tears were becoming,
his worth appealing, combined with physical beauty.
Diores also strongly supported Euryalus:
if first prize went to Salius, Diores
would lose—the palm and prize he'd won would be nothing.
Aeneas spoke like a father. "Boys, you will surely
retain your winnings. No one will change the palms or
          arrangement.
350   But let me pity the fall of an innocent comrade."
After speaking he gave Salius the hide of a massive
Gaetulian lion with claws of gold and mane overflowing.
Now *Nisus* protested! "If pity and prizes
go to a stumbling loser, where are the presents
earned by Nisus? I rate the praise of a first-place
crown—if Luck were a friend of Salius and Nisus."
While speaking he pointed to still-wet grime on his body
and smeared face. Aeneas, an excellent father,
smiled and ordered a shield brought out—Didymaon's
          achievement,
360   once pulled by Greeks from a sacred portal of Neptune.
He gave an exceptional man an exceptional honor.

Lethal Fists

Now that racing had ended and palms were awarded
Aeneas announced, "I speak to anyone present
with strength of heart and spirit: come forward and hold out
fists for straps of leather." He showed awards for the boxing:
a steer flecked with fillets and gold for the winner;
a sword and prize helmet to comfort the loser.
Without delay Dares offered his bulging
strength, he stood there as men openly murmured:
370   Dares alone had once contended with Paris;
he'd beaten Butes too by a mound where the once-great
Hector lay. Butes had brought his enormous

girth from Bebrycia, home of Amycus' people,
but Dares had knocked him flat and he'd died in the tawny
dust. Holding his head up high for a fistfight,
Dares displayed broad shoulders, sparring with two hands,
both arms lashing the air, jabbing and hooking.

The Gauntlets of Eryx

Who would challenge? No one in all the assembly
dared to approach the man or slide hands into gauntlets.
380 Quickly assuming therefore that all had conceded
the winner's palm, Dares stood at the feet of Aeneas,
holding the bullock's horn with his left hand and asking,
"Son of the Goddess, if no one dares or believes he can fight me,
why should I stand here? How long is it right to delay things?
Order my prize led off." All of the Trojans
voiced agreement: the man should take what was promised.
Here Acestes gravely chided Entellus,
sitting on green couches of grass next to each other.
"Entellus, our strongest champion once! Your title was empty?
390 Letting a fine prize be seized with no struggle—
what patience! Where is our God and your teacher,
Eryx? Do we remember all of Trinacria's glory
and Eryx for nothing? The trophies that hung from your ceiling?"
Entellus: "The love of glory and praise has not left me.
Fear I shrug off. But cold and aging have slowed me,
thinned my blood, wearied and numbed the strength of my body.
If youth were mine still—the youth of that proudly
posturing upstart—if I were young at this moment,
you'd hardly need some fancy bull or reward to induce me:
400 I'd scorn prizes and fight." But just as he finished
he threw a pair of immensely heavy gloves in the center.
Eryx had used them briskly and often in fistfights,
tough hides stretched on his knuckles and forearms.
They stunned the mind: a dense layer of seven
bull's-hides, stiffened with lead and stitches of iron.
And stunned most, Dares himself had doubts about fighting.
The high-spirited son of Anchises maneuvered the heavy,
thonged folds of the gloves this way and that way.
Shortly the older man addressed him with feeling.
410 "What if someone could see the gloves and the armor
itself of Hercules now and a grim fight on this coastline?
Eryx wore my weapons once—your brother, Aeneas.
Look: fetid blood-spots and brain-flecks are still here.

He faced Hercules' might; I used them myself once,
when better blood gave me strength, and the envy
of Age had not yet scattered grey on my temples.
Now, if Dares of Troy objects to our weapons
and kindly Aeneas agrees, with King Acestes' approval
we'll even the match: I'll forgo Eryx's gauntlets—
420 don't be afraid, Dares—and you, the gloves of your Trojans."
Done, he removed a double cape from a shoulder,
baring a huge frame, imposing muscle and tendon.
He stood on the sand dead center, and stood there immensely.
The son of Anchises brought out matched gloves like a father:
the same gauntlets were strapped on the hands of both boxers.

Styles of Fighting

Quickly they squared off, each man alertly on tiptoe,
fearlessly lifting an arm in the air first to the Sky-Gods.
Keeping their heads high and back from the jabbing,
they mixed and punched at punches, feinting and flicking:
430 Dares quick on his feet, confident, younger,
Entellus weighty and strong, though his knees were unsteady,
large joints shaky and slow, and his breathing was labored.
The men threw plenty of hard blows that were wasted.
A few drubbed a ribcage, causing a massive
chest to rumble. Soon occasional punches
struck a temple or head. Cheeks smacked from the harder
impact. Heavy Entellus remained in position,
only dodging a blow by watching and weaving.
Dares, like someone bombarding the heights of a city,
440 or laying siege to a mountain fort with his missiles,
probed for openings here and there, and continued
pressing from every angle sharply, but vainly.
Now Entellus rose up high with a right hand
and hooked it downward, but Dares had spotted it coming
and nimbly avoided the blow by sidestepping quickly.
Entellus had thrown strength at the wind—and moreover
the man ponderously slipped and fell, his lumbering body
flat on the ground like a hollow pinetree that often
topples, uprooted on high Erymanthus or Ida.

The Rage of Entellus

450 Trinacrian people and Trojans anxiously jumped up,
shouts went to the sky, and Acestes, the first to come running,
lifted his old friend from the ground in compassion.

Hardly deterred or upset by the fall, the contender
returned to the fight fiercer. Anger stirred up his power:
awakened strength and shame ignited his manhood.
He hotly drove Dares backward through all the arena,
pounding him now with right and left combinations.
No pause, no rest—like volleys of hail from a stormcloud
banging a rooftop, hard blows from the champion's
460 both hands repeatedly pummeled Dares and spun him.

A Deadly Demonstration

Aeneas paternally stopped the fight. He could hardly
allow such fierceness of spirit, the rage of Entellus,
to go on longer. Aeneas rescued the worn-out
Dares and offered a few words to console him.
"My sorry friend, what stark madness captured your spirit!
You must see the Powers have changed to help your opponent:
yield to the Gods." That word ended the fighting.
Dares, led by some loyal friends to the roadstead,
dragged along weak-kneed, shaking a groggy
470 head, spitting clumps of blood mixed with some broken
pieces of tooth. Friends were called and accepted his helmet
and sword. The palm and bull went to Entellus.
The winner, proud of the bull now and elated,
spoke out: "Son of the Goddess and all of you Trojans,
look at the bodily strength I had as a young man:
see what death you called Dares away from."
He stopped and stood there directly facing the bullock.
That prize for the fight stood still. Raising a right hand
high he aimed between the horns at the midpoint:
480 the gauntlet struck, fractured the skull and spattered the brains
        out.
The bull sprawled on the gound, quivered and died there.
Entellus prayed from his heart over the carcass.
"Eryx, the bull is yours. I offer a better
life than Dares' death. I've won. I'm finished with gauntlets."

Bird Target

Next Aeneas called on those who were thinking
perhaps of competing with fast-flying arrows. He set out
prizes and lent a large hand in dismasting
Serestus' ship. A fluttering dove at the masthead
hung by a cord, the high target for bowmen.
490 Participants gathered and threw their lots in a welcome

brass helmet. Hippocoön, Hyrtacus' youngster,
came up first and foremost; people applauded.
Mnestheus followed—earlier one of the ship-race
winners, the green olive circling his forehead.
Your brother Eurytion, famous Pandarus, came up
third: when Pallas told you once to damage a peace-pact
you twirled a spear first in the midst of Achaeans.
The last one left at the helmet's base was Acestes,
daring to try his hand in an action of young men.

A Rare Bowman

500 Each man bent a bow for himself in a forceful
show of strength. They drew out arrows from quivers.
The first to pierce the winged breeze by twanging a bowstring,
sending an arrow skyward, was Hyrtacus' youngster:
it flew off and stuck in the fronting wood of the masthead.
Timber shook and the bird's terrified feathers
flapped. Everyone loudly yelled and applauded.
Mnestheus eagerly stood up next. Bending the bow back,
he sighted along the shaft and directed it upward.
He failed to strike the bird itself with an arrow,
510 sadly, but severed the linen cord which had knotted
its leg to the high mast. The bird which had hung there
was free and raced for a dark cloud by riding a Southwind.
Quickly Eurytion now, whose bow had been ready,
the arrow nocked for a while, called on and vowed to his brother.
He scanned the sky, empty except for the happy
bird beating its wings for that stormcloud. He struck it:
the bird dropped, abandoning life in the starry
air and falling, returning the arrow embedded.

The Omen of Fire

Only Acestes remained—and the palm had been taken.
520 Still he shot an arrow high in the air to exhibit
a father's power and skill. The bowstring was humming
when suddenly a sign confronted their vision, predicting
future greatness. A major event would confirm it
later and frightened prophets would sing of the omen.
The arrow burst into flame when it flew through a hazy
cloud and inscribed a trail of fire as it dwindled
and died in the thin air. A shooting star will be torn from
the sky often that way, and trail out hair when it passes.
Men of Troy and Trinacria, spirits astonished,

530 stood there praying to Sky-Gods. Their leader, Aeneas,
accepted the sign. Embracing a happy Acestes,
he loaded the man with rich prizes and told him,
"Take them, father. The great King of Olympus—
that was no chance sign—wants you to lead off the honors.
Accept this present from ageless Anchises, my Father:
an image-embossed wine-bowl given by Thracian
Cisseus once to my Father himself as an ample
gift, a proof of his own love and remembrance."
He stopped and circled Acestes' forehead with laurel
540 greens. First and foremost he called him the winner.
Eurytion graciously bore no grudge at the honor,
although he alone had shot the bird from the heavens.
Next the man who'd severed the cord came to be honored.
Last, the one whose winged arrow had stuck in the masthead.

The Boys' Parade

Before the contest ended, Aeneas paternally
called for Epytus' son, a loyal companion
and guide of young Iulus, and spoke to him closely:
"Go to Ascanius quickly now, see if the young men's
troops are formed and prepared to maneuver their horses.
550 Tell him to lead the corps in his grandfather's honor
and show off their weapons." Aeneas ordered the pressing
crowd to withdraw from a wide course to open a circuit.

Faces of Old Troy

The boys came marching together while parents were watching.
Horses' bridles glinted. All of the people
of Troy and Trinacria cheered and admired when they passed by.
Each had crowned his hair with a circlet, according to custom,
and each one carried two steel-tipped lances of cornel.
Some had shouldered a burnished quiver, or twisted
gold around their chests, high, like flexible collars.
560 Three groups of horses in all, each with a roving
leader: two groups of six boys in each section
glittered in columns and followed respective commanders.
A little Priam, recalling his grandfather's good name—
your famous bloodline, Polites, would father Italians—
led the first squadron of jubilant youngsters.
The leader rode a fine, white-spotted Thracian,
pasterns white, and white high on the forehead.
Atys was next—his bloodline would lead to the Atii household—

little Atys, a boy loved as a boy by Iulus.
570 Last and finest-looking by far was Iulus
himself on a mount from Sidonia given by radiant
Dido once—a sign of her love and remembrance.
The rest of the boys rode Trinacrian horses
of old Acestes.
Parents welcomed the shyly nervous youths and applauded.
They saw their old parents of Troy in these faces.

Ascanius Leads

Each horse and rider gladly and ritually circled
the whole course with relatives watching. A shout in the distance
came from Epytus' son, then a whip-crack—the sign to be ready.
580 They answered by racing apart, three squadrons dissolving
and breaking ranks. Signaled again they went wheeling
about, trained their lances and rode at each other.
First they moved in one, then another direction:
opposing groups intertwined in alternate circles,
making as if to engage in actual combat.
Now bare-backed and fleeing, then turning their lances
to charge, at length they made peace and cantered together.
As men once talked on Crete's heights of the Labyrinth's
tricky and winding path which moved past a thousand
590 deceptive by-paths and blind walls (unredeemable error
obscured the signs to be followed) eluding observance:
the sons of Troy constructed a similar tangle
of mounts prancing and playing at war and evasion.
They looked like dolphins in splashy Carpathian waters
or swimming and veering at play in Libyan whitecaps.
Ascanius, first to revive the games when he circled
Alba Longa with walls, would make the equestrian
march a custom, teaching ancient Latins the practice,
just as he rode himself with young Trojan companions.
600 Alba would teach her sons; and far in the future
powerful Rome would keep the games to honor her fathers.
The boys are still called "from Troy" and their columns are
     "Trojan."

Juno and Iris

So far events had taken place to honor Anchises.
But Luck now changed. She couldn't be trusted.
While various ritual games went on by the death-mound
Juno, Saturn's daughter, bringing Iris from heaven,

breezed along to the Trojan fleet on an Eastwind,
plotting things. An old bitterness filled her.
Iris traveled fast through a bow of a thousand
610   colors: seen by no one she quickly descended,
watched and circled the large crowd on the shoreline.
She saw the abandoned port—the fleet was unguarded.
Trojan women, apart on the beach at a distance,
mourned Anchises' loss, all of them gazing
at deep water and weeping. "So much sea and exhaustion"
(they spoke as with one voice) "and still water confronts us."
They longed for a city. Work at sea had oppressed them.

Burn the Ships!

So Iris flew in the center, aware of her power
to injure. She doffed the dress and form of a Goddess
620   to look like Beroe, the old wife of Doryclus
from Mount Tmarus, where parents once had children of stature.
She mingled among Trojan mothers around her
and said, "What misery not to have died by an Argive
hand in that war, dragged by the walls of our fathers!
What doom will Luck prepare for such miserable people?
Already the seventh year has passed since Troy was demolished.
Still we trace each coast and channel, every unfriendly
rock and star, chasing a fugitive Italy,
borne on the sea's breadth and tossed by its rollers.
630   But here's land of our brother Eryx and friendly Acestes:
who'll stop us from building a walled town for our people?
You House-Gods rescued from Greeks at Troy in a futile
gesture, will walls never be called Trojan? I'll never
see Hector's rivers, the Simois, Xanthus?
No: come with me now to the damned ships and together
we'll burn them! Cassandra appeared in my sleep: the form of the
        seer
gave me a flaming torch, 'Home for you Trojans
is here,' she said, 'stay here.' It's time that we acted:
the signs are clear, no stalling, the four altars of Neptune
640   himself—look!—they'll give us torches and spirit."

Fear, Doubt and Desperation

While speaking she avidly seized a dangerous firebrand,
raised it high first, and with all her power she swung it
and threw it. She stirred minds and astounded the Trojan
women's hearts. One of their number was Pyrgo,

the eldest; she'd nursed many sons in the palace of Priam:
"That's not Beroe, mothers—not the Rhoeteian
wife of Doryclus—look at the marks of a Goddess:
the burning eyes, grace and spirited footstep,
even the tone of voice and facial expression.
650 I just left Beroe now myself: she's an ailing
woman alone, upset to be missing the contests,
unable to pray duly and honor Anchises."
She stopped speaking,
mothers began to doubt, their glances were hostile:
they eyed the ships, torn between painful attachment
to land right there and to realms the Fates had provided.
When Iris rose on balanced wings into heaven,
flying by cloud, trailing the grand arch of a rainbow,
the women were more struck by the omen and driven
660 to panic. They yelled and grabbed torches, some from an altar,
some from a nearby hearth. Shoots and smoldering branches
flew as Vulcan raged, nothing restrained him:
painted afterdecks, oars and benches were smoking.

Ascanius Rebukes the Women

Shortly Eumelus brought back word of the burning
ships to the stadium seats by the tomb of Anchises.
People turned and saw a floating, darkening ash-cloud.
Ascanius, glad to be leading mounted formations,
quickly and eagerly dashed on his horse to the troubled
camp—his trainers breathless, unable to stop him—
670 "What's this madness now," he called out, "where are you off to,
you wretched women? These are no enemy campsites
you burn but your own hopes. I'm your Ascanius,
look!" He threw an empty helmet before them,
worn when he'd charged figures during the war-game.
Aeneas rushed up now with a column of Trojans,
and women scattered in fear. They littered the shoreline,
fled into woods or furtively looked for a hollowed
rockpile somewhere, ashamed of their acts in the daylight.
They changed, recognized family, and Juno was struck from their
bosoms.

Jupiter's Rain

680 Fire hardly checked its wild assault for that reason:
flame and smoke thrived under the caulking,
puffed and seeped through wet planks, and a clammy

heat gnawed at keels. The whole fleet could succumb to
the sickness. Heroic effort and streams of water were futile.
Aeneas reverently pulled the cloak from his shoulders,
reached to the sky and called on Gods for assistance:
"All-powerful Jupiter! Don't detest to the last man
your Trojan people. Not yet—not if your ancient
kindness can pity human struggle. Grant that our vessels
690   be saved from the fire, Father: rescue a remnant
of Troy from death. Or kill what's left with your furious lightning
if that's my desert: use your hand to destroy us."
He'd hardly finished when drops fell from a darkling
cloud strangely growling with thunder, it rattled
the entire field and hillside, thick and violent torrents
rushed from the whole sky, night-dark and gusty
with Southwind. Stern-decks filled, oak which had blackened
soaked up water: every flame was extinguished.
All but four ships were saved from the fire-plague.

More Trojans Left Behind

700   Aeneas, still the father, stunned by this bitter
setback, shifted now this way and that way.
He felt intense concern. Should he stay on Sicilian
land and forget the Fates? Or seize an Italian beachhead?
An old man named Nautes, singly instructed
by Pallas of Triton—she'd made him known for the depth of his
          knowledge
by telling him either the meaning of powerful anger
in heaven or things the Fates' order demanded—
used that voice now to comfort Aeneas.
"Son of the Goddess, follow the Fates backward or forward.
710   Whatever happens, all good luck must be earned by endurance.
Your friend of divine and Trojan roots is Acestes:
take advice for your people, join with him freely,
offer him those left from the burned ships and the others
tired of huge adventure—things that concern you.
Weed out older men, women exhausted
from sea travel, whoever is weakening, troubled
by danger and wearied: they'll raise walls in this country,
calling their town, if the name is permitted, Acesta."
Talk like this from an old friend was disturbing;
720   Aeneas felt deeply divided by all of his worries.

Anchises' Voice

When sable Night reached the zenith, led by her horse-team,
Anchises' fatherly form appeared to have glided
down from the sky abruptly. He spoke to Aeneas
with vigor: "Once you were dearer than life, when my lifetime
lasted, my son. Since Troy's fate overwhelms you,
I've come by Jupiter's order. He routed the fire from
your ships: high heaven surely can pity.
Take the advice which old Nautes graciously offered.
Bring to Italy only men you have hand-picked,
730   the strongest hearts. You'll have to conquer a rugged,
harsh people in Latium. I want you, before that,
down in the Hell-God's home to meet with your father
in deep Avernus, my son. I'm not with the somber,
evil shadows of Tartarus: pleasant and holy
meetings are mine in Elysian Fields. A virginal Sibyl
will lead you here when black rams have been slaughtered.
You'll learn of a future city and all your descendents.
For now, good-by. Humid Night has wheeled by a midpoint
of travel and curt horses of Dawn are breathing behind me."

Another Troy to Leave

740   He stopped and retreated like thin smoke in a crosswind.
Aeneas asked, "Why do you hurry and rush off,
who do you run from? What prevents our embracing?"
He said no more. He stirred the ash of the sleepy
hearth-fire, humbly reverenced Troy's House-Gods and white-
        haired
Vesta's inmost shrine with meal and ritual incense.
Quickly he called for his friends and foremost Acestes.
He told them his dear father's message and Jupiter's order.
At last in his own mind he'd reached a decision.
Discussion was brief: Acestes complied with the order.
750   They transferred women, those who longed for a city;
hearts with no great need for distinction could stay here.
Others renewed benches, replaced planking on vessels
consumed by fire, and adjusted oarlocks and rigging:
fewer in number but brave and eager for battle.
Aeneas meanwhile sketched a plan for the city,
using a plow. He assigned houses and ordered
a place called "Troy" and "Ilium." Pleased with the kingdom,
Trojan Acestes marked out a forum and called on the elders

760 to draft laws. On Eryx's peak, close to the starlight,
they founded a shrine for Cyprian Venus. A priest and an ample
sacred grove remained by the tomb of Anchises.

Sacrifices, Farewells, Departure

For nine days everyone feasted and honored
the altars. The sea lay flat, breezes were gentle.
Then the Southwind blew and re-called them to water.
Loud laments rose on the curved shoreline where people
embraced each other. They waited a night, then a full day.
Now some mothers, the very persons the water
had once seemed harsh on its face to, its name unendurable,
wanted to leave and tolerate every burden of exile.
770 Aeneas had kind and friendly words to console them,
sadly entrusting them all to his blood relation, Acestes.
He finally ordered a lamb killed for the Stormwind,
three bulls for Eryx, and cables loosened in order.
Head trimly circled with leaflets of olive,
standing high on the bow holding a wine-bowl,
Aeneas dropped entrails and streams of wine in the water.
Winds came up astern to attend their departure.
Competing crews, lashing waves, swept through the water.

Venus Implores Neptune for Help

The mind of Venus meanwhile labored with worry.
780 She sought out Neptune; complaints poured from her bosom:
"Juno's heavy anger and unappeasable passion
drive me, Neptune, to try every entreaty.
No length of time, no one's goodness can soothe her;
Jupiter's rule, the Fates—nothing can break her.
She's not content to destroy with unspeakable hatred
Troy and the Trojan people, to drag a remnant of Trojans
through every ordeal: she'll even harry a beaten
Troy's bones and cinders. Who knows the cause of such fury?
She may. You saw yourself her recently massing
790 Libyan seas, her suddenly working and tangling
water and sky, her vainly trusting Aeolian whirlwind.
What brashness—in Neptune's realm!
See how she drove Trojan mothers to malice,
to wreck ships of the fleet—the act is revolting.
She forced their friends to leave them in foreigners' country.
I ask, for a final few, for safe time on your water.
Let them arrive in Laurentum and gaze on the Tiber.
The Fates may grant them a city: I ask it be granted."

Divine Assurance Qualified

The deep sea's Lord and son of Saturn responded,
800 "It's wholly right, Cytherean Lady, to trust in my kingdom.
It gave you birth, and earned your trust: I have often
controlled mad or frothing ocean and heavens.
I cared no less on land for Aeneas, the Xanthus
and Simois bear me out: in Troy when Achilles
chased and pinned to a wall your winded detachments,
offering thousands to Death and damming the groan-filled
river, the Xanthus could not discover a channel
to roll seaward. I myself rescued Aeneas
in cave-like mist when he faced the stronger Achilles—
810 his God no match for that strength—though I wanted to uproot
Troy's foundation, laid by this hand, for its falsehood.
I'm still of the same mind. Away with your worry:
your men will arrive safely in port as you wish near Avernus.
But one must die. They'll search the seas but he'll vanish.
A single life for many."

Sea Spirits on a Calm Sea

That word calmed and cheered the heart of the Goddess.
Neptune yoked wild horses with gold and he fitted
their frothy bits: reins slackened completely,
the sky-blue chariot lightly flew on the wave-tops.
820 Water calmed under the muttering axles.
Swollen waves flattened, cloud ran from the far-flung
sky and various friends appeared: sea-forms like giant
whales, the groups of old Glaucus, Ino's Palaemon,
scampering Tritons, the whole squadron of Phorcus.
Thetis remained to the left with chaste Panopea,
Melite, Spio, Cymodoce, Thalia, Nesaea.
A lush gladness now jolted the anxious,
fatherly heart of Aeneas. Quickly he ordered
every mast hoisted and sail hung on each yard-arm.
830 They all worked as one: tacking together
to port and to starboard next, canvas unfurling
and sail-yard turning, re-turning when gusts pushed at the
        galleys.
Palinurus guided them all, conducting the close-ranked
line: ships were told to follow his movements.

An Ominous Visit from Sleep

Already a dewy Night had fingered the halfway
point in the sky, sailors calmly relaxing,
loose-muscled, sprawled on hard seats by the oarlocks,
when Sleep softly glided down from the highest
stars, dividing night-air and ruffling some shadow,
840 looking for you, Palinurus. Bringing a somber
dream to a harmless man, the Sleep-God resembled
Phorbus and settled high astern. His speech was a wordstream:
"Son of Iasus, Palinurus! The sea is conveying
your fleet by itself. Winds are steady. It's time to be resting.
Lay down your head—take your tired eyes from their labor.
I'll take your place myself for a while at the tiller."

The Helmsman Lost

Palinurus hardly moved an eye as he answered,
"Me? You want me to turn my back on the gentle
waves of a quiet sea? Place trust in that monster,
850 even consigning Aeneas to treacherous sea-wind?
Clear skies have tricked or beguiled me too often."
He kept a tight grip on the helm as he answered.
He never lost his fix on the stars for an instant.
The Sleep-God then rustled a branch near his temple,
wet with Lethe drops and the Styx's hypnotic
power: the man's vision swam and failed though he fought it,
a sudden calm had hardly begun to relax him
when Sleep, hovering, sheered off a section of stern-deck
and tossed helmsman and helm both in the water
860 headlong. The man called to his friends often but vainly.
Sleep flew into thin air and ascended on wingbeats.
The squadron still pursued its course through the water
safely, carried by Neptune's fatherly promise, unfrightened.
The fleet already approached a cliff of the Sirens—
dangerous once, with white bones by the hundred—
a raucous and constant pounding of rocks in the distance.
Aeneas realized the ship was yawing and drifting,
her helmsman lost. He steered himself through the night-dark
sea, often sighing, struck by the loss of a shipmate.
870 "Ah, Palinurus—too sure of a moderate sea-swell
and sky! You'll lie stripped on some alien beachsand."

VI

THE UNDERWORLD

Reaching Italy

Aeneas wept while speaking, slackened the reins of his galley
and glided ashore at length at Cumae, a port of Euboeans.
Prows were turned seaward, anchors securing
the ships fast with their bites, and the shoreline was bordered
with rounded hulls. Men who'd yearned for Italian
soil leaped out. One group searched for the fire-seed
hidden in veins of flint while another collected
wood near dens of beasts, finding and pointing to rivers.
Aeneas, recalling his duty, made for the lofty
10   heights where Apollo presided, close to the spacious and private
cave of a feared Sybil through whom the Delian Prophet
breathed his great mind and will, revealing the future.

Daedalus and the Labyrinth

Trojans went under the golden roof and grove of Diana.
According to legend Daedalus fled from the kingdom of Minos,
daring to trust himself to the sky on his rapid
wingbeats, making his cold, unlikely way to the Arctic
and finally touching down on this hilltop at Cumae.
On first returning to land, Apollo, he offered
his oar-like wings to you, and built a magnificent temple.
20   Androgeos' death was carved on the doors, and the wretched
Athenians, forced to pay by surrendering seven
sons each year: an urn stood there, lots to be drawn out.
The island of Crete rose from the sea on the portal

facing. Here was brutal love for a bull, Pasiphae
furtively mounted, a two-formed fetus inside her—
the Minotaur, man and beast, reminder of sexual outrage.
Here was its home, a work of unwindable tangles.
But Daedalus pitied the deep love of a queen, Ariadne,
loosened the tricky knots of the building for Theseus,
30 guiding his blind feet with thread. Icarus also
would play a great part in this great work—if his father's
grief had allowed it: twice he tried to capture that downfall
in gold and twice his hand failed him. Trojans were reading
all this closely now when Achates (sent on before them)
arrived with Diana's priestess, the Sybil of Phoebus
named Deiphobe—Glaucus' daughter. She spoke to their leader:
"Those are not the pictures you need at this moment.
It's proper to sacrifice now: seven bullocks that never
were yoked and seven hand-picked ewes. It's our custom."
40 Aeneas' friends followed the ritual order
promptly. The priestess called them on high to her temple.

Apollo's Arrival

A cave had been cut in a huge mass of Cumaean
rock: a hundred wide paths converged on a hundred
mouths where sounds could rush out—the Sybil's responses.
The men came to an entrance. The virgin commanded,
"It's time to demand the God's word. Look—my Apollo!"
Her face and color changed at once while she spoke at the
        entrance,
her breasts heaved, her hair lost its arrangement
and wild fury filled her heart: she seemed to be taller
50 now that the God's will gave her more than a human
voice and breathed close. "You're slow in your prayer?
Aeneas of Troy," she said, "slow to make vows? But before then
the great mouth of our sky-struck house will not open."

Will Troy's Bad Luck Now End?

She fell silent. Cold tremors ran through the Trojans'
rugged bones. Their leader earnestly poured out a prayer:
"Phoebus, you always pitied the hard labor of Trojans.
You guided the hand and Trojan arrow of Paris
straight for Achilles' flesh. With you as my leader
I entered seas bordering vast lands, the Massylian
60 people's far interiors, broad fields at the Syrtes.
At last we cling to a fleeting Italian beachhead.

Let Troy's bad luck follow this far and no farther!
Every God and Goddess offended by Trojan
strength and glory: let it be right, now, that you pity
Troy's people. And you, most holy of seers
who know the future: I claim the kingdom that's owed by
the Fates: give us Latium, rest for the people
of Troy, for our wandering Gods' disquieted powers.
I'll found a temple of solid marble for Phoebus,
70   Diana as well. I'll name festal days for the Sun-God.
And priestess, majestic shrines wait in our kingdom
for you: I'll place your oracle told to my people
and all your mysteries there. I'll dedicate hand-picked
men to your service. But here don't trust incantations
to leaves—the rush of a playful wind may disturb them—
sing them yourself, please." He ended the prayer.

Apollo Speaks through the Sibyl

Now the seer, not yet yielding to Phoebus,
dashed through the large cave as if able to shake off
the great God from her chest. But all the more he oppressed her,
80   mastered her wild heart and mouth: he gripped and subdued her.
The hundred large doors of her cavern were swinging
wide by themselves and winds carried the Sybil's responses:
"At last are you done with extreme danger on water?
Worse remains on land. Trojans will enter
Lavinia's realm—drop that heartfelt anxiety—
but wish you'd never arrived. I see you in battle,
war's horror, foaming blood on the Tiber.
You won't be lacking a Simois River, a Xanthus,
Greek-like camps and a new Achilles emerging in Latium,
90   born himself of a Goddess. Juno will never
be far from you Trojans. How you'll scrape for advantage like
        paupers,
pleading with every city and people in Italy!
A foreign wife again makes trouble for Trojans:
a marriage again to a foreigner.
Don't concede to the trouble. Fight it more boldly
wherever Luck permits. Your pathway to safety
first is cleared by a Greek city: you'd hardly expect it."

A Prayer for Reunion

So the Cumaean Sibyl chanted ambiguous,
frightening words in her shrine, wrapping truth in her darkness,

100　doubling the cave's noise. Apollo had shaken
　　　the reins and twisted a spur in her breast to incite her.
　　　Soon as her wild, frenzied outcry diminished,
　　　Aeneas, the leader, began: "None of that hardship,
　　　virgin, is new in form or appears unexpected.
　　　I've known it all: I've pondered or lived it beforehand.
　　　I ask one thing. It's said the gates of the Ruler of Darkness
　　　are near, and a murky swamp from the Acheron River's
　　　overflow. Let me go down: see the face of the Father
　　　I love: teach me the sacred path: open the portals.
110　I saved him myself from fire and a thousand pursuing
　　　enemy spears. He escaped from a mob on my shoulder.
　　　My close partner at sea, in all of our travels
　　　he bore each threat from the sky and water, exceeding
　　　the strength and duties of age even when sickly.
　　　The man prayed and gave commands in fact that I humbly
　　　seek and approach your entrance. Pity a father
　　　and son, I ask your indulgence. Your power is total:
　　　Hecate gave you control of Avernian woodland
　　　to use it. If Orpheus could summon Eurydice's shadow,
120　trusting a Thracian lyre's melodious strumming:
　　　if Pollux could save a brother by dying another
　　　way, descending and rising again—why should I mention
　　　Hercules, Theseus? I'm of high Jupiter's bloodline."

The Golden Bough

　　　He uttered that strong prayer while gripping the altar.
　　　The seer answered, "You *are* of the bloodline of heaven,
　　　Trojan son of Anchises. Going down to the Underworld's easy:
　　　the Hell-God's dark door is open morning and evening.
　　　The climb back to higher air, retracing your footsteps:
　　　there's the work, the struggle. A few have been able,
130　raised by fire-like courage to heaven, the son of some Sky-God,
　　　or helped by Jupiter's love. Woods are all intervening;
　　　the River Cocytus glides and circles, a pitchy meandering.
　　　Still if you love so much and intensely desire to
　　　enter the Styx's water twice, to witness the pallor
　　　of Tartarus twice, if mad labor enthralls you,
　　　listen and do this first. The leaves and the supple
　　　bend of a golden bough hide in a shady
　　　tree, a sacred prize of the Underworld's Juno.
　　　Forest completely obscures the bough in a shadowy valley.
140　No one's allowed to enter the Underworld's coverts

before pulling that goldhaired child from its tree-trunk:
Proserpine's ordered the fine gift to be carried
down to herself. Once you've broken the first off,
a second golden bough will sprout similar leaflets.
Look up high, therefore; soon as you find it,
pull with your hands. The bough will easily follow
if God's word has called you. Otherwise nothing
will wrench it free, not the best muscle or iron.

The Brashness of Misenus

"But now your friend is dead. A body's unburied.
150 You could not know, sadly. The corpse dishonors your vessels
while you seek guidance here and muse at our doorway.
Carry the man to a tomb first. Bury him duly.
Lead out black rams: make them your first expiation.
Only then will you see the Styx River and forest,
a realm uncrossed by the living." She sealed her mouth and was
            quiet.
Aeneas left the cave with a mournful expression.
Eyes downcast, he mentally puzzled over
this blind turn of events. A friend he trusted, Achates,
walked along, side by side, sharing the worry.
160 Between themselves they exchanged a number of questions.
What friend did the seer refer to? What corpse could be needing
burial? Soon they arrived and regarded Misenus
there on the dry beach, taken by death without pity.
A son of the Wind-God, a standout at stirring companions
with trumpet calls igniting the War-God, Misenus
had joined with powerful Hector, gone into combat
with Hector's group and excelled with spear as with bugle.
But after Achilles victoriously stripped Hector of spirit
Misenus gave what leadership, courage and friendship
170 he could to Aeneas of Troy, following no one inferior.
Now by chance with a hollow conch he'd rumbled the seacoast,
madly challenging Gods, calling and blaring.
An envious Triton had seized the man (if the story
deserved belief) and plunged him in surf among boulders.

Another Burial

So everyone circled now and wept for him loudly,
Aeneas with special devotion. They followed the Sibyl's
command promptly, still in tears: they erected
a tomb and altar with timber, worked and raised it to heaven:

they went to an old pine-stand close to a mammal's
180 deep burrow, felled both pitch-pine and ash-tree.
Oaks grunted at axe-blows, wedges split up the oak-logs,
and huge cords of rowan tumbled down from the mountains.

Help from Two Doves

First indeed in all that work was Aeneas,
encouraging men, wielding tools that the men used.
He pondered it all himself sadly and deeply,
gazing at deep forest. He happened to pray there:
"If only that tree with the golden bough could appear here,
right in this vast forest! Clearly the Sibyl was honest,
Misenus: she spoke of your death too truthfully, sadly."
190 By chance a pair of doves appeared when Aeneas
had just finished: they veered from the sky and alighted
on green moss within view. The greatest of leaders
recognized Venus' birds and prayed to them gladly,
"Guide me, somehow: set a course through the air-flow,
find a way to the grove where that priceless bough overshadows
the rich earth. And you, my Goddess and Mother,
don't fail me in time of doubt." He stopped speaking and walking:
he noted a sign they made, the course they elected.
The doves kept feeding, only flying before him
200 so far as his eye could follow. He kept them in focus.
In time they reached the malodorous throat of Avernus,
they climbed quickly and glided down through the air-waves,
both perching high in the tree they had looked for:
a second color, gold brilliance, shone through the branches,
the way mistletoe blooms in woodland in winter
cold, its new foliage circling a slender
tree (not the parent) with berries of yellow.
Golden leaves appeared that way in the oaktree's
green. Metal tinkled softly in breezes.
210 Aeneas gripped it at once, eagerly pulling.
It gave slowly. He brought it back to the home of the Sybil.

Pyre and Memorial

Trojans meanwhile mourned on the shore for Misenus
nonetheless, going through last rites for ungrateful
ashes. First they built a huge pyre out of chopped-up
oak and tacky pine. They plaited the sides with a darker
wood, leaning the death-tree against them, the cypress.
Armor gleamed on top of the pyre in adornment.

Men heated cauldrons, fire bubbled the water;
others washed the cold body and oiled it.
220 Moaning, weeping their last, they settled the body
back on a couch. They draped it with purple, familiar
clothes of the man. The large bier was supported
(a somber task) and torches applied, in the way of their fathers,
with eyes averted. Piled-up presents of incense,
oil poured in bowls, and meal were cremated.
After the ashes fell, the death-fire diminished,
wine moistened the thirsty dust and the remnants.
Corynaeus gathered the bones. A bronze jar would enclose them.
Three times with clean water he circled the people,
230 sprinkled them lightly with flowering branches of olive
in ritual cleansing, and finally offered some verses.
Aeneas conscientiously raised an enormous
tomb enclosing the man's oars, weapons and trumpet.
That windy hill is now known as Misenus,
keeping a friend's name alive through the ages.

Prayers to the Hell-Gods

With all that done they quickly followed the Sibyl's
command: by a deep cave with enormous and jagged
mouth, guarded by oil-black pools and a nighttime of forest,
where hardly a single bird could navigate safely
240 or fly overhead—such was the vapor that seeped from
the dark mouth and rose to the dome of the heavens
(Greeks called the place *Aornos*, "The Birdless")—
the priestess stationed four of her black-backed
heifers first and poured wine on their foreheads.
Clasping hair near a horn she snipped off the topmost,
placed it on ritual fire, the first of her offerings,
and loudly called: "Hecate! In heaven and hell you have power."
Men cut the throats and caught the arterial
gush in bowls. Aeneas slaughtered a black-wooled
250 lamb himself for Night, the mother of Furies,
and Earth, her great sister; a calfless cow for the Hell-Queen;
then, for the Styx's King, he started an altar
service at night, piling thick beef on the sacral
fire and pouring fatty oil on the sizzling entrails.

The Hour to Descend

And see, under the first glare of the rising
sun the ground lowed underfoot, forested ridges

began to move, dogs peered and whined at the shadows.
"The Goddess is coming," the seer yelled, "you must leave us,
all you men not purified, leave the forest completely!
260 Aeneas, take to the path, pull your sword from its scabbard:
you'll need spirit now and steady emotion."
She broke off and wildly flung herself in the open
cave. Aeneas, resolute, followed his leader.

Invocation to the Lower Powers

Lords of the spiritual empire! Shadow and Silence,
Chaos, Phlegethon, mute stretches of Midnight,
make it right to say what I've heard: give me the power
to bare things deep in the earth covered in vapor.

Real and Unreal at the Entrance

They moved through obscure darkness, desolate shadow,
past empty houses of Dis, unoccupied throne-rooms,
270 the way a path moves through woods when moonlight is doubtful
or sparse, when Jupiter hides the sky or obscures it,
when black Night deprives the world of its color.
Before the entrance, Grief and vindictive Anxiety
smoothed their beds in the gullet itself of the Hell-God.
Wan Disease was here with comfortless Aging
and Fear. Crime-encouraging Hunger and grimy
Poverty, forms frightful to witness. Death and the throes of
Death. Lethargy, Death's brother, and sickly
minds' Giddiness. War, the bringer of Death, on the threshold
280 opposite. Furies on iron couches. Mad Revolution,
her hair a tangle of blood-soaked fillets and serpents.
A huge elm in the center extended shadowy branches
like old arms. They say dozens of idle
dreams are at home in all that foliage, clinging.
More prodigies lay beyond it, a mélange:
Centaurs at doors of stalls, Scyllas doubly contorted,
the hundred-handed Briareus, the Hydra from Lyrna,
fiercely hissing. Chimaera, armed with its flame-spears.
Gorgons, Harpies, and Geryon's three-bodied shadow.
290 Suddenly clutching a sword, trembling in terror,
Aeneas held out its fine edge to those that were nearest.
Had not his well-taught friend told him the bodies
were hollow forms of reality, tenuous flittings,
the man would have vainly charged, blade swiping at shadows.

Charon and the Styx River

A path led down from there to Acheron's water
and Tartarus. Churning, seething with mud in a monstrous
vortex, a whirlpool dumped tons of sand in Cocytus.
A boatman guarded the river's flow: Charon was frightful,
in dire filth, the beard on his chin like a jumble
300 of grey briars, the eyes like motionless firelight.
A soiled and knotted coat hung from a shoulder.
He punted a ferry himself, took care of the canvas,
and carried people across in the rust-colored vessel.
Now old, he'd aged raw and green, as a God does.
A crowd came running and thronging the banks of the river:
men and mothers, the forms of great-hearted heroes
relieved of life, boys and unmarried daughters,
children placed on pyres before the eyes of their parents:
dense as leaves falling and drifting in forests
310 in autumn at first frost, or birds flocking to seashore
from whirlpools at sea when the cold season pursues them
over the waves and sends them to sun-loving country.
They stood there begging to ride first on the water.
Hands reached out, they longed for the opposite shoreline.
The dour boatman picked out this one and that one,
keeping many others far back on the gravel.
Aeneas, deeply moved and alarmed by the uproar,
spoke out: "Tell me, virgin, why is that crowd by the river?
What do the spirits want? What keeps that number away from
320 the bank while others move through the indigo water?"
The aging priestess briefly answered Aeneas:
"Son of Anchises, surely the son of a Goddess,
the deep marsh you see is a pond of the Styx and Cocytus.
Even Gods fear to swear and renege by its power.
The large crowd you see is helpless, unburied.
Charon, the boatman, takes on those who are buried.
No one may cross that grumbling stream from this anxious
side before his bones find rest in some death-mound.
Souls wander and flit about the bank for a hundred
330 years. Then Charon takes them. They ride the waves they had
        longed for."

Palinurus Reappears

Anchises' son walked slower. He stopped there,
pondered all the unfair luck, pitying deeply.

He saw, in the crowd lacking burial honors,
a sad Leucaspis, Orontes (the Lycian squadron commander),
both borne from Troy on gusty sea till a Southwind
tumbled their ships and men in the water, and swamped them.
And look: Palinurus, the helmsman—guiding himself now.
Checking stars on the recent voyage from Libya
he'd dropped astern, got thrown, surrounded by water.

340   Aeneas could just make out the somber man in that heavy
gloom. He spoke up first: "Which of the Gods, Palinurus,
tore you from friends and plunged you deep into water?
Tell me! We never found Phoebus deceptive
before that time, when he mocked my heart with his answer,
saying you'd reach the coast of Italy safely,
unharmed at sea. How could that promise be truthful?"

Desperate Cries for Help

The other: "Phoebus' oracle never deceived you,
son of Anchises, my leader: no God plunged me in water.
Sharp and random violence broke off the tiller.

350   Charged with holding our course, I clung to the steering
and flew off, dragging it with me. I swear by the bitter
sea, Aeneas, I feared much less for my body
than yours, the steerage gone, an overboard helmsman—
your ship could capsize in deep, gathering white-caps.
For three wintry nights a violent Southwind
rushed me along on huge waves. From high on a roller's
crest on the fourth dawn I recognized Italy.
Swimming ashore gradually, reaching for safety,
I hooked my hands on the jagged ledge of a sea-cliff,

360   clothes heavy and drenched—when barbarous people
struck me with daggers, foolishly thinking of booty.
Wind and wave toss and keep me there on that shoreline.
I beg you, by all the breath and light of the precious
sky, your father, your rising hope in Iulus:
save me from all this wrong. You can, you're unconquered:
look for Velia harbor and throw soil on my body!
Or, if a way exists for the Goddess, your Mother,
to show you—I'm sure you're ready to enter the Styx's
broad river and marsh with power from heaven—

370   give your hand to a wretch: take me over that water!
Help me to rest in peace at least as a dead man."

Underworld Law

The seer began to speak as he begged in that manner,
"Why such painful desire, Palinurus, such longing
to see the grim Styx's flow? You are unburied:
how can you pass to the Furies' banks before you are asked to?
Stop hoping to bend the Gods' law with your begging.
Take this word to console you—your fall was a hard one—
people far and wide in neighboring cities,
urged by signs from the sky, will atone for your death by erecting
380 a tomb and offering gifts each year at the death-mound.
The place will have a permanent name—Palinurus."
Her promise relieved his hurt for a time and diminished
his heart's gloom. He smiled to hear of the place-name.

Charon's Challenge

Aeneas, pursuing the course he'd started, came to the river.
Soon as the ferryman saw him there from the Styx's
water, passing mute scrub and close to the streambank,
Charon aggressively shouted, challenging quickly:
"Whoever you are, approaching our river in armor,
stop walking there: say why you should visit
390 a land of Shadow, languid Midnight and Nightmare.
To carry living flesh in my Styx ferry is sinful.
I hardly enjoyed taking Hercules over
the water, or Theseus, no, or Pirithous—
though Gods bore them and men could not beat them.
One of them wanted to chain Tartarus' watchdog,
drag him trembling away from the throne itself of our Ruler;
the others tried to escort our Queen from the bed of her husband!"

Acknowledging the Golden Bough

The seer of Amphrysian Phoebus answered him shortly,
"Don't be troubled. No one here is deceitful.
400 Our weapons have no force. Your monster-like watchdog
may bark in his cave forever to terrify bloodless
ghosts. Your queen will remain chaste at the door of her uncle.
Aeneas of Troy, known for filial love and for war-work,
wants to meet his father's shade in Erebus' darkness.
If no one sign of his great devotion will move you,
here's a bough you'll know." She opened a vestment,
revealing the gold. Charon's puffed-up rancor subsided.
Protesting no more, amazed at that venerable offering—

an ominous branch no one had seen in a long time—
410 he swung the coal-blue ferry around to the bank and approached
       them.
First he dislodged from the long benches the other
souls who'd sat there. Clearing the boat's gangplanks, he took on
the bulk of Aeneas. The ferry groaned under the living
weight—swampwater spurted through stitches and fissures.
At length he safely ferried the man and the priestess
across the river to grey sedge and featureless mudflat.

The Watchdog Subdued

Cerberus shook this place with three-throated barking,
a huge beast crouched in a cavern that faced them.
The Sibyl, seeing his necks already bristling with serpents,
420 threw some scraps of fruit, drugged and honeyed to make him
sleep. Savagely hungry he gaped and snapped at the pieces
with all three mouths. The large hindquarters buckled;
he sprawled on the ground, immensely stretched through the
       cavern.
Aeneas passed the entrance, the watchdog unconscious,
and quickly left the riverbank no one re-crosses.

Pain and Judgment in the Underworld

They soon heard voices, a deafening outcry
of spirits weeping, children deprived of joy on the very
threshold of life by Luck, removed on a darkling
day from their mothers' breasts and plunged in some bitter
430 death. Nearby were spirits condemned to die through the charges
of perjurors, given their true place by lot or by judgment
now: Minos presided, shaking the urn at the head of
a silent court. He studied each life and its evil.
Other places were held by innocent, downcast
people who'd caused their own deaths, hating the sunlight,
ditching their lives. How they were willing to labor
hard now in higher air and suffer as paupers!
Gods' laws blocked them. Dreary, unloveable water
constrained them: the nine-coiled Styx intervened and enclosed
       them.

Dido Once More

440 Not far from there, spread out in every direction,
appeared Fields of Mourning (the name they were known by),
where people consumed by love's ruthless infection

kept to themselves on footpaths covered by myrtle
woods. In death too their anxiety lingered.
Here were seen Phaedra, Procris, wretched Eriphyle,
showing the wound her son had cruelly inflicted.
Evadne and Pasiphae walked with a friend, Laodamia.
The Nymph Caeneus, once a boy, now was a woman
again, changed by the Fates back to her earlier figure.
450 Among them, roaming that far-flung woodland, was Dido,
Phoenicia's woman, her wound fresh. Soon as the Trojan
leader stood up close and saw through the shadows
her dusky form (as a man, when the month is beginning,
sees or thinks he sees the moon rising through cloud-trail),
he shed some tears. He spoke fondly and gently:
"Unhappy Dido, the story I heard was correct then?
I heard you had died, sought out death with a sword-thrust.
And I—my God—I caused your death? I swear by the starlight,
by Gods in the sky, the Power in Earth's depths, if there's any:
460 I never wished, my queen, to sail from your seacoast.
Gods compelled me—just as I'm driven to travel
now through Night's depths, through briar and shadow.
They drive by their own rules. How could I figure
my leaving would bring such deep distress to your spirit?
Please don't go—don't walk from where I can see you—
what do you run from? The last words I'm permitted to tell you—"
Aeneas tried, in tears, to calm and subdue her.
She looked grim. Her womanly spirit was burning.
She turned and kept her gaze fixed on the stubble.
470 Her face had changed, once he began to address her,
no more than flint would, or hard Marpesian rock-stands.
She finally tore herself away like an enemy,
running for shadowy woods where Sychaeus, her husband
at Tyre, could match her love and respond to her caring.
Aeneas remained stunned by her death's unfairness. He followed
a long way, pitying. He wept when she moved off.

Fields of Warriors

He trudged back to the way provided. Soon he was reaching
far fields arranged for people famous in battle.
He met Tydaeus here, Parthenopaeus
480 (in well known armor), the pale form of Adrastus.
Trojans were here, killed in war and deeply lamented
above on earth. Aeneas watched them all in a drawn-out
line and sighed. Thersilochus, Medon and Glaucus

(Antenor's three sons). Ceres' priest, Polyboetes.
Idaeus, still tending weapons and chariot.
They stood around, left and right, spirits in clusters.
Unsatisfied now with merely a glimpse of Aeneas,
they gladly walked along, stopped him and asked his reason for
    coming.
But Greek princes and cordons of King Agamemnon,
490 seeing the man's weapons gleam through the shadows,
trembled, acutely afraid. They moved off—as they'd headed
once for their ships—or tried projecting their voices
feebly, the shouts they started belied by their gaping.

War's Atrocity

Aeneas could see a son of Priam, Deiphobus,
totally mangled here. Lips viciously cut off,
lips and both hands, the ears ripped from their temples
and torn off, nose cropped: a scandalous maiming.
Aeneas could hardly recognize the man as he shivered,
covering ghastly wounds. He spoke up first as a friend would:

500 "Deiphobus, strong in war, from the high bloodline of Teucer,
what person chose to inflict such barbarous torture?
Who could allow it—on *you*? They told me a rumor
that last night: weary of slaughter and killing Pelasgians,
you fell on top of a mixed-up litter of corpses.
Later I built an empty tomb on Rhoeteum's
coast myself. I called aloud three times to your spirit.
Your name and weapons guard the place. But I never discovered
your body, my friend, or gave you rest in the land I was leaving."
Priam's son: "My friend, nothing's neglected:
510 you settled it all for the dead shade of Deiphobus.
My own bad luck and the capital crimes of a Spartan
woman plunged me in pain: Helen left these mementoes.
Remember, we wasted ourselves in trivial pleasure
that last night—we cannot help but remember—
after the fatal horse came running and leaping
up Troy's heights, its belly loaded with weapons
and soldiers. That female pretended to dance. Leading some
    Trojan
women and shouting, 'Euhoe,' holding the largest
torch in their midst, she actually signaled Greeks from our
    fortress.
520 Exhausted from worry, meanwhile, heavy and drowsy,

I lay on my wretched bed. Deep and pleasureable stillness
covered my body, resembling the stillness of dead men.
My prize wife had earlier cleared arms from the building,
even pulling a sword I trusted from under my pillow.
She opened the house doors and hailed Menelaus,
hoping of course that here was a fine gift for her lover,
that talk of the old mistakes now would be smothered.
Why delay it? They rushed in the bedroom, adding a single
crime-mongering friend, Ulysses. God, if you let me
530 demand rightful vengeance, turn on the Greeks with my torment!
But you—it's your turn—tell me what happenings brought you
alive here. Did seas force or confuse you?
Some God's warning or will? What luck has oppressed you,
to come to a place of disquiet, sunless and dismal?"

The Sibyl Hurries Aeneas

During their talk Aurora had driven already
across the zenith, coursing through sky in her rose-colored
      chariot.
All the allotted time might have gone in that manner
had not the Sibyl spoken briefly—her warning was friendly:
"Night comes on, Aeneas. We lose hours to your sorrow.
540 Here's the place where the road divides into two paths:
the right one leads to the walls of powerful Pluto—
our path to Elysium; the left one leads to the ruthless
Tartarus' depths—criminals' pains are incurred there."
Deiphobus told her, "Don't be harsh, magisterial priestess.
I'll go—and re-fill the number of shades back in that darkness.
Go and enjoy better luck, you pride of the Trojans!"
He said that much, turned while speaking, and left him.

Tartarus and its Punishments

Aeneas abruptly noticed a cliff on the left side.
He saw a thick wall, three belts of fortification,
550 ringed by a river whose rapids were burning and boiling—
the Underworld's Phlegethon, rolling a clatter of boulders.
Enormous gates were in front, solid columns of iron.
No human force, no Sky-God himself in a battle
could wreck them. Against the sky stood a tower of iron;
a Fury, Tisiphone, sat on top, wrapped in a bloody
coat. Day and night she guarded the courtyard.
Groans were audible now and cracks of relentless
whips, dragged chains, the grating of metal.

Aeneas paused in terror, gripped by the uproar.
560 "Tell me, virgin priestess, what forms of evil are driven
to punishment here? The rising din is outrageous."
The seer began, "Famed leader of Trojans,
by Law no pure spirit may cross that criminals' threshold.
When Hecate made me rule the groves of Avernus,
she taught me the Gods' vengeance herself and led me through all
          this.
Rhadamanthus of Crete governs that hardest of kingdoms.
He hears out tricksters, checks them, and forces confessions.
Each one sinned in the world above with a furtive and empty
pleasure, delaying regret too late, till the death-hour.
570 Instantly straddling the guilty spirit is vengeful
Tisiphone, armed with a stinging whip: while her left hand
waves fierce snakes, she calls for a horde of her sisters.
At length a feared gate opens on screeching
sockets and hinges. Imagine what sort of a watchman
sits at the entrance, that form guarding the doorway:
fifty black and monstrous mouths of the Hydra—
it holds a fiercer place inside. Then Tartarus opens
itself, a headlong plunge far down into darkness,
twice as far as your view to the sky or the air on Olympus.
580 Titans are there, Earth's primordial children,
downed by thunderbolts, rolling around in the deepest
holes. I saw twin giants, the sons of Aloeus,
who strove to demolish the breadth of Jupiter's heaven
by hand, to thrust him down from the heights of his kingdom.
I saw Salmoneus too paying a brutal
price for copying Jupiter's fire and the sound of Olympus:
drawn in a four-horse chariot, shaking some torches,
borne in triumph through Greek crowds and the city
at Elis' center, he'd claimed for himself Olympian worship.
590 Madman! To mimic a stormcloud's inimitable lightning
with brass wheels and the stamp of horn-footed horses!
The all-powerful Father hurtled a fire-spear
from massed cloud—not some torch or a luminous, smoking
pine—its violent whirlwind twisted him headlong.
I saw Tityus also, foster child of everyone's Mother,
the Earth. He lay outstretched, the body extended
nine full acres. A vulture, monstrous and hook-beaked,
skimmed his ageless liver, tissue ripe for the torment
constantly: the bird grubbed deep in his ribcage
600 for meat, giving no rest to the flesh: it always recovered.

Why mention the Lapithae, Pirithous, Ixion,
threatened by black granite apparently tilting
and falling right now? Or men on high festival couches
with gold-gleaming legs, with dishes arranged for a monarch's
delight before their eyes? An elderly Fury
lounging nearby stops their hands from touching the table:
she leaps up, cocking a torch, her outcry like thunder.
Here are those who hated a brother while living,
struck a father, or tangled dependents in hoaxes.
610 More—the largest crowd—came upon riches,
lived alone and shared no wealth with their children.
Some were killed for adultery, or followed a traitor
in battle, daring to break faith with a master.
Now they're jailed and waiting punishment. Don't be too curious
how they're punished, what form or fate overwhelms them.
They roll great stones or hang from the turning
spokes of wheels. Theseus miserably sits there:
he'll sit forever. Phlegyas, saddest of all men,
reminds everyone, loudly calling through shadows:

620 'BE WARNED: LEARN JUSTICE: STOP SCORNING THE
     SKY-GODS.'

One man sold his country for gold and inflicted
despotic rule. Another rigged laws for a price, or unriggged them.
One man forced forbidden sex on a daughter.
They all dared to offend grossly, and did as they dared to.
If I had a hundred mouths and tongues and a hundred
iron voices I could not number all of the evil
forms or cite the name of everyone's sentence."

The Presentation of the Golden Bough

Having said all this the aging priestess of Phoebus
added, "But come now. Take to the road. Finish the labor
630 you started. Hurry—I see a wall raised by the Cyclops'
forges ahead—an arched portal confronts us.
There we'll place the gift we were told to beforehand."
She ended. They walked the dim roadway together,
covered the ground intervening and came to the portal.
There at the entrance Aeneas sprinkled his body
with fresh water. He set the bough at the doorway that faced him.

Entering the Elysian Fields

Done, finally, the office performed for the Goddess,

they came to a joyful place, green and delightful
groves of contented people, the homes of Elysium.
640 Headier air was here; a lilac color appareled
fields that knew their own starlight and sunlight.
Men on the grass trained their bodies for wrestling
or grappled on tawny sand, competing in matches.
One group sang songs, tapping their feet to a dance-time.
A Thracian priest in a long garment was keeping
time as well on the seven clear tones of his lyre-strings,
plucking now with a finger, now with an ivory plectrum.
Teucer's old nation was here, a beautiful people,
great spirits of leaders born in a better
650 age, like Ilus, Assaracus; Troy's patriarch, Dardanus.
Aeneas admired from a distance the armor and empty
chariots, upright spears in the ground, and the scattered,
loose-reined horses cropping fieldgrass. The credit
a man might take for sword or horse-team while living,
for careful shining and feeding, followed him down into earth-
    depths.
Left and right Aeneas saw on the fieldgrass
men feasting while singing, enjoying a paean in chorus
under a scented laurel. From there the Eridanus
River's fullness rolled above them through forest.

Musaeus Helps the Sibyl

660 Some had suffered wounds in war for their country.
Some were devoted priests during their lifetime.
A few were sacred prophets who'd sung things worthy of Phoebus.
A few had worked to discover a way of enhancing
life anew, and deserved remembrance for service.
A white headband circled everyone's temples.
The Sibyl spoke up now when they crowded around her,
Musaeus above them all—he stood in the center,
the large crowd noting his out-standing shoulders.
"Tell us, you glad spirits, and you, exceptional seer:
670 what part of your world holds Anchises? We came here,
crossing wide Underworld water, to see him."
Musaeus made a brief response to the Sibyl.
"No one's home is fixed. We live in the shaded
groves, on couches of stream-banks, or occupy meadows
freshened by brooks. But you, if will and heart will support you,
climb this hill. I'll find you the readiest footpath."
He finished and walked before them. Higher, he showed them

fields of light. They left the hilltop behind them.

Reunion of Father and Son

Anchises now like a father was earnestly gazing
680 at souls confined in a deep green valley and destined
for higher light. By chance he reviewed and considered
a whole line of dear people—descendants'
future luck (and bad luck), customs and art-work—
just when he saw Aeneas approaching directly
there on the grass. He raised both hands in excitement,
words fell out, tears dropped from his cheekbones,
"You finally came? The love a father had hoped for
survived your hard road? Am I favored to witness
my son's face, to hear and respond to familiar language?
690 I really thought so—my heart knew of this future!
I marked our time. All my care did not fail me.
To welcome you here, my son, from such wide lands and such
          driving
seas! What country expelled you, what desperate danger?
How worried I was the Libyan kingdom might harm you!"
Aeneas answered, "Father, your sad apparition
often met me and urged me to strive for this region.
Our fleet stands in the Etruscan Sea. But give me your right hand,
please, Father—don't withdraw—let me embrace you."
Large tears wetted his face while he pleaded.
700 Three times he reached for the figure's neck to embrace him:
the image eluded his grasp each time. Reaching was futile—
he moved like a dream with wings or a stirring of breezes.

Gathering at the Lethe River

In time Aeneas could see in a separate valley
a grove apart where forest and copses were rustling.
The Lethe River flowed by peaceable homes there
and large masses of people came running and circling,
just as bees in clear summer might settle
on various blooms in a meadow, swarming and circling
white lilies, making a whole countryside murmur.
710 The sudden, unexplained vision was causing
Aeneas to shudder; he asked what waters were those in the
          distance,
who the men were, filling the banks like an army.
His father Anchises: "Spirits destined for other
bodies by Law: they've come to that river, the Lethe,

for carefree water, a long drink of oblivion.
In fact I've wanted to tell you, to show you in person
now for a long time our line of descendants,
to celebrate fully together your sighting of Italy."
"But Father, must we think some spirits go soaring
720   upward from here, again reverting to heavy
flesh? Why such mad desire for daylight and sadness?"
"I won't keep you uncertain, my son. I will tell you."

The Great Wheel of Life and Death

Anchises began to reveal each phase of a cycle.
"First a Spirit inside them nourishes heaven
and earth's marshy plains, the luminous orbits
of moon, stars and sun: Mind streams through their members
completely, stirs their mass, and unites with voluminous Body.
Then come species of birds, animals, people,
prodigies borne on the marbled surface of ocean.
730   That Force is fire-like: the source of that seed is celestial,
until weights of bodily sickness retard it:
earth-bound joints and death-bound members can dull it.
So people fear and crave, they grieve or they're giddy,
they see no higher air, confined in jails of their darkness.
Even when life's last glimmer has left them,
harm can still remain: not all the body's contagion
leaves their wretched selves entirely: things which are deeply
wound together for years must grow mysteriously grafted.
Therefore they work off old wrongs. They are punished,
740   paying debts by hanging exposed in the empty
wind. Others are washed in a violent whirlpool.
Some are purged by fire of the last of their malice.
We all endure our own spirit's correction.
Then we're sent through wide Elysium, many remaining
in glad fields for long days till they finish a cycle
of time that frees them of hard imperfection, leaving awareness
pure as the highest air and simple as firelight.
All the others roll the wheel of a thousand
years. A God then calls them in long lines to the Lethe,
750   clearly to help them start forgetting and want a return to
the arched sky, to turn back to the body."

Future Kings of Rome

Anchises finished and drew his son and the Sibyl
together right through the crowd's boisterous center.
He climbed a mound from where he could scan all of the spirits'
long lines and study the men's faces approaching.
"Come, now. Honor at last will follow the children
of Troy. Descendants remain for Italy's people:
brilliant spirits to come with our own reputation!
Let my words present them. I'll teach you your future.
760 See that youth who leans on a spear with no spear-point?
He holds by lot the place closest to daylight: he rises
to higher air first from our mix with Italian bloodlines:
Silvius, surname of Alban kings, and the last-born
son your wife Lavinia rears in the forest
when you are old. But a ruler, and father of rulers:
at Alba Longa he'll help our people to conquer.
Next is Procas, whom Troy's descendents will honor;
Capys and Numitor; Silvius Aeneas, reviving
your own name—and just as outstanding in honor
770 and battle—if Alba will ever yield to his power.
Look at those men! What youth and strength they're displaying,
their shaded temples carrying citizens' oak-leaves!
Some will build Nomentum, Gabii, the town of Fidenae;
some, citadels high on the hills of Collatia,
Pometia, Camp Inuus, Bola and Cora.
Names will appear where land is nameless at present.

The Glory of Rome Itself

"Even Mars' child will join his grandfather-comrade:
Romulus, Ilia's boy, born of Assaracus'
blood. See that standing double crest on his helmet?
780 The Gods' Father himself marks him now with distinction.
Look, my son: Rome's glory comes from that omen.
Matching the world in rule, Olympus in spirit,
Rome will surround her seven hills with a single
wall, proud of her men and children—recalling our Mother
Cybele riding her chariot, crowned with her turret, through
     Phrygian
towns, exulting in son-Gods, embracing her hundred
grandsons, all Sky-Gods holding heights on Olympus.
Look there, focus your eyes now on our people,
your own Romans: Caesar and all of Iulus'
790 lineage under the great axle-tree of the heavens.

Augustus

"And this man, a man you've heard promised so often,
Caesar Augustus: a God's own son who will settle
a Golden Age once more on Latium's meadows,
ruled by Saturn before. He'll open the empire
to India, Africa, lands lying beyond the ecliptic,
beyond the sun's annual journey, where Atlas
turns the world wheel on his back while it's burning with inlaid
stars. Already Caspian kingdoms dread his arrival,
Scythian land shudders at answers from heaven—
800   seven mouths of the Nile are anxiously foaming!
Even Hercules never covered such country
transfixing the bronze-hoofed deer, quieting forests
on Mount Erymanthus, and scaring the Hydra with arrows—
no, not Bacchus in triumph, vine-shoots for reins on his chariot,
driving tigresses down from the high ridges of Nysa.
And we're still slow extending our power through action?
Fear prevents us from settling Ausonian country?

Other Rulers to Come

"Who's in the distance, crowned with tendrils of olive
and carrying relics? The grey beard and hair of a Roman
810   king, I'm sure. With laws he'll strengthen the infant
city, though sent from the poor district of little
Cures to rule an empire. Next in succession,
disrupting the country's leisure, goading inactive
men to war, comes Tullus—his army still unaccustomed
to winning. Ancus, a braggart, follows behind him—
too pleased already with breezes of popular feeling.
Want to see the Tarquin kings? And the vengeful,
proud spirit of Brutus? The man who'll recover the fasces,
first to receive Consular power, the Lictor's
820   brutal axe? Sons will wage war on that father:
wretched, he'll cause their punishment—all for the beauty
of freedom. Whatever the future makes of his action,
love of the land prevails and intense longing for honor.

Caesar will War with Pompey

"Here are the Decius and Drusus families. Look at Torquatus'
grim axe. And Camillus, recovering standards.
But those two men you see matched in glittering armor,
of one mind now with the death-world around them,

my God, what war between themselves when they make it
to life's light, what slaughter of ranks they will foster!
830 The father comes down from Alpine redoubts, a fort at Monoecus;
the son-in-law marshals Eastern forces against him.
No, my children: don't get used to such conflict:
don't turn such fighting force on your fatherland's entrails.
You stop first—you come from a race on Olympus—
throw down your spear, my grandchild.

Rome's Obligation to Govern

"A man known for killing Greeks will be Corinth's
conqueror, driving a winner's chariot high up the Capitoline.
There's the wrecker of Argos and Agamemnon's Mycenae:
he'll kill the seed itself of war-strong Achilles,
840 avenging Troy's fathers and outraged shrines of Minerva.
Who'd leave your greatness, Cossus and Cato, in silence?
Or Gracchus' family? The twin Scipios—lightnings
of war demolishing Carthage! Fabricius, little
but *strong*. Serranus, planting seed in a furrow.
And where do you take my tired spirit, you Fabians?
Only Maximus saves our state by delaying.
Others may hammer bronze into delicate breathing,
drawing—I'm sure it's true—life-signs from marble.
Some plead causes well; some track with a stylus
850 paths in the sky and predict what stars will be rising.
Ah, but you Romans, remember to rule people, to govern,
there's your art—to make peace like a custom,
to spare humble men and war on the pompous."

Loss of the Young Marcellus

Anchises told them (both were amazed) more, like a father:
"Watch Marcellus, known for exceptional war-wealth,
marching in triumph, a man taller than all men.
He'll shore up Rome at a time of noise and confusion,
a horseman who'll trample Carthage and Gaul in rebellion.
He'll hang captured weapons three times for his father Quirinus."
860 Aeneas now caught sight of a beautiful youngster
in brilliant armor, walking along with Marcellus.
His face lacked joy, however; his glances were downcast.
"Father, who's that person attending Marcellus?
A son? Some other eminent family member?
What loud friends are around him! His form itself like a painting!
But night-like dark and sad shade have enclosed him."

Anchises, a father, began to weep when he answered.
"My son, don't press for such deep family sorrow.
The Fates will merely show this boy to our nation—beyond that
870 allowing nothing. You Gods, Roman expansion
must seem too strong if a gift like this one should linger.
What loud mourning of people will move from the Campus
of Mars through the whole city! What funeral sorrow
the Tiber will see gliding past the still-recent death-mound!
No one child from a Trojan clan will encourage
so much hope in Latin grandfathers. Romulus' country
will never pride itself in such a descendent.
Ah, for the old trust and goodness, hands undefeated
in battle! No one man could have met him in armor
880 safely, whether he'd face the enemy walking,
or digging spurs in the sweated flanks of a stallion.
Sad, pitiful boy. If hard Fates can be broken,
you'll be Marcellus. Fill my hands with some lilies:
I'll scatter violet blossoms at least for a grandson,
heap up gifts for that spirit, and offer a futile
service." So they roamed through all of the aery,
wide fields of that world, regarding each subject.

The Coming War in Italy

Anchises led Aeneas through every particular,
firing his heart with love for future distinction.
890 Then he informed the man of battle approaching,
he told of Laurentian people, the town of Latinus,
and how to escape or endure hardship that faced him.

Leaving tthe Underworld

Two gates of Sleep are there: according to legend,
the one of horn offers an easy exit to actual
spirits; the one of ivory, polished and shining,
sends to the sky elusive Underworld fancies.
When done speaking Anchises walked his son and the Sibyl
together and saw them out through the ivory gateway.

Reunion with Friends

Aeneas cut a trail to the ships. Rejoining companions,
900 he soon sailed straight up the coast to the port of Caieta.
Anchors were thrown from prows. The ships stood on the beach-
        sand.

VII

WAR BEGINS IN LATIUM

A Loving Remembrance

You also brought fame to our coastline, Caieta,
nurse of Aeneas, a lasting name when you died here:
your honor still preserves the place, and your good name
marks your bones in great Hesperia—something of glory.
Aeneas lovingly rendered the proper and final
rites. He raised a death-mound. After the high seas
calmed he set a course and sailed from the harbor.

Sailing and Noise at Night

Winds held until nightfall. Radiant Moonlight
approved the journey: the sea glowed with tremulous brilliance.
10   He scraped a shore—that close to the island of Circe,
the Sun's wealthy daughter. She filled inaccessible
forest with constant song and her opulent ceilings
glowed at night from scented cedar and firelight.
She wove on a fine loom, the shuttle went whistling.
Angry lions audibly groaned as they fiercely
fought their chains, growling and snarling through midnight.
Bristling swine and bears thrashed in their cages.
Huge wolves howled for the loss of their manhood.
A cruel Goddess, Circe had changed their appearance
20   with strong herbs, giving them animals' bodies.
To keep the God-revering Trojans from suffering outrage
by nearing that frightful shore or making the harbor,
the Sea-God filled their sails with following breezes
and helped tham accelerate past that turbulent water.

muse invoked Erato ↗

147

A View of the Tiber

Soon, when rays reddened the sea, and Aurora
glowed in the deep sky, her chariot rosy then yellow,
all the wind's breath subsided abruptly.
Oars worked through a flat surface of water.
From out at sea now Aeneas could make out
30   spreading woodland, now the Tiber pleasantly flowing,
yellow, laden with silt, quick-running eddies,
breaking in surf. Around and above it were shorebirds
in fair number, familiar with banks and bends of the river:
they charmed the sky with song or glided past tree-tops.
Aeneas told his men to alter course for this landfall.
They gladly swung their bows and approached the shadowy river.

Prayer to the Goddess

Tell me now, Erato, what were those times like? ——
Who ruled in ancient Latium's country when Trojan
forces first landed a fleet on Ausonian beachsand?
40   Let me record their wars right from the outset:
you're my Goddess: help your seer tell of the fearful
shock of battle, ranks driving, the killing of princes,
Tuscan hordes, all of Hesperia mustered
for war. A great world order was born here:
mine is a major task.

Bees in a Swarm

               King Latinus was aging
now: he'd ruled peaceful town and field for a long time.
Born (we hear) of a Nymph of Laurentum, Marica,
and Faunus, whose father was Picus, who claimed that his father
was you, Saturn—the ultimate source of this bloodline.
50   Latinus had no male heir. The Fates had decided:
a first-born son had been lost when young, in his boyhood.
Only a daughter sustained the august family bloodline.
Now fully mature she was ready for marriage.
Many had sought her hand from all of Ausonia,
from great Latium. But first and foremost was Turnus,
handsome, with strong father and grandfathers, favored
and deeply loved by the queen, as a son by a mother.
But various Gods' omens alarmed and opposed her.
A laurel tree in the high central court of the palace,
60   its hair held in awe, sacred for many

years, found by the father himself when Latinus
built his first fort, they say, honored the Sun-God.
People took their name from the tree—the Laurentians.
One day bees swarmed (it's amazing to tell this):
riding a humid breeze and humming intensely
they'd settled high on its crown, their feet interlocking:
the swarm hung from a bough abruptly, like leaflets.
Quickly a prophet announced: "I see a stranger arriving,
force that comes from the same source as the bees have:
70   men ruling the same place high on our fortress."

Fire in Lavinia's Hair

And more. While tending an altar with purified pinewood,
standing close to her father, the virgin Lavinia
seemed (it shocked them) seized by a fire that enveloped
her long hair: flames crackled through all of the headdress,
burning her regal hair and burning the jeweled
and famous crown. Wrapped in a luminous golden
smoke she scattered that Fire-God through all of the building.
Terrified people talked of the marvellous portent.
Prophets predicted the girl herself would be famous,
80   Fate-full; but monstrous war would confront the community.

Faunus Answers at Night

The king, moved by the signs, went to consider
the holy word of Faunus, his oracle-father,
high in a grove of the wide Albunean forest,
where sacred springs echoed and musk was exhaled from the
    shadows.
Here Italians and all the Oenotrian people
had come for answers when doubtful. Bringing his presents
here a priest might lie through the still night on some outstretched
skins of slaughtered sheep. He'd beg for a vision,
watch the crowded flight of astonishing figures,
90   hear a mélange of voices, relish the discourse
of Gods and speak to the Acheron's depths, to Avernus.
Here the father, Latinus himself, prayed for an answer.
He'd killed a hundred full-grown sheep according to custom;
spread on the outstretched hides, he lay on the victims'
fleece; a voice came from the deep forest abruptly:
"Don't try making your daughter the bride of a Latin,
my son: put no faith in the wedding you planned on.
Sons-in-law will come from abroad who will carry

[handwritten marginal note: Lavinia / Latinus' daughter]

our name and bloodline to heaven. Their grandsons will witness
100 the whole world at their feet. They'll guide it and govern,
sea to sea, where the Sun looks down as it circles."
So Faunus, his father, warned him there in the stilly
dark. Latinus himself could hardly keep quiet—
Rumor already had circled, flown to the farthest
Ausonian town, when the sons of Laomedon's people
moored their fleet on the green banks of the Tiber.

A Prophecy Fulfilled

Aeneas, with ranking chiefs and a handsome Iulus,
settled himself under high boughs of a willow.
Ready to eat, they'd set some food on their wheat-mats
110 along the grass, even as Jupiter prompted:
they'd piled some rough fruit on this matting of Ceres.
By chance when all was eaten they turned to the paltry
breads of the Goddess. Hunger and poverty drove them:
they seized and chewed, rashly and wrongly, the rounded
crusts, the last wide squares—Fates had prepared them—
and Iulus joked, "Look, we're eating our tables."
That's all he said. But the first end of their hardship
was heard in that voice. First Aeneas picked up on
his words, covered Iulus' mouth, and stunned by the Powers
120 quickly proclaimed: "I greet you, land that is owed me
by Fates! And you, faith-full House-Gods of Trojans:
here is your home, our country. My Father Anchises
told me the Fates' secret and now I'll repeat it:
'My son,' he said, 'when hunger drives you to unknown
land and food runs low, when you chew on your tables,
have hope: although you're exhausted, you're home. And
        remember—
build earth-works and houses first with your own hand.'
Here was that hunger, the last pang that was waiting,
putting an end to our grief.
130 Come on, be glad, then! Look to the light of the sunrise,
to learn of the place and find people who live here,
who've raised walls: we'll search far from the harbor.
For now lift your cups to the Gods in libation,
call on my Father Anchises and pour wine on the tables."

Surrounded by Gods

After speaking he circled his temples with leafy
shoots and prayed to Earth, first among Godheads;

to local spirits, to Nymphs and rivers remaining
unknown, to Night and the rising Night's constellations.
He duly invoked Jupiter, Ida's Lord, and the Mother,
140 Cybele; Anchises in Erebus, Venus in heaven.
Three times clearly the all-powerful Father
thundered—his personal sign—high in the sky's revelation
of airy cloud trembling and burning with golden
light. And the word was spreading through Trojan gatherings
     quickly:
the day had arrived: they had found the walls that were
     promised!
Enthused by each great sign they began celebrations
again: they placed and crowned wine in their wine-bowls.

Exploring, Visiting, Building

When rising Dawn lighted the land and another
day with her lamp, they left the campsite to seek out
150 towns and people, markers and coasts. The Numicus River's
pools were here, there the Tiber. Some daring
Latins must live nearby: the son of Anchises commanded
a hundred envoys picked from each order to visit
the king's august walls: crowned with leaflets of Pallas
they'd bring gifts to the man: they'd sue for peace for the Trojans.
The men moved off at a quick-paced trot to comply with
their orders. Aeneas himself established a trench-line
and built up walls of earth—his first home on that shore-line—
shaped like a fort, circled with stakes and embankments.

Trojans and Latins Meet

160 Already the young delegation had covered the distance:
they saw the towers and sheer walls of the Latins.
Boys and fine young men in front of the city
worked in the dust, training chariot horses.
They bent stiff bows or tensed shoulders to hurtle
rugged spears; they competed in racing or boxing.
A messenger mounted a horse to announce to the aging
king that tall men had arrived in unusual
dress. Latinus ordered these men to be summoned
into the palace. He sat on the central throne of his fathers.
170 His home was immense, with a hundred high and majestic
pillars. The home of Laurentian Picus, it stood on the city's
heights where trees and their fathers' faith had inspired them.
Here each king had duly welcomed the scepter

first and lifted the fasces. Here, in a senate-and-temple,
were seats for holy feasting, where rams had been slaughtered,
and elders resided at long continuous tables.
Indeed figures of old grandfathers stood here,
a series in antique cedar: Italus, lordly Sabinus,
the vineyard master whose form guarded a billhook;
180 elderly Saturn, both faces of Janus:
all in the vestibule. Others were kings from a distant
past who'd suffered war-wounds defending their country.
Many weapons too hung from the sacred
door-frames: rounded war-axes, helmets with feathers,
captured chariot parts, massive bars from a city
gate, shields and spears, prows broken from warships.
Picus himself presided with Romulus' crooked
staff, robed tucked up, a shield in his left hand—
Picus, that breaker of horses. His wife Circe had struck him
190 down with a golden rod: gripped by lust she had changed him
with drugs to a bird: she'd sprinkled his feathers with color.

A Kingly Welcome

Sitting inside that God-filled home on his fathers'
throne, Latinus told the Trojans to enter the building.
He spoke up first in a friendly tone when they entered:
"Tell me, you sons of Dardanus—yes, we remember
your city and people, we know what course you steered on the
          water—
what do you want here? What cause or need could compel you
to sail all that blue-green sea to Ausonian beaches?
Did storms drive you? Mistakes you made in your travels?
200 Deep-sea sailors often encounter such problems.
Now that you rest in our port, on the banks of our river,
accept our welcome. We Latins, remember, are Saturn's
people—not by force of law or some bindings
but freely. We keep to our ancient God and tradition.
In fact I recall, though years have darkened the story,
the old Auruncans told of Dardanus growing
here on a farm, then leaving for Phrygian cities,
Samos in Thrace, which men called Samothrace lately.
He came from nearby Corythus, a Tuscan location;
210 now a gold palace and throne have received him in star-set
skies, increasing his number of God-worshipping altars."

Asking for Help

He stopped speaking. Ilioneus responded.
"Majesty, eminent son of Faunus, no darkling
storm at sea forced us to come to your country.
Our course was not confused by the stars or the shoreline.
We're all borne to your city deliberately, freely,
though forced from another kingdom, once the supremest
viewed by the sun, coming from far-off Olympus.
Jupiter founded our nation: Dardanus' children
220 are glad to call Jupiter Grandfather: kingly Aeneas
of Troy, who brought us here, is of high Jupiter's bloodline.
How fierce was that storm from mad Mycenae that poured on
the plains of Mount Ida! Europe and Asia were driven
by Fates—a world was forced to collide with a world there.
Even at Earth's extremes they've heard of the conflict,
where Ocean is turned back and the immoderate Sun-God
centers and cuts off a long tract from four others.
After the storm, conveyed on desolate sea-ways,
we searched for a plain home for the Gods of our country,
230 some harmless coast with water and air open to all men.
We won't disgrace your kingdom. And word of your kindness
will carry weight: such acts won't die or be thankless.
It won't bring shame to have taken Troy to Ausonia's
breast—I swear by the hand and Fate of our forceful
Aeneas, tested in friendship and armed confrontation.
Throngs of people from many nations have wanted
to join us themselves. So don't feel scorn if we offer
a hand first, if we come with wreaths and proposals.
God's word—a rule of its own—has impelled us
240 to look for this ground. Dardanus sprang from your country,
and loud commands of Apollo urged us, recalled us
to Tuscany, back to the Tiber, the sacred Numicus fountains.
We've also brought some modest signs of our former
stature, relics taken from Troy when it burned down.
Anchises gave fatherly thanks with this gold at an altar.
Priam carried this mace when he summoned the people
and set down laws rightly. This ritual turban
and robes are the work of Trojan women."

The Joy of Latinus

As Ilioneus finished, Latinus was keeping
250 his looks lowered, eyes on the floor and unmoving.

Now he became restless and tense: much as that purple
embroidery touched him—the mace of Priam was touching—
he wondered about the marriage bed of his daughter.
He deeply pondered old Faunus' prediction:
had Fates impelled or removed Aeneas from foreign
rule to be called his son, his equal in power?
Signs had suggested the prime strength of that future
household—the whole world could be seized by their army.
At last the king was happy: "May Gods bless this beginning,
260 foretold by themselves! All that you ask, Trojan, is granted.
I won't scorn your gifts. As long is the king is Latinus
Troy won't lack for a breast of rich field and abundance.
And surely Aeneas himself should come if he really
longs to be called our friend, he should join in your welcome
soon, and not be afraid—our faces are friendly!
Part of my plan for peace is to grasp the hand of your leader.
So now take my word back to Aeneas.
I have a daughter; words from the shrine of my Father
with many signs from heaven, forbid her to marry
270 a local man. Sons-in-law will arrive from
a foreign land, we're told, a bloodline to carry the Latin
name to the stars. The man the Fates demand is Aeneas,
I think. If truth lies in foreboding I'll want him."

Regal Horses

Finished, the father selected a number of horses
(his tall stables had three hundred that stood there and glistened):
he ordered a horse led out at once for each of the Trojans.
They marched in a quick-footed line, decked out in purple.
Gold halters hung from their chests, and their covers
had gold stitching; the bits they chewed on were golden.
280 For absent Aeneas: a paired chariot horse-team
bred by a Sky-God—fire blew from their nostrils—
Circe had smartly engendered these hybrids in secret
by mating her mare with a stud of her father Apollo.
With all that praise and wealth from Latinus, Aeneas'
men returned high on their mounts to tell of the peace-plan.

Juno Returns

But look—coming from Argos, Inachus' country,
the cruel wife of Jupiter, riding an air-wave,
spotted the Trojan ships from far in the heavens.
From Sicily's Mount Pachynus she knew Aeneas was happy:

290 she saw him raising roofbeams, trusting this country
     already, ignoring the fleet. She paused. Agony siezed her.
     She shook her head and angrily blurted the words out:
     "You hateful weeds of Troy, with your Fates' opposition
     to *our* Fates—couldn't you die on some plain of Sigea,
     be caught and enslaved, or couldn't you suffer cremation
     when Troy burned? You found an escape through the center
     of every fire and force. I presume my power is worn down
     finally, I rest or doze, my hatred depleted.
     How I dared to pursue them—forced them from homeland,
300 grimly blocked their escape on each of the sea-lanes—
     I used up the strength of sea and sky against Trojans!
     But how have the Syrtes helped me, monster Charybdis
     or Scylla? Trojans live where they want, by the Tiber,
     saved from the sea and from me. The War-God could ravage
     a giant people, the Lapiths, and even the Father of Sky-Gods
     yielded ancient Calydon once to a wrathful Diana.
     What Lapith or Calydon crime deserved such a judgment?
     While I, the mighty wife of Jupiter, sadly
     able to dare anything, any maneuver,
310 I lose to Aeneas. Well, then. If none of my power
     is strong enough I'll surely ask for help—from wherever.
     The Gods above won't bend? I'll trouble the Hell-Gods.
     I can't keep Troy from the Latin throne? Let it happen—
     the Fates are fixed, Lavinia's the wife of Aeneas—
     ah, but to stall some things, add to the action,
     that I may do. And smash both kingdoms and people!
     Let father and son-in-law unite: it will cost them
     their own blood, Rutulian and Trojan. Your dowry, Lavinia:
     War waits as your bridesmaid. If Hecuba carried
320 a torch in her womb and gave birth to a wildfire,
     Venus now has also delivered a Paris,
     a funeral torch once more for this Troy's restoration."

Daughter of Night

     No sooner done she made for the land like a hoarfrost
     and summoned that grief-builder, Allecto, from Under,
     her dreaded Fury's throne in darkness, with mournful
     war in her heart, rage, deceit and criminal plotting.
     Even her father Pluto despised her, her sisters
     in Tartarus hated the fiend—she changed her face and her savage
     form that often—black snakes could spring from her forehead.
330 Juno addressed her with words that whetted her malice.

"Virgin daughter of Night! Do some work that you owe me—
a task to prevent my honor and name in a region
from fading or cracking. Stop the sons of Aeneas
from crowding Italy's land, surrounding Latinus with weddings.
You're able to arm single-spirited brothers to duel;
you twist homes with hatred; you carry a killing
fire into buildings and lash them—a thousand destructive
skills and names are yours. Look in your fertile
heart. Plant war-seeds and frustrate this peace-pact.
340 Let men crave and demand weapons rashly and seize them."

Maddening Snakes

So now Allecto, stained with Gorgonian venom,
made for Latium first, the Laurentian ruler's
high buildings. She calmly sat by the door of Amata,
the queen, who fumed over the Trojans' arrival.
She fretted and feared for the loss of Turnus in marriage.
The Goddess flung one of her blue-black and hair-like
snakes: she prodded it close, close to the heartbeat,
tempting the queen to upset all of her household.
Gliding under her clothes, curling a gentle
350 breast (and hardly felt there), the viper unnerved her
and breathed out maddening poison. Sometimes resembling
a long choke of twined gold, sometimes a chaplet's
long ribbon, it linked with her hair or strayed on a shoulder.
Although at first the malaise, like a damp and venomous seeping,
stunned her senses and wound her bones in a fever,
her mind and heart were not yet fully ignited.
She spoke to the king softly, much like a mother.
She often wept for her daughter's wedding a Trojan.
"*Must* Lavinia now go to a Trojan in exile?
360 You're her father: don't you pity yourself or your daughter?
He won't pity a mother—he'll trick and desert us
and head out to sea with the first Northwind, a virgin his booty—
the way that Phrygian shepherd slipped into Sparta
and took to Troy Helen, the daughter of Leda.
What of your sacred trust, the ancient concern for your household?
How often you gave your hand to Turnus, your kinsman!
If Latins must look for sons-in-law from a foreign
land and that's final, if Faunus' command must oppress you,
any country I think is certainly 'foreign'
370 that's free of our rule. And *that's* what the Gods were revealing:
If Turnus' house were traced to the very beginning

you'd find Acrisius, Inachus, men from central Mycenae."
No use. She tried talking things out with Latinus
but saw him standing against her. The serpent's infection
reached her innards, frenzy wandered throughout her
now and made her wretched. Seized by exorbitant terror
quickly she ran through the large town in a panic:
the way a top will often twirl from a whipping
string when boys wrapped in a game get it spinning
380   in wide arcs through an empty courtyard—they drive it and lash it
around in the yard while younger boys are astonished,
puzzling about, amazed at the whirr of the boxwood,
taking life from a string-pull. Driven as quickly
the woman ran through the center of town, stirring up people.

Bacchic Frenzy

She even assumed the Wine-God's will in a forest,
adding worse mischief, starting a greater derangement.
She fled into wooded hills, hiding her daughter,
hoping to stall nuptial fire or slip from the Trojans.
"Bacchus," she called, "only your Godhead can merit
390   this virgin! Look," she yelled, "she's raising your supple
vine-rod and growing sacred hair, circling and dancing!"
The story spread. Mothers' breasts burned with resentment.
The same fire drove them all to look for new dwellings:
they left home, surrendering hair and neck to the breezes.
Some went filling the sky with tremulous dolor,
they wore pelts or toted vine-circled spear-shafts.
The frenzied queen lofted a blazing torch in their center,
chanted the wedding song of her daughter and Turnus,
and rolled her bloody eyes. Abuptly she shouted
400   wildly, "You mothers from all over Latium, listen:
if thanks remain in your good hearts for a wretched
Amata—if care for mothers and justice can gnaw you—
loosen your hair-bands now and join me in ritual."
So there in the bush, with beasts' lairs all around them,
Allecto goaded the queen like Bacchus in every direction.

Turnus and Calybe

After she'd whetted that fury enough to begin with,
jumbling the plans of the whole house of Latinus,
the dour Goddess ascended swiftly on coal-black
wings to the daring Rutulians' bulwarks, a city
410   founded by Danae (they say) with Acrisian settlers,

driven there by a headlong Southwind. Elders had called it
Ardea once; the great name of Ardea lasted;
its luck did not. Here Turnus already
had slept through half the dark night in the palace.
Allecto doffed her harsh mien and her Fury's
form and changed herself to an elderly woman.
Wrinkles cut through the dirt on her forehead, and white hair
grew intertwined with fillets and leaflets of olive.
Becoming Calybe, an old seer in the temple of Juno,
420 she came up close to speak. Turnus was watching.
"Turnus, you've gone through so much work—and for nothing?
Your own scepter passed to a Trojan outsider?
You sought a dowry and bride with your blood, but Latinus
denies you: he wants a foreign heir for the kingdom.
You went and faced danger, thankless and laughed at
for trying to sprawl Tuscan ranks and pacify Latins.
A strong daughter of Saturn, Juno, commanded
my speaking openly now in the still night as you lie here.
Move, then: arm your men: get ready for battle.
430 March through the gate gladly: set fire to the painted
ships of Phrygian leaders camped by our beautiful river.
Great and powerful Gods insist. Even Latinus,
unless he gives you a bride and stands by his promise,
may soon test and feel the weapons of Turnus."

Allecto Revealed

The man responded in turn by mocking the seer.
"I've heard of some ships," he said, "borne on the Tiber's
water. It's not as you guess. Things haven't escaped me.
Don't paint such stark terrors. Imperial Juno
has not forgotten our cause.
440 But you—muddled in dust—age has drained you of vision.
You work up empty concern, mother. When royal
armies move, you play the vain and terrified prophet.
Worry about God's face: watch in your temple.
Let men make war or peace—and war when they have to."
At every word Allecto's anger grew hotter.
A sudden tremor shook the man's body while speaking:
his eyes fixed on the Fury's dozens of hissing
snakes: revealing her form, rolling her flamelike
eyes, she pushed him back when he stammered and struggled
450 to speak again. She pulled two snakes from her hairline
and cracked a whip, her mouth raving with warning:

"Yes, I'm muddled in dust, age drains me of vision!
When kings make war I play with fantasized terror!
Look again: I'm here from the house of fear-filling sisters:
I carry war and death in my hands."

A Maddened Turnus

She stopped and threw fire at Turnus. She fastened
a darkly smoking brand—it glowed at his breastbone.
Monstrous fear broke his calm, sweat had completely
covered the man, every bone-joint and member,
460   he shouted madly, scrambled for arms in the bedroom and
        building,
he seethed with lust for a sword and the mad evil of battle
but most with rage: the way the roar of a stick-fed
fire builds at the brass ribs of a cauldron
when water boils, leaping inside and then outside—
spray spits up high and mixes with steam-cloud,
the top overflows and dark smoke flies into heaven.
Turnus damned peace. He commanded a march on
King Latinus. He told the best young men to get ready
to fight, to guard Italy and drive troops from the border:
470   they'd find themselves a match for both Latins and Trojans.
After the speech he vowed to the Gods and invoked them.
Rutulians rallied, goading each other for battle,
some moved by the grace and outstanding beauty of Turnus,
some by his ancestor-kings or his own brilliant achievements.

Hunting Dogs

While Turnus filled Rutulians with spirit and courage
Allecto hurried on Stygian wings to the Trojans.
She eyed the place. She'd trick them otherwise: handsome
Iulus was driving game into traps on the shoreline:
the Underworld virgin suddenly scattered disorder
480   by tingling the dogs' snouts with an odor they knew of—
away they ran for a stag. Here was a primal
cause of trouble that fired farmers' instinct for fighting.
The stag was a splendid beast with magnificent antlers,
taken by Tyrrhus' boys from the teats of its mother
to nurse on their own. (Their father Tyrrhus had guarded
broad lands of the king whose livestock obeyed him.)
The stag got used to the care and command of a sister,
Silvia. Soft wreaths embellished the antlers.
She washed his wild coat in a clear fountain and brushed it.

490 He let her touch him; he took to the mistress's table.
He roamed the woods and returned himself to the building,
a home he knew at night, whatever the hour.

Ascanius Wounds the Stag

The fierce hunting dogs of Iulus had flustered
the stag when it roamed afield. By chance it had floated
down a stream and lay on a green riverbank, cooling.
Ascanius, hot with desire now for a notable honor,
arched a bow himself and aimed on the arrow.
Some God steadied his hand. The weapon went whistling
hard at the deer's flank, striking the belly.

Silvia's Call

500 The wounded animal fled to familiar surroundings,
entered a stall bleeding, moaning and filling
the whole place like a man dolefully begging.
First the sister, Silvia, palms beating her forearms,
called for help. She shouted to vigorous fieldhands
who gathered quickly (a virulent sickness, Allecto,
hid in their quiet woods): armed with a tempered
stake or heavily knotted club—whatever they spotted
they picked up—anger made it a weapon. And Tyrrhus,
breathless with rage, called out crews—by chance he'd been using
510 a large axe and wedge to chop oak into quarters.
Ah, and the cruel Goddess found time for more trouble.
She made for the steep roof of a stable and sounded
the rural alarm from its peak. She strained her Tartarean
chords through a curved horn: suddenly every
grove shuddered and deep forest re-echoed.
Even the distant pond of Diana responded,
the pale and sulfurous Nar River, the springs of Velinus.

Fighting Breaks Out

Mothers trembled and pressed sons to their bosoms.
Farmers, truly enraged now, ran to the summons
520 the feared horn had given: they gathered from all sides,
grabbing weapons. Young Trojans had also
rushed from the open camp to the aid of Iulus.
Lines were drawn. No longer a quarrel of rustics
wielding bumpy staffs or fire-blackened stake-points:
steel would decide it. A darkly broad harvest of two-edged
weapons bristled. Bronze, provoked by the sunlight,

gleamed and threw flashes back at a cloud-trail:
a wave begins that way, with a white-capping sea-wind,
rising gradually higher at sea to an upright
530 crest that mounts from the trough's base to the sky-heights.
Abruptly a man in the front row toppled. An arrow
had whistled and struck the eldest descendant of Tyrrhus,
Almo. The wound clogged his voicebox and bloodied
the throat and tongue: his thin windpipe was glutted.
Men fell around him now: the aging Galaesus,
who'd offered to make peace, one of the fairest
persons, once the richest Ausonian farmer,
with five herds of sheep, five of cattle returning
to barns, and a hundred plows working the pasture.
540 While men faced off and fought through that meadow
the strong Fury, who'd kept her promise and spattered
the first fighters with blood, sending some to their death-rites,
turned from Hesperia now. She whirled through the heavens
to find Juno and proudly tell of her triumph:
"There—for you a dispute's matured into anguish and battle.
Tell them to make friends or join in a treaty
now that I've splashed Trojans with blood of Ausonians!
I'll add more strife if you really desire it.
I'll bring neighboring towns in the war with some rumors:
550 I'll fire their hearts with love for the maddening War-God.
They'll come to help from everywhere. Fields will sprout with my
      weapons."

Juno's Caution

But Juno answered, "Enough lying and terror.
War can stand on this pretext; the close combat is bitter.
The first blades provided by chance have been covered
with fresh blood. Now *there* is a marriage—a solemn
rite for King Latinus and Venus' excellent household!
But you—the Father and Ruler of highest Olympus
would hardly want you roaming freely through heaven.
Leave the place. If luck should change in the struggle
560 I'll manage myself." Saturn's daughter had spoken:
Allecto rose on wings hissing like serpents
and left the steep sky for her home by the River Cocytus.
A place near high mountains in Italy's heartland,
renowned and recalled in many realms, is a valley
called the Ampsanctus. Dark flanks of a forest
enclose each side with dense brush, and a river

roars through rocks in the center, rushing and twisting.
There's also a fearsome cave with manifest air-holes
for grim Dis, and a monstrous chasm that opens
570 a sickly mouth where the Acheron bursts out. The Fury's
power and hate hid here. Earth and sky were disburdened.

Crowds Pressure Latinus

Saturn's regal daughter meanwhile was adding
a further touch to the conflict. A large number of shepherds
had rushed from the field into town, carrying dead men—
young Almo, the grimed face of Galaesus—
they called on Gods and begged Latinus to witness.
Turnus, ringed by torches and protests of killing,
doubled their fear: he claimed if the Trojans were called to the
          kingdom,
their Phrygian stock would be poison: they'd drive himself from
          the palace.
580 And men whose mothers were leaping in faraway woodland,
struck by Bacchus to dance there (Amata's name was no light one),
now gathered from every side to belabor the War-God.
The whole crowd called at once for a blasphemous conflict,
counter to Gods, counter to warning and omen.
They stood grumbling around the house of Latinus.
The king however remained like a sea-cliff, immobile:
just as a sea-cliff, when built-up rollers are breaking,
retains its mass against surf which is mounting
and snarling around it in vain: while foam and surrounding
590 rocks make noise it repels the seaweed flung at its body.
Still he lacked strength to dismantle their sightless
plan. Things went on as cruel Juno had wished them.
The father repeatedly called on Gods, on the answerless air-flow:
"We're broken by Fates," he said, "some storm-wind transports
          us.
You wretched people will pay plenty for sinful
bloodshed. And Turnus, a tragic punishment's waiting
for all your crime. You'll vow too late to the Powers you worship.
For me, rest has begun. A whole harbor is waiting.
I'm only robbed of a happy death." He stopped and sequestered
600 himself in the palace, abandoning matters of statecraft.

Juno and the Gates of War

Hesperian Latium started a custom which Alban
towns kept sacred, which now Rome as the greatest

power maintains when first preparing for battle,
whether they haul by hand the grief-spreading War-God
to Thrace or head for Arabia, Hyrcania, India,
following Dawn eastward, seizing Parthian standards:
the twin gates of War (as people have called them),
revered in faith and fear of the truculent War-God,
locked by a hundred bronze bars in a durable iron
610 grip, Janus always guarding the entrance:
when elders preside and judge fighting is certain,
the Consul himself, wearing the robe of Quirinus
in Gabine style, opens the clangorous portals
and calls out War. Young men echo the summons
and brass horns exhale in a raucous consensus.
Latinus now was urged to follow the custom,
to open the dismal gates and declare war on the Trojans.
The father refused to touch them. He turned from the duty,
shocked and revolted. He hid himself in the darkness.
620 Ah, but the Queen of the Gods, gliding from heaven,
pushed at the gates herself: the daughter of Saturn
twisted the hinges and snapped the iron frames of the War-God!

Ploughshares into Swords

A formerly calm and placid Ausonia flared up,
some men ready to march through fields, others to harry
tall horses through dust—all clamored for weapons.
One man polished a light shield or a gleaming
spear-point with oil; another whetted an axe-edge.
They reveled in hoisting a flag or blaring a trumpet.
Even some large cities organized forges
630 to make new weapons: stony Atina, confident Tibur,
Ardea, Crustumerium, towered Antemnae.
They scooped out safe helmets, fashioned the willow
frames of shields, softened metal for breastplates
of bronze, shaped and polished silver for leg-guards.
All their love of plowing, their pride in a sickle,
yielded to smelting swords of fathers in forges.
Already a bugle called—the watchword for battle was moving.
One man left home nervously clutching a helmet.
Another prodded a testy horse-team, or sported
640 triply gold-meshed armor, a sword and shield that he trusted.

The Poet Prays for Help

Open Helicon now, you Muses, enlighten my singing:
what kings were provoked to war, what armies behind them
filled the field? Even in those days Italy prospered
in rich land and men, and glittering weapons.
Truly you can recall them, Goddesses: tell me,
for hardly an air or wisp of their glory has reached us.

Mezentius and Lausus

First to enter the war was a God-scorner, Mezentius.
A rugged man from Tuscany's coast, he'd armed some contingents
and rode next to a son, Lausus. No one was finer
650 appearing except Turnus, the man from Laurentum,
than Lausus. Hunter of wild beasts, breaker of stallions,
he led (though in vain) a thousand men from Agylla's
town walls. He deserved a happier homeland
and rule. He hardly deserved a sire like Mezentius.

A Son of Hercules and Rhea

Next Aventinus, handsome son of a handsome
Hercules, showed off horses and chariot honored
with prize palms on the grass. A design of his father
stood on the shield: a hundred vipers girding the Hydra.
The priestess Rhea had borne him in secret and brought him
660 to shores of light on a wooded Aventine hillside:
God and woman had joined after Geryon's killing
when conquering Hercules reached a field in Laurentum
and washed bulls from Spain in Tuscany's river.
The army carried cruel pikes and staffs into battle
or wielded the slender sword and spear of the Sabine.
Aventinus marched with a huge hide of a lion
around him, white fangs and a scraggly, fearsome
mane his headdress. He'd often entered the palace
coarsely dressed, shouldering Hercules' clothing.

Catillus and Coras

670 Twin brothers who'd left the city of Tibur
(their city and people named for a third brother, Tiburtus),
Catillus and Coras were Greek young men and aggressive.
They rode in the front rank with dense weapons around them

the way a pair of Centaurs, born of some stormcloud,
gallop down from the high ridge of a mountain
like Othrys or snowy Homole—stretches of forest
give them room and the brush yields where they crash through.

Caeculus and his Farmhands

The man who built the town of Praeneste was present,
born to Vulcan among cattle at pasture
680 and found by a hearth (every age has believed it):
Caeculus. A spread-out legion of farmhands had joined him,
men from Praeneste's heights and fields of Gabinian
Juno, living where cold Anio water
splashes Hernican stone and bank. Anagnia's bounty
had fed them with fatherly streams like yours, Amasenus.
Not all had a shield and sword or a clattering horse-team:
most had grey shots of lead for slinging, or carried
a pair of spears in each hand. Sand-colored wolfskin
covered their heads like caps. They walked with the left foot
690 bare, the right foot strapped crudely in rawhide.

The Untried Troops of Messapus

Messapus arrived, a horse-tamer and son of the Sea-God.
His motto: "No one's fire and sword will defeat me."
Not used to war, his people had rested a long time;
he'd briskly told them to form ranks and rehandle their weapons.
Some were Fescennine columns, Aequans, Faliscans;
some held Soracte's heights or Flavinian farmland,
Ciminus Mountain and Lake, or the groves of Capena.
They marched in paired rows and sang of their leader,
like white swans that often appear in a hazy
700 sky returning from feeding—pleasantly singing,
their necks long, their rhythmic beat on the Cayster
River and all its marsh.
No one would think that bronze-clad legion of marchers
formed a grand army, but rather a stormcloud
of raucous sea-birds driven from deep water to beach-dunes.

Clausus and the Sabines

Look at the old and high blood of the Sabines—
Clausus driving a column, the image himself of an army!
His family later will spread through Latium, the Claudian
       household,
after Rome will share power with Sabines.

710 A huge number had joined him: Amiterneans, people
from old Cures, Mutusca—olivetree country—a swelling
crowd from Eretum, Nomentum's walls, the land near Velinus,
Rosea, men from the rugged Tetricus' hillside
and Mount Severus, Casperians, Forulians, people
who drink from the Tiber, Himella and Fabaris Rivers,
men dispatched from chilly Nursia, Latins and Ortines,
and those cut off by the bad-luck Allia River.
Their numbers matched the rolling Libyan sea-swells
when wild Orion falls on the water in winter,
720 or ears of corn warmed by the sunlight in early
summer in golden Hermian or Lycian pasture.
Shields clashed and the ground shook from the thud of their
        marching.

A Hater of Troy

Halaesus next: Agamemnon's son and a hater
of Troy's name, he'd teamed chariot horses for Turnus
and hauled out a thousand churlish clans who were turners
(with hoes) of Massican soil blessed by the Wine-God.
Fathers had sent them from high hills in Aurunca
or nearby Sidicine flatland. Some were from Cales,
or homes by the shallow Volturnus River. An Oscan
730 group and also a band of Saticulans carried
slender spears fitted with tough cords for retrieval.
Guarded by light shields, they had curved swords for infighting.

Oebalus and his People

And you, Oebalus: don't be unmentioned and absent
now from my song! They say a Nymph named Sebethis
gave you in birth to Telon who ruled Teleboan Capri
in old age. Not content with his father's
land, the son had already conquered the widespread
Sarrastrian people, the plain soaked by the Sarnus,
men who'd settled in Rufrae, Batulum, fields of Celemna,
740 and those below Abella's walls in appletree country,
accustomed like Teutons to flinging objects in battle.
They'd covered their heads with bark torn from their oak-trees.
Their bronze shields and bronze projectiles were gleaming.

Ufens

The hills of Nursia sent *you* into battle,
Ufens—widely renowned and lucky in warfare.
Your men were unusually rough Aequicolans, used to
hard ground and hunting often in woodland.
They worked the land armed, always collecting
new booty and glad to live off their stealing.

A Doomed Priest

750 A priest, too, came from Marruvian people,
helmet plaited with leaves of blossoming olive:
Umbro, the bravest man sent by a ruler, Archippus.
He often cast sleep on venomous adders
or foul-breathed watersnakes just by humming and stroking—
he stilled their anger and skillfully countered the poison.
But Umbro would cure no blow from a Trojan
spear: he'd find no help for that wound in a sleepy
song or in herbs culled on a Marsian mountain.
Angitia's groves would mourn his loss, and the glasslike
760 water of Lake Fucinus.

Remembering Hippolytus and Phaedra

A splendid son of Hippolytus entered the conflict—
well-known Virbius, sent by his mother Aricia.
She'd raised him around Egeria's woodland and marshy
banks, where fat-dripping altars placate Diana.
Hippolytus died, the story goes, from the plotting of Phaedra
(his blood they say fulfilled a curse of his father),
when bolting horses tore him apart. But returning
to sky and stars he reached the air of the Sky-Gods,
revived by Apollo's herbs and the love of Diana.
770 Then all-powerful Jupiter, galled that a human
should rise to life and light from Underworld shadow,
thrust with his own lightning that son of Apollo,
the skilled inventor and healer, down into Stygian water.
Diana, however, cared for Hippolytus, hiding
the man in a secret home with help from the Wood-Nymph
    Egeria:
alone in Italian woods he'd live out a lifetime
unknown, changing his name to Virbius later.
That's why hard-hoofed horses are kept from the sacred
grove and shrine of Diana: horses had scattered

780 the man's parts on that shore when sea-beasts alarmed them.
     Hardly deterred now, the son labored a sweating
     chariot team on the plain, in a hurry for battle.

A Leader of Leaders

     Outstanding among those chiefs was the figure of Turnus.
     Holding a sword as he rode, by a whole head he was tallest,
     the high helmet triply crested: Chimaera's
     form sat there, jaws afire, spewing like Etna's,
     appearing to rage and rumble more like a death-fire
     when more blood flowed and fighting intensified.
     Io was carved on the smooth shield, with her rising
790 horns in gold, at the time she bristled and turned to a heifer.
     The strong design had the girl's guardian, Argus,
     and, poured from a chased urn, the Inachus River, her father.
     A stormcloud of infantry followed Turnus, their shielded
     columns filling a whole field: young ones from Argos,
     groups from Aurunca, Rutulia, historic Sicanus,
     Labicans' painted shields and Sacranian forces,
     men who'd worked the Tiber valley with plows, or the sacred
     banks of the Numicus River, Rutulian hillsides,
     a ridge on Circe's island, the farmland protected
800 by Tuscan Jupiter, green glades enjoyed by Feronia,
     where Satura's dark swamp lies, and the chilly
     Ufens River winds through lowland to hide in the sea-bed.

A Rustic War-queen

     A Volscian woman came behind them: Camilla
     drove her cavalry, bronze-flowering squadrons
     led by a war-queen. The woman had never accustomed
     her hand to a wool-staff or wicker basket: she'd suffered
     in hard battle. She outran the wind when she sprinted,
     whether she flew by the tallest unplucked stalks of a cornfield,
     hardly bruising the delicate ears when she raced by,
810 or dashed through the middle of mounting surf as if hung there,
     hardly wetting her nimble feet in the water.
     Every youngster emerged from house and field to admire her,
     joined by a crowd of mothers who gazed at her movements,
     openly struck by her spirit. Monarchial purple
     covered her smooth shoulders. Her hair had been gathered
     in gold by a clasp. She carried her Lycian quiver
     herself and a rustic myrtle shaft with its spear-point.

VIII

AENEAS IN ANCIENT ROME

Will Diomedes Help?

Soon as Turnus hoisted flags of war from Laurentine
heights and a hoarse trumpet sounded its warning,
soon as he slapped his high-strung horse and clanged on his
  armor,
every heart in Latium instantly shuddered:
young men swore oaths of tumult and terror,
raging madly. The main leaders, Ufens, Messapus
and God-scorning Mezentius, organized forces;
every broad field was emptied of farmhands.
Venulus, sent to the city of great Diomedes,
10   asked for help: Trojans had settled in Latium,
Aeneas' fleet had arrived, bringing their conquered
House-Gods and claims, in accord with Fates, that Aeneas
would rule. Scores of clans had joined with the Trojan
leader and spread his name widely through Latium.
What end he desired from that start, if Fortune approved him,
what war he'd wage, Diomedes might fathom
clearer than either King Latinus or Turnus.

Confusion

So much for Latium. Aeneas, the Laomedontian leader,
could see it all. A wide sea of anxiety tossed him.
20   His mind restlessly shifted this way and that way,
taken in different directions, everything turning—
just as the light from a bronze bowl of water will sparkle

when struck by the sun or the moon's radiant image—
quickly it flies through the air in every direction,
reaching the highest ceiling and striking the panels.

A Vision of the God Tiber

Night came. The depths of sleep held the surrounding
country and creatures, tired birds and the livestock.
Aeneas lay on a bank under the chilly
axle-tree of the sky, disturbed like a father
30   by grim war-scenes. His body relaxed in the small hours.
A God himself appeared: the beautiful Tiber
River rose like an old man in the poplar
leaves, face thinly veiled in some blue-grey
linen, hair covered by shadowy marsh-reed.
Each word, when he spoke, eased the concern of Aeneas.
"Son of divine stock, savior of ancient
Troy from Greece, you've brought your city back to our country:
Laurentine soil and Latin fields have been waiting!
Don't leave: this home is truly your own and your House-Gods'.
40   Don't feel threatened by war: all of the swollen
anger of Gods will subside.
And lest you think this dreamlike vision is empty,
you'll find a huge white sow by a riverbank oak-grove,
a litter of thirty young ones lying around her—
white piglets there on the ground taking her nipples.
There's the site for your city and sure rest from your labor.
After a thirty-year cycle Iulus
will found right there the renowned city of Alba.
My word is not to be doubted. Now, this pressure you're under:
50   I'll briefly teach you how to emerge as the winner.
Arcadians rule the coast. Descendents of Pallas,
they follow the flag of a friend and ruler, Evander.
They chose a site among hills for founding their city
and named it after an ancestor—Pallanteum.
They wage constant war with Latium's people.
Take them as friends of your camp: join in a treaty.
I'll lead you myself to their bank upstream on my river:
I'll help your crew overcome the current's resistance.
Up then, son of Venus! Soon, when the starlight is fading,
60   offer Juno the right prayers and master
her angry threats with lowly vows. You may honor
my flow when you've won: I'm the full current you see here,
trimming the bank, cutting through beautiful farmland:

the blue-green Tiber, a river loved by the Sky-Gods.
My home is widest here; my headwaters rise among hill towns."

Thanks to the Gods

The River-God stopped, dove down in a deeper
pool and vanished. Sleep and nighttime were ending:
Aeneas rose and watched the glow of the rising
sun in the sky. Cupping his palms, ritually holding
70   river water, he poured out prayer to heaven:
"Nymphs of Laurentum, Nymphs at the source of our water,
and you, sacred River, fatherly Tiber,
accept Aeneas finally, protect him from danger.
Whatever lake or fountain contains you now, may you pity
our setbacks, whatever soil you gracefully spring from.
I'll offer you gifts always, praise you forever.
Horned River, King of Hesperian waters,
just stay close—closer to firm up your power."

Sacrifice of the White Sow

When finished he picked two ships from the fleet and equipped
      them
80   with oars, manned them with friends and armed them with
      weapons.
But look: an omen suddenly jolted his vision:
he saw a white sow in some bushes with piglets,
all in white—they lay in a riverbank thicket.
Aeneas reverently carried and placed mother and litter
on Juno's altar—yours, powerful Juno—and killed them.

Upstream on a Still River

All that long night, Tiber diminished
his full flow. The current moved slower and stopped there:
it lay like a still pond, resembling a peaceful
lake or watery field—reducing the labor of rowing.
90   The journey began with hurrying shouts of approval,
well-oiled keels glided along the marveling water.
The woods marveled as well, unaccustomed to brilliant
shields of men and painted hulls on the surface.
The oarsmen pulled all day and night. They grew weary
of rounding wide bends, watching the varied
forest cover, and slicing through weeds in the quiet
water. A hot sun had climbed halfway to heaven
when walls were seen in the distance, a citadel, scattered

buildings and homes. Rome much later would equal
100 the heavens' power; but now Evander's holdings were meager.
Prows were swung in quickly to make for the city.

A Greeting from a Young Prince

By chance that day the Arcadian king was rendering yearly
tribute to Gods, to Hercules' name, in a spacious
grove outside the wall. Together with Pallas,
his son, all the best young men and a senate—not wealthy—
he burned incense. Warm blood steamed on an altar.
But now, when tall ships were seen in the shady
foliage, gliding with oars at rest for a landing,
men took fright at the scene and turned in a hurry
110 to leave their table. Pallas boldly forbade them
to break up the rites. Personally seizing a weapon,
he ran to a hill and called from a distance: "You strangers—
what makes you travel this less known way? Where is your
        homeland?
What course did you set? Have you come for peace or a battle?"
High on the stern Aeneas spoke like a father,
his hand extending peaceful branches of olive.
"Troy bore us. The swords you see are unfriendly
to Latins: their pride and aggression forced us to flee here.
We look for Evander. Bring him a message that chosen
120 Dardan leaders have come looking for friends in a conflict."
Struck by the great name of Troy, Pallas responded,
"Step out, whoever you are. Speak to my Father
in person, enter our house, a guest of our House-Gods."
He took the man's right hand and firmly embraced him.
They walked along, the grove and river behind them.

Common High Bloodlines

Soon Aeneas spoke to the king as a friend would:
"Best man born of the Greeks: Fortune has willed me
to seek your help and hold out branches plaited with fillets.
I don't fear you, in fact, as Arcadian leader
130 of Greeks, with roots joined to both of Atreus' children.
Rather my own stature, holy signs from the Sky-Gods,
our Fathers' close blood, the world-wide scope of your honor
and Fates have all compelled me freely to join you.
Dardanus, Ilium's first founder and Father,
born, in the Greek account, of Atlas' daughter Electra,
sailed to Troy—the same Atlas who fathered Electra,

who greatly supports the sky's globe on his shoulders.
Your own father was Mercury: glorious Maia
conceived him on cold Cyllene's ridgeline and bore him;
140 and Atlas, the same sky- and zodiac-lifter,
fathered—if things we hear can be credited—Maia.
So. A single bloodline splits into each of our households.
Sure of all that, I made no clever initial
test through an envoy. I offer my body in person:
I'm here myself, a humble man at your threshold.
A single Daunian nation threatens us both with a cruel
war. If we're expelled they anticipate nothing
can stop them from bringing all of Hesperia under
their yoke: they'll rule from the northern sea to the southern.
150 Accept our trust. Give yours. Our men are the staunchest
fighters: young spirits, but toughened by action."

Evander's Warm Welcome

Aeneas was done. All the time he had spoken
the king had searched his eyes and face, all of his body.
Now he answered briefly. "Bravest of Trojans,
how gladly I welcome and know you! How well I remember
the words and face of your great father, Anchises!
I still recall the son of Laomedon, Priam,
heading for Salamis, seeking the realm of a sister,
Hesione. From there he left for cool Arcadian country.
160 I was a boy then, cheeks the color of blossoms.
I marveled at Troy's leaders, I marveled at Priam
himself; but the tallest figure of all was Anchises.
My boyish heart and mind burned with a longing
to speak to the man, to join my hand to his own hand.
I went to him eagerly. I led him to Pheneus' city.
When leaving he gave me a rare quiver with Lycian
arrows, he gave me a chlamys with gold interwoven,
and two gold bridles—now they're owned by my Pallas.
So: the hand you want will join in your treaty.
170 When first light returns to our country tomorrow
you'll leave here pleased with my help—my resources will aid you.
Celebrate, meanwhile: because you've come here in friendship,
Grace our annual rites. It's wrong to postpone them.
Now is the time to get used to the fare of your ally."

Feasting

He ordered cups and food brought back when he finished.
He settled the Trojans himself on a grassy embankment.
He offered Aeneas a seat especially inviting:
a maple throne spread with the hide of a lion.
Hand-picked youths competed at bringing the roasted
180 flesh of bulls from the priest's altar, loading the labor
and gifts of Ceres in baskets, and serving the Wine-God.
Aeneas and all his Trojan following feasted
on lustral innards and long chines from the bullocks.

Monster and Half Man

After their hunger dwindled and appetite settled,
King Evander said, "This annual worship,
our banquet custom and deeply numinous altar,
are not the result of ignorance, flat superstition
or aging Gods. My Trojan guest, we were rescued
from great danger: we keep up rites for one who deserves them.
190 First look at that cliff with ledge overhanging
and widely scattered boulders. A home in the cliff-wall
stands empty where rocks collapsed, a massive destruction.
A cave had been there, a hole deep in the hillside:
the den of Cacus, a frightful monster and half-man.
Untouched by the sun's rays, that soil was reheated
often by fresh blood. Brashly fixed to the entrance
were men's wan heads that hung there pale and decaying.
Fathered by Vulcan the Fire-God, the monster could cough up
black smoke from his mouth, and his bulk was enormous.

Cacus Provokes Hercules

200 "Time eventually brought us the arrival we'd longed for—
a God's help. One of the greatest avengers,
proud of killing and plundering Geryon's triple
form, Hercules came here driving cattle in triumph.
His huge bulls occupied valley and stream-bed.
But Cacus' wild, mad spirit would never
leave some crime or deceit untried or untested.
He pulled from their stalls four superbly proportioned
bulls and the same number of beautiful heifers.
Then, to prevent the tracks from pointing correctly,
210 he dragged them tail-first, reversing signs of the movement.
He hid them far back in the stone dark of his cavern.

He'd left no trail to the cave for anyone searching.

The Thief is Exposed

"When Hercules meanwhile moved his herd from the stable
after they'd fed enough and were ready to leave there,
some cows mooed on leaving—in fact they were filling
all the hillside and grove, complaining and moaning.
And one of the cows in Cacus' horrible dungeon
mooed back—wrecking the hopes of her jailer.
Was Hercules burned and galled—he actually darkened
220 with anger! Quickly he grabbed a heavily knotted
club and made for the windy, steep side of the mountain.
Now for the first time our people were seeing
Cacus afraid. Faster than Eastwind he ran off
to hide in the cave with panic winging his footsteps.
Once inside he snapped the chain on a giant
rock designed by his father the Fire-God to hang there
in iron: it dropped and blocked the entrance entirely.

Final Vengeance

"Imagine: Hercules gets there, spirited, raging:
he glares at the entrance, turning this way and that way,
230 teeth grinding. Three times, furiously sweating,
he circles the whole Aventine hillside and batters
the stone entrance. In vain. Tired, he sits in a gulley.
A sheer granite spire, eroded on all sides,
rose on top of the cave. A lofty perspective,
it offered nesting at times to hideous vultures.
Its peak leaned to the left, over the river.
Hercules pushed against it: he cracked it and loosened
the deep base. Suddenly all of it toppled:
the great sky rumbled back at that cracking,
240 the startled river jumped its banks, and its current
reversed: the huge den of Cacus was roofless!
His home lay bare, the cave's deep shadows uncovered,
as though the earth had quaked violently downward
disclosing a grey realm below, the Underworld region
repugnant to Gods, who peer from above at the monstrous
chasm where dead men cringe at the downrushing sunlight.
Caught in the sudden glare, unexpectedly cornered
now in the scooped-out cave, Cacus howled—what an eerie
cry!—while Hercules pelted him hard from the cave-top with
    sundry

250   weapons and missiles. He struck him with big tree-limbs and
           boulders.
       Then, with no escape from the danger, that monster's
       mouth heaved up dense cloud—it's amazing to speak of—
       and quickly the whole den roiled in a blinding
       smoke. Vision dwindled, a fog-heavy midnight
       formed in the cave, and fire mixed with the darkness.
       Nonetheless a spirited Hercules jumped down
       himself through the fire, leaping headlong where densest
       smoke billowed and black fog seethed in the cavern.
       In darkness he seized Cacus who coughed out his futile
260   flames, he held him knot-tight, squeezed till he emptied
       the throat of blood, and forced the eyes from their sockets.
       The entry stone pulled back, the dark cavern lay open.
       Dragged-off bulls which Cacus denied he had stolen
       came to light. The deformed cadaver was hauled out
       feet first. Our hearts could not get enough: we inspected
       the horrible eye-holes and face, the savage's bristled
       and hairy chest, the throat whose fire was extinguished.

Rites in Remembrance

       "Since then our people have gladly offered this tribute
       and kept a feast-day. Potitius started the service;
270   Pinarius' family kept up Hercules' worship,
       placing the altar himself in this grove—we are used to
       calling it Maxima—may it be Maxima always!
       Come then, gentlemen. To praise and honor such power,
       circle your hair with leaves and lift up your goblets.
       Call on our common God. Freely offer libations."
       He stopped and covered his hair in shadowy poplar,
       Hercules' two-toned leaves, hanging like pendants.
       He filled a ritual cup and everyone quickly
       and gladly called on Gods, pouring libations.

Songs in Remembrance

280   Meanwhile Evening approached, borne down from Olympus.
       Priests were walking now, Potitius leading,
       dressed in the proper pelts and carrying torches.
       They started feasting again. They carried the welcome
       gifts to tables and piled a full plate on each altar.
       The Salian family approached and sang at a smoking
       shrine, their temples ringed by leaflets of poplar.
       One group younger, another older, they honored

Hercules' actions in song: crushing and tearing
two big snakes when a child (a stepmother's monsters),
290 wrecking by hand outstanding cities in wartime
(like Troy and Oechalia), then completing a thousand
hard tasks (at the word of unscrupulous Juno)
for King Eurystheus. "You," they sang, "are unbeaten:
you slaughtered the cloud-born Centaurs, Hylaeus and Pholus,
the monster at Crete, the huge, rock-sheltered Nemean lion.
Lakes of the Styx feared you, the watchdog of Orcus
kept to his bloody cave with bones he had half chewed.
No one's form scared you, not even the tallest,
Typhoeus, grasping a spear. Your thinking was steady
300 when Lyrna's Hydra, that mob of heads, had you surrounded.
We greet you, Jupiter's true son, adding your beauty
to God's: graciously walk with us all in your worship."
That was the song they sang, especially calling
to mind the fire exhaled by Cacus himself in the cavern.
The whole forest echoed with song: hillsides re-echoed.

Rome's Hard Beginnings

From there they all moved back to the city,
divine matters done with. The king, burdened with old age,
walked by a friendly Aeneas while leaning on Pallas,
his son. He eased the walk with mixed conversation.
310 Aeneas gazed in open wonder at all the surroundings,
the place absorbed him, he gladly inquired about every
detail and listened to stories of old generations.
King Evander, the Roman citadel's founder,
told him, "Native Nymphs and Fauns lived in our forest
with hard trunk-like men born of the oaktrees,
who knew nothing of custom and culture, the teaming
of oxen, storing food and dividing resources.
They lived on pungent bark and scraps from their hunting.

A Brief Golden Age

"Saturn first arrived from the sky of Olympus,
320 an exile. He'd lost a realm and fled from Jupiter's weapons.
He gathered the untaught people scattered on mountain
heights and gave them laws. He wanted the country
called Latium, since he'd 'lain' safe on our sea-coast.
They call it a Golden Age under that monarch,
he ruled so calmly. The whole nation was peaceful.

The Curse of War and Greed

"Later times were soon discolored and poorer
due to war's madness and love of possessions.
Ausonian bands arrived and Sicilian people.
Names in Saturn's land were often discarded.
330 Harsh kings like Thybris, in form like a monster,
gave his name to Italy's river, the Tiber.
(It lost the old true name, the Albula River.)
Irresistible Fates, an all-powerful Fortune,
drove me from native land and chased me through utmost
seas to place me here. The Nymph Carmentis, my Mother,
urged me on, with fearsome warnings begun by Apollo."

Place-names of Rome

He'd scarcely finished and come to a shrine when he pointed
straight at a gate which Romans call the Carmental—
a name that honors the ancient Song-Nymph, Carmentis.
340 A future-predictor, she'd first sung of Aeneas'
coming greatness and Pallanteum's distinction.
He showed where Romulus briskly restored the Asylum,
a large grove. And under a cool cliff was a grotto,
the Lupercal—after Pan's usual name on Lycaeus.
The king noted the sacred trees of Argiletum,
recalling the "death of Argus," a guest of Evander.
He showed the Tarpeian Rock and Capitol hillside,
later in gold, now a tangle of thickets.
Primal awe of the place already had troubled
350 country people; they trembled near the rockpile and bushes.
Evander said, "The brush and forested hilltop
are home for a God but which is uncertain. Arcadians
think they've often seen Jupiter shaking
a dark shield in his hand and massings the stormclouds.
And there, do you see that pair of towns with their jumbled
walls? An older people's reminders and remnants:
this one built by our Father Janus, that one by Saturn;
one we call the Janiculum, the other, Saturnian."

Simple Shelter

After he said all that they entered the modest
360 home of Evander. They'd noticed cattle were dotting
the Roman Forum—moos in our elegant Ship's-Keels!—
before they came to the throne-room. The king: "Hercules entered

this room accepting a plain house in his triumph.
Be daring, my guest: scorn wealth, imagine you're worthy
of God as well! Don't visit the poor with unkindness."
He stopped and led the way under the crowding
structure's roof. He showed the tall Aeneas some bedding:
a leaf support covered by Libyan bearskin.

Venus and Vulcan

A rush of her dark wings: Night mantled the country.
370   But motherly Venus fretted. With plenty of reason:
Laurentians threatened, a harsh tumult had stirred up.
She turned in her golden bed to Vulcan, her husband.
With airs of divine love she began to address him.
"While Greek kings were wrecking Troy in that conflict—
a citadel destined to fall to enemy burning—
I asked for no help, none of your skillful maneuvers
or arms for my wretched people. I never intended,
my dearest husband, to use your labor for nothing,
although I owed Priam's children a great deal
380   and often wept at Aeneas' arduous struggle.
Now by Jupiter's order he holds a Rutulian beachhead.
Now I ask you humbly for weapons and sacred
strength. I ask it mother for son: Nereus' daughter
could move you with tears; so could the wife of Tithonus.
Look at those tribes gather, the barring of city
gates, the sharp swords that could slaughter my people."

Divine Persuasion

The Goddess finished. Vulcan paused. She caressed him
here and there, a white arm gently embracing.
The fire he caught was quick and familiar, a well-known
390   warmth that spread through his marrow and caused him to
          shudder,
as flame will often run through a fissure in stormcloud
and flash light with a burst of shuddering thunder.
His wife smiled, aware of her lovely beguiling.
Her lord answered, won by the Goddess's passion,
"Why look for a distant pretext? Faith in your husband,
Goddess—where has it gone? Had you cared in the same way,
my arming Troy had also been right in the old days.
Neither your all-powerful Father nor Fates could have stopped it:
Troy would have stood for ten more years, Priam surviving.
400   But now if you're ready for war and determined to try it,
whatever concern my skill can show I will offer—

things I can make with molten iron and alloy
strengthened by fire and bellows. No more of your pleading—
or doubting your own force." The words he had spoken
yielded now to a lover's embrace, and the restful
sleep he desired, at peace on the breast of his consort.

Like a Roman Wife

In time the need for sleep abated. The journey
of Night was half over: the hour when a woman
might rise for Minerva to earn a living with slender
410   spindle, stirring drowsy sparks at a fireplace,
adding night to her work-hours, tiring the servants
with long shifts by firelight, keeping her husband's
bed chaste and providing for small sons' education.
The Fire-God rose in the same brisk way at that early
hour from a soft bed to work at the forges.

Naked Cyclops

An island rises close to Sicily's coastline,
next to Aeolian Lipari: smoldering, steep-sided, rocky.
A cave is cut out below for the forges of Cyclops.
Etna's caves drum from that strong pounding of anvils.
420   A moan sounds and resounds in the cavern with noises
from steel bars and fired furnaces' breathing.
They call it Vulcan's home—Vulcania Island.
The Fire-God came down here from the heights of Olympus.
Cyclops worked in the huge cave at their iron—
Brontes, Pyracmon, Steropes—all of them naked.
Their hands had formed in part the forks of a polished
lightning such as Jupiter hurls by the hundred
to earth from the broad sky. Part was unfinished:
they added three swirling spokes of a rainstorm,
430   three of wet cloud, red fire, and quick-flying Southwind.
They mixed dread and noise next in the lightning,
awe-filled brilliance and angry following firestorms.
Elsewhere they rushed work on the bird-quick wheels of a chariot,
used by Mars to terrify people in cities.
They worked on a shocking breastplate, the armor of furious
        Pallas:
they struggled to polish the gold, scaly like snakeskin,
a twisted serpents' design, with Gorgon herself on the Goddess's
chest—the neck was cut but the eyeballs were rolling.

New Arms for Aeneas

"Put all the work you've started aside, Cyclops of Etna,"
440 Vulcan told them. "Give me all your attention.
Build arms for a strong-willed man with your powerful,
dexterous hands. *Now* for that masterful knowledge,
quickly, no dawdling!" He said no more and the Cyclops
nimbly set to work, all of them sharing
by lot. Gold and bronze flowed in the channels.
Wound-inflicting steel melted in mountain-size forges.
They formed an immense shield, in itself a protection
against each Latin weapon: a welding of seven
round layers. While air was pumped by a bellows
450 that inhaled and exhaled, bronze was tempered in hissing
tanks of water. The cavern groaned with the banging,
Cyclops raising their strong arms in a cadence,
turning the bronze with gripping tongs while pounding together.

Morning Colloquy

While Lemnos' Lord rushed his work on the Aeolian shoreline,
nourishing light stirred the lowly house of Evander.
Birds warbled and cooed under the roof-eaves.
The old king rose, put on a tunic
and wrapped the soles of his feet in Tuscany sandals.
He tied a Tegean sword to one side and a shoulder.
460 He flung back on his left side the hide of a panther.
A pair of guard-dogs that stayed by the doorway
preceded him now, keeping pace with their master.
He made for the private room of his house-guest, Aeneas.
The king remembered their talk, the help he had promised.
Aeneas had also risen early that morning.
His friend Achates joined him; his son Pallas, Evander.
They all met, joined hands and sat in a central
room to enjoy an open lengthy discussion.

Tyranny and Torture

The king spoke first.
470 "Greatest Trojan leader! I'll never acknowledge
Troy's kingdom really lost while you're living.
Our help and power in war are feeble in contrast
with your great name. The Tiber crowds us on one side;
armed Rutulians press and rattle our walls on the other.
Still I'm ready to send large clans to your campsite,

wealthy people from where chance unexpectedly offers
you safety: Fates brought you here and demand it.
Not far away is a city founded on ancient
bedrock—Agylline homes—where Lydian people,
480 superb fighters, formerly lived on the Tuscan
ridge. They flourished for years till a tyrant, Mezentius,
finally ruled them proudly. The arms of a savage—
but why dwell on the crimes of a despot, the doings
of madmen? Let God dispose of that head and his household!
The man in fact would force a dead body on living
flesh, mouth to mouth, finger in finger—
his kind of torment. Running with poisonous slaver,
embraced horribly, slowly the victim was murdered.
People wearied at last of the criminal madness.
490 They armed, surrounded the king's house and attacked it,
butchered his toadies and hurled flames at the rooftop.
The man escaped the slaughter. He fled to some friendly
Rutulian soil, where the army of Turnus protects him.
So all of Etruria rose in justified fury,
led by the War-God, demanding the tyrant be punished.

New Leadership

"Aeneas, I'll make you leader myself of their thousands.
The whole shore jostles with ships, with crewmen who murmur
and call for war-flags. An old prophet restrains them,
singing the God's word: 'You chosen Maeonian people,
500 prime strength of the men of old: justified rancor
supports your fighting; Mezentius merits your fury.
But no Italian, by right, may rule your assembly:
choose a foreign leader.' So now the Etruscan
army slumps in the field, alarmed by word from the Sky-God.
Tarchon himself sent me a king's delegation
with scepter and crown, asking I take up the ensigns:
'Come to our camp, seize the throne of the Tuscans!'
But cold and age have slowed me, drained me for decades.
Faded strength prevents me from ruling with courage.
510 I'd urge my son but a Sabine woman's his mother:
he's part Italian by birth. But you, with your Trojan
bloodline and youth, with Fates' will in your favor,
you step forward: lead Troy and Italy strongly!
I'll also unite you here with my hope and my comfort,
Pallas. Let him get used to the burden of battle
with you teaching, doing the grave work of the War-God:

to see and admire from his youth the acts of Aeneas.
I'll give my son two hundred Arcadian horsemen,
oak-hard, hand-picked; Pallas will bring you as many in *his*
  name."

Thunder and Weapons in the Sky

520 He'd scarcely finished—Aeneas, the son of Anchises,
looking downcast along with trusted Achates,
mulling with sad hearts the oncoming struggle—
when Venus his mother gave them a sign from the open
sky suddenly: a flash and shudder of thunder
came through the air, everything seemed to be sinking
abruptly, a Tuscan trumpet blared on the air-waves.
They looked up: thunder crashed over and over,
they saw in a clear expanse of heaven some weapons
that reddened clouds in the sky and hammered like thunder.
530 Many were struck dumb. But the Trojan commander
recognized the sound his Goddess-Mother had promised.
Now he said, "My friend, you certainly need not
ask what change that sign portends: Olympus demands me.
My Goddess-Mother promised to send me an omen
if war threatened: she'd bring me weapons from Vulcan,
help from the sky.
But oh, what slaughter of sad Laurentians will follow!
You'll pay me dearly, Turnus. Dozens of shields in the water,
helmets and strong bodies of men will roll in the lordly
540 Tiber. Let them call up troops and shatter the peace-pact."

Departures

No sooner done he raised himself from the high-ranked
chair and stirred the sleepy embers at Hercules' altar
first, then gladly visited yesterday's Hearth-God
and little House-Gods. Evander, according to custom,
picked and sacrificed full-grown sheep; so did the Trojans.
Aeneas walked to the ships next, rejoining companions.
He chose a number of men who'd follow in battle—
the specially brave ones. The rest of the company floated
downstream slowly on flat, welcoming water:
550 they told Iulus of future events, his father's arrangements.
Trojans heading for Tuscan fields were presented
with mounts—a special breed was led to Aeneas, a lion's
tan hide on its back, the claws golden and shiny.
Rumor instantly spread and flew through the village:

horsemen had rushed to the shore of the king of the Tuscans.
Fretful mothers doubled their prayers, anxiety
drew closer to danger, the War-God's image was growing.
Soon the father, Evander, hugged his departing
son. He could not weep enough as he spoke out:
560 "If only Jupiter now would bring back my past years—
the time I cut down front-line troops at Praeneste
itself and piled up shields and triumphantly burned them!
This hand sent King Eurylus down to the Hell-God.
His mother Feronia gave him three lives when she bore him—
a frightening story—triple armor to get through:
he had to be killed three times. Still I deprived him
of all three lives. This hand stripped him of armor!
If then were now, I'd never be pulled from your pleasant
embrace, my son. Our neighbor Mezentius never
570 would throw scorn on my head or widow our city's
women, cruelly killing scores of our people.
But all you Gods and you, greatest Ruler off Sky-Gods,
Jupiter: I ask that you pity an Arcadian monarch:
hear a father's plea. If Pallas can come back
safely thanks to your power—if Fates can preserve him
so I might see him alive, returning to join me—
I beg to live. I'll suffer, be hard, whatever the burden.
But Goddess of Luck, if you plan some unthinkable downfall,
let me be torn right now from bitter existence
580 while hope is unsure, concern for the future uncertain:
while you, my dear son, my only and final
joy, hold me. May no graver message be wounding
my ear." The father poured out words at this final
parting, and fainted. Servants took him to shelter.

Off to War

Shortly men on horseback rode through the open
gates, Aeneas in front with trusted Achates
and other Trojan leaders. Pallas, surrounded
by men, striking in chlamys and colorful armor,
looked like the Morning Star rising from Ocean's
590 depths, more loved by Venus than all of the star-fires,
lifting that sacred head, scattering darkness.
Mothers who stood on the wall anxiously followed
the cloud of dust and gleaming brass of each column.
Well-armed men pushed through scrub, taking the shortest
path, raising shouts when lines were assembled.

Chariots drummed on the dust-ridden flats with their hoofbeats.

Tarchon's Camp

A large grove lay by a cool river at Caere,
widely revered by faith-filled fathers. Hills were around it,
a circle of dark and surrounding evergreen forest.
600 The story goes that the first people to settle
in Latium's country, ancient Pelasgians, offered a festal
day and this grove to their God of pasture and livestock, Silvanus.
Not far from here Tarchon had quartered the Tuscans
in camp safely. Every corps could be surveyed
now from a high hill, their tents filling the farmland.
A lordly Aeneas approached with the men he had chosen
for war. Tired, they looked to themselves and their horses.

Weapons from the Sky-Gods

Ah, but Venus appeared, a radiant Goddess
in aery cloud, carrying presents. Soon as she spotted
610 her son in a valley apart, alone by a chilly
stream, she abruptly appeared before him and told him,
"Look: my skilled husband's work which I promised:
it's finished, my son. You'll soon have no hesitation:
challenge proud Laurentians and fierce Turnus in combat."
After speaking she reached for her son to embrace him.
She set the brilliant arms by an oaktree before him.

Vulcan the Designer

Glad to be greatly honored by gifts from the Goddess,
unable to relish the weapons enough by mere looking,
he marveled and turned each piece with a hand or an arm-swing:
620 the crested and fearsome helmet throwing up fire-horns,
the death-carrying sword, the bronze-stiff and blood-red
breastplate, massive as blue-black thunderheads reddened
by hot rays of the sun and reflecting them far off,
greaves of polished gold and purified silver,
a spear, and all the shield's indescribable plaiting.
The Fire-God had worked events in Italy and Roman
triumphs there on the shield. Aware of the coming
age, knowing the prophets, he'd carved Ascanius' future
family tree, what wars would be waged in what order.
630 He'd also designed the moss-green cave of the War-God:
a wolf lay there with twin boys at her nipples,
playfully tugging and fearlessly licking their mother.

The wolf bent her neck gracefully backwards
to stroke them in turn, her tongue grooming their bodies.
The artist had added Rome nearby and the lawless
rape of the Sabine women attending the rounded
Circus' great games when war suddenly broke out:
Tatius' vigorous Cureans fought with Romulus' people.
Later the same two kings ended the conflict:
640 standing armed by Jupiter's altar and holding
ritual bowls, they killed swine and joined in a treaty.
Nearby on the shield was Mettus, drawn into pieces
by four-horse teams. (Alban, stick to your promise!)
Tullus dragged the liar's guts through the forest,
dotting leaves of bushes with dew-looking blood-drops.
Porsenna was here too commanding that Tarquin
return from exile. He laid massive siege to the city.
Future sons of Aeneas fell on swords for their freedom.
Porsenna seemed like an outraged man or a menace,
650 what with Cocles daring to damage the bridges
and Cloelia breaking her chains and swimming the river.

Rome's Future on the Shield of Aeneas

On top of the shield was Manlius, guarding Tarpeian
heights, holding the Capitol's hilltop while standing
before the temple. Romulus' palace bristled with recent
thatching and here, flying through gold-plaited columns,
a silver goose warned of Gauls at the entrance.
And Gauls arrived: protected by forest at nighttime,
the gift of a covering darkness, they captured the fortress.
Their hair on the shield was gold, gold as their clothing,
660 their striped coats gleamed and gold had encircled
their white necks. Every man brandished an Alpine
pair of spears. Long shields guarded their bodies.
Vulcan had carved in relief the Salians dancing,
bare Lupercans with wool-ringed helmets and shields which had
          fallen
(they say) from the sky, and chaste mothers conducting
relics on gentle coaches through Rome. He had added
distant thrones of Tartarus, high gates of the Hell-God,
crime and punishment: you, Cataline, dangling
from overhanging rock and dreading looks from the Furies.
670 The just were apart, Cato giving them statutes.

Civil War at Sea

The central design was a sea-scape in rising and far-flung
gold, though a sky-blue sea was foaming and white-capped.
Glistening dolphins careered in circles of silver,
tales thrashing the waves and cutting through sea-froth.
Two fleets in bronze were visible there in the center.
The Battle of Actium, look: Mars had aligned them,
all of Leucate's golden water seething and glowing,
Caesar Augustus leading Italians in battle:
joined by people and elders, House-Gods and Great Gods,
680 he stood high on the stern. His fine temples emitting
twin flames, he bore a crest displaying the star of his father.
Nearby Agrippa was proudly launching a squadron,
wind and God behind him, a sign of his war-pride
gleaming from temples—a crown studded with ship's-beaks.
Antony came with foreign wealth and a mélange
of weapons: he'd conquered Dawn's people on ruddy
shores and sailed with Eastern forces from Egypt
and farthest Bactra. That curse, an Egyptian wife, was behind
    him.
They all charged at once—the water completely
690 roiled, torn by pulling oars and three-pointed rammers.
They headed for deep water. You'd think the Cyclades Islands
were loose and swimming, or high mountains colliding with
    mountains:
the towered, manned and attacking ships were that massive.
They hurled flaming hemp and fast-flying missiles
of iron. Neptune's fields turned red from the slaughter.
The queen, dead center, not yet seeing the serpents
who'd kill her, called on her men with a rattle of Isis.
Prodigy-Gods of every kind, like the dog's-head, Anubis,
held out weapons against Venus, Minerva
700 and Neptune. Mars raged in the midst of the action,
engraved in iron, with grim Furies above him.
Discord roved and gloated, her mantle in tatters.
Bellona, with bloodied whips, followed behind her.
Watching Actium, arching a bow, was Apollo,
high overhead—every Egyptian and Arab,
all the Sabaeans and Indians turned in a panic.
The queen herself seemed to be calling for sea-wind,
for more sail *now*, for loosening mainsheets.

Vulcan had made her blanch at all the carnage around her
710 and coming death. She rode on the water with Northwind.
Facing the queen, the grief-struck form of a splendid
Nile-God opened all the folds of his clothing:
that sea-blue lap with its hidden streams called to the losers.

Triumph in Rome

Caesar rode through Rome, the city of triumph.
A triple victor, he vowed to Italy's Gods an eternal
gift: three hundred superb shrines through the city.
Streets were a clamor of games, rejoicing and cheering.
At every temple and altar mothers were dancing;
bulls were sprawled on the ground or killed at an altar.
720 Caesar sat by the white portal of Phoebus
acknowledging people's gifts attached to majestic
door-posts. A long line of conquered subjects
filed past—a welter of languages, dress-styles and weapons.
Vulcan had formed Nomads here and the loose-robed
Africans, Leleges, Carians, arrow-bearing Gelonians.
He'd formed the Euphrates, now flowing more gently,
Morins from far north, the Rhine with its double
fork, wild Scythians, the Araxes, offended by bridges.

Shouldering the Future

Admiring the shield by Vulcan, this gift from his mother,
730 Aeneas enjoyed the design, unsure of its meaning.
He raised and shouldered the fame and fate of his children.

IX

WAR AT THE TROJAN FORT

Turnus is Goaded Again

While all that happened far off in that region,
Saturn's daughter Juno sent down Iris from heaven
to brash Turnus. By chance Turnus had sat down
in sacred ancestors' lowland, a grove of Pilumnus.
Rose-mouthed Iris, Thaumas' daughter, addressed him:
"Turnus, what none of the Gods dared to assure you,
although you wished it, look—a day's rotation has brought you!
Leaving friends, fleet and campsite, Aeneas
has looked for Evander's throne, a Palatine scepter.
10   What's more, he's reached the farthest Corythan cities
and armed gathered throngs of Lydian fieldhands.
Why delay? Now is the time: call out your horses
and chariots, hurry: shake that campsite and seize it!"
She stopped and rose on paired wings into heaven,
trailing through clouds the grand arch of a rainbow.

An Army on the Move

The man knew her; he raised both hands to her starry
home while he followed the Goddess' flight, and he asked her,
"Iris—you grace the sky—who sent you down to this country?
Who drove you through clouds? That sudden storm of your
        brilliance—
20   where does it come from? I see the sky where it opens
and stars roam the zenith. I'll follow your lofty
sign wherever you call me to war." Soon as he finished

189

he went to the river and cupped fast-flowing water.
He prayed and vowed repeatedly, burdening heaven.
Soon the entire army moved through an open
field, a wealth of horse and gold-embroidered apparel.
Messapus controlled the vanguard, the princes of Tyrrhus
the rear, and Turnus the largest force in the center
(grasping and twirling a sword, by a whole head he was tallest):
30 the way the deep Ganges rises from seven
quiet streams, or the Nile recedes from the lowland,
hiding its own rich flow in the channel.

Alarms

Now the Trojans could see that gathering dustcloud:
a bleak, sudden darkness rose on the flatland.
Caicus called out first in front of the earthworks.
"What's that mass of roiling smoke and darkness, you people?
Swords, quickly! Bring arrows, climb on the bulwarks,
the enemy's here, wake up!" Clamoring Trojans
swung and locked each gate then filled up the wall-tops.
40 Aeneas, their best fighter, had told them on leaving
to do just that: if luck went bad in his absence,
to form no rash column or trust to the open
field, but stay in camp, walled and protected.
Even if anger and shame urged them to combat,
still they should block the gates, following orders,
armed and sheltered in towers, awaiting the enemy.

A Wolf at the Sheepfold

Turnus, racing ahead of a slow-moving column,
followed by twenty hand-picked riders, abruptly
reached the fort. He rode a white-spotted Thracian;
50 the gold helmet he wore was crested with crimson.
"Who will join me first, you men, to challenge the Trojans?
Look"—he whirled a spear in the air and he threw it—
the battle's gambit. He proudly rode on the open
field where friends took up the war-cry, responding
with shrill screams, perplexed at the dull hearts of the Trojans,
who dared not move on the field and openly face down
armed men—they stayed in camp. So Turnus went circling
the walls widely on horseback, avidly looking for access,
just like a wolf at a full sheepfold, lying in ambush
60 or growling at chinks, enduring the pelting of downpour
and midnight wind. While lambs are safe with their mothers

and bleating loudly, he snarls, shamelessly angry
and gruff: they're out of reach, hunger has maddened
and tired him for hours, his mouth unbloodied and thirsting.
Turnus glared at the camp's wall with a flared-up
anger just like that: hard pain burned in his marrow.
Where could he try to enter? How could he drive out
Trojans ringed by ramparts and spread them on flatland?

Burn the Ships!

The fleet lay to one side joined to the campsite,
70   guarded by mounds of earth and the flow of the river.
He'd strike it. He called for fire from cheering companions
and briskly filled both hands with crackling pinewood.
They all worked hard—the presence of Turnus compelled them—
till each young man was armed with a blackening firebrand.
They seized hearth-fires; smoke from torches and glowing
ash lifted, a skyward mix for the Fire-God.

The Poet Invokes his Muse Once More

What Power, you Muse, prevented the burning of Trojan
ships? Who kept the intense heat from those vessels?
Tell me—there's old, constant faith in the story.

Cybele's Protection

80   Back in time when Aeneas first constructed a navy
near Mount Ida, preparing to head out to deep sea,
they say the Gods' Mother herself, Cybele, offered
a plea to great Jupiter: "Grant to your loving
Mother, my son, a request now that you've conquered Olympus.
For years I've loved one pine forest especially,
a grove on the highest ridge where my rites are conducted,
evergreen-dark and mixed with shadowy maple.
I gladly gave my trees to Troy when Aeneas
lacked a fleet. Now I'm troubled; anxiety pains me.
90   Ease my fear and grant your Mother a prayer:
let no set course, no wind or waterspout shatter
or sink them. Let them be strong: they rose on my mountain."

Jupiter's Promise

Her son, however, who turned stars of the cosmos:
"Mother, where would you call the Fates from? What are you
      asking—
that mortal and man-made ships be granted immortal

rights, and Aeneas blandly pass through uncertain
danger? What God is allowed such absolute power?
No: the ships will complete their task, reaching Ausonian
ports one day. But those that escape from the sea-storms,
100 bringing the Trojan prince to land in Laurentum,
will change their earthly shape: I will command them
to turn into Sea-Nymphs to rove like Nereus' daughters,
Doto and Galatea, their breasts breaking the sea-foam."
He stopped and swore by the Styx, the stream of his brother,
by banks burning with pitch, that darkening maelstrom.
He nodded, then; the nod rumbled all of Olympus.

Newborn Sea-Nymphs

At length the promised day arrived and a cycle
owed to the Fates ended: the fury of Turnus
warned that Mother to ward off fire from her sacred
110 ships. First a strange glow in the eastern
sky dazzled the eyes and a grand cloud with Idaean
dancers rushed overhead. A voice terrified people,
it fell through the air and filled ranks of Rutulians and Trojans:
"Don't be afraid, men of Troy, my ships are defended,
you need not man or arm them. Turnus will burn up the ocean
before my sacred pine! My ships, I release you.
Go as Nymphs of the sea: your Mother commands it."
Every ship suddenly broke her riverbank cable
and moved like a dolphin, nosing downward and upward,
120 heading for deep water. A marvellous omen:
each had stood with its bronze prow by the river:
now each had a girl's form, carrying seaward!
Rutulian spirits were stunned. Even Messapus
trembled; his horse-team fretted. The Tiber had slowed down,
calling its march to the sea back and murmuring harshly.

Another Reading of the Omen

Turnus however remained courageous and cocksure.
Aggressively rousing spirits he challenged them outright:
"The omen's *against* Troy! Jupiter's hauled off
their usual refuge himself: the ships are not waiting
130 for fire and Rutulian sword; so now, with no sea-road
or hope of escape, the Trojans have lost half their resources!
But we hold the land—with thousands of people
bearing Italian arms. No sign will dismay me,
whatever divine response the Trojans come up with.

We granted their Fates and Venus enough when the Trojans
touched fertile Ausonian land. And how will we stop them?
With Fates of my own: this *sword* will destroy that disgusting
race! They'd steal my bride—not only Atreus' children
have felt that threat—but not only Mycenae can take up
140 arms. One fall was enough? Yes: if they'd only
sinned once, and come to despise afterward every
female. Now their men put faith in this dirt-pile,
stall us with trenches—a paltry space before death comes!
It gives them spirit. But haven't they seen what the Sea-God
built by hand—their Phrygian city—crumbling and burning?
You, my hand-picked swordsmen: who will demolish
that rampart? Join me, charge that simpering campsite!
I need no thousand ships or armor from Vulcan
to beat down Trojans—even if *all* of the Tuscans
150 called them friends. They need not dread a Palladium's
clumsy theft at night, nor a killing of bastion
guards on the heights: *we* don't hide in a horse's
belly or darkness: we circle walls with fire in the daylight!
I'll hardly make them think we're Pelasgian youngsters,
or Greeks delayed for ten winters by Hector.
But men, the better part of daylight has left us
now: take what remains to relax and be happy.
Our action has gone well. Prepare for battle, be ready."
He gave the task meanwhile of blocking each entrance
160 with men at watch and circling the walls with fire to Messapus,
who picked fourteen Rutulians, each with a hundred
soldiers behind him, to stand by the Trojan embankments.
The men's gold and purple helmets were gleaming:
taking turns they ran to a post or they left it,
stretching on grass to drink wine, holding a brazen
bowl while a campfire blazed. Sentries idled a sleepless
night in gambling.

The Trojans' Anxiety

Armed Trojans watched from bulwarks above them.
They held higher ground but they worried and bustled,
170 inspecting gates, building buttresses, walkways,
weapons in hand. Mnestheus pushed them and eager
Serestus—appointed the men's principal leaders
by lordly Aeneas if any misfortune should threaten.
Along the wall the whole contingent was watching
in turn by lot, each man assigned to a lookout.

Nisus Plans Boldly

One gate watchman was Nisus: a spirited fighter,
the son of Hyrtacus, sent by Ida the huntress
to join with Aeneas, adding his light-weight arrows and quick-
    thrown
spear. Nearby was a friend, Euryalus: no one
180 who followed Aeneas in Trojan arms had such beauty.
Boyhood showed on his face—young and unshaven.
These two loved each other, whether they charged in
a skirmish or held the same post by an entrance.
Nisus wondered, "Do Gods, Euryalus, addle or heat up
our minds? Or men make gods of their dangerous cravings?
My mind has nudged me now for a long time into combat,
some ultimate test. My brain won't rest and be quiet.
Look at the trust in things the Rutulians maintain:
some little fires pulsing, sentries relaxing
190 with wine or sleeping, silence everywhere. Listen
now to my thoughts. One idea is recurring.
All our people and elders have called for Aeneas'
return: men should reach him with clear information.
If elders will give you all I ask for—the action and honor
will satisfy me—you'll see me find an escape-route
under that hill to the walled city of Pallanteum."

Euryalus Will Not Be Left Behind

Stunned and amazed at such great longing for honor,
Euryalus spoke at once to his feverish comrade.
"So: you'd run from your friend at the height of an action,
200 Nisus? Sent alone in the worst possible danger?
Not so. My Father Opheltes, accustomed to battle,
taught me different when Troy struggled with terror
from Greece. I never acted with you in this manner.
I followed our noble Aeneas' Fates to the limit:
here, this spirit disdains the light of the living
and sees life as a small price for the honor you strive for."

The Specter of a Mother's Loss

Nisus, responding: "I never feared in fact you were lacking.
But no, it's wrong: let great Jupiter bring me
back to your cheers—or whoever regards the action with favor—
210 but if some God, as you often see in a crisis,
if some bad luck or God or accident takes me,

I'd want you to live. You're young: you deserve to be living.
Let those who drag me from battle or ransom my body
place me in common ground. If Fortune prevents that,
let rites be performed and a tomb adorned in my absence.
No, let me not cause your sad mother unbearable
grief, boy—the only mother of many
who dared to follow, who scorned the city of mighty Acestes."

It's Decided

But the other: "Weave your logic—it's empty and futile.
220 My mind won't fail now or change its position.
Let's hurry," he said, rousing a watch to relieve them,
to take their turn at once. Euryalus, leaving
the post, walked as a friend with Nisus to look for their leaders.

Escape Plans

Through all that country various animals rested.
Cares were soothed and beasts unmindful of struggle.
But leading Trojan commanders, men who were hand-picked,
held a high council that dealt with critical pressures.
What should they do now? Who'd bring word to Aeneas?
They stood there, leaning on long javelins, holding
230 shields, in the central camp. Nisus together
with young Euryalus quickly asked for a hearing—
a serious matter, worth their time. So Ascanius
welcomed the nervous pair first and commanded
Hyrtacus' son to speak. "Hear us, you men of Aeneas,"
Nisus said, "judge us fairly, regarding not only
our youth but our plan. Rutulians, winey and sleepy,
are still, relaxed. We've seen a way to escape them:
it lies at a fork by the gate closest to water.
Fires are fewer there, stars darkened by pitchy
240 smoke. Allow us to take this chance. If you do so,
you'll see us return soon from the search for Aeneas
at Pallanteum's walls—and a huge slaughter completed,
with loot from corpses. Trails won't blur our sense of direction:
we've seen in a hazy valley the settlement's outskirts.
We hunt there often; we know each bend of the river."

Trojan Wonder and Thanks

Aletes, weighed with age, mature in his insight:
"Gods of our Fathers, Troy's in your power forever!
You're not prepared, not yet, to annihilate Trojans—

not when you bring us men of such spirit and steady
250 courage." He grasped the hands and shoulders of both men
while praying, eyes and cheeks moistened by weeping.
"What's worthy, you men, what prize for such laudable instincts?
How can we pay you? Gods must give you the finest
reward first—and your own nature. The love of Aeneas
will pay you the rest, and soon. My leader Ascanius,
grown up now, will always remember your service."

Pledges Never Fulfilled

Ascanius broke in, "Yes: only my Father's
return will save us, you men. I swear by our House-Gods,
Nisus, by great Assaracus' House, by shrines of the white-haired
260 Vesta: whatever faith and fortune are due me
I place in your lap. Re-call my Father and bring him
in view: once back he'll change our sadness to nothing.
I'll give you a pair of goblets finished in silver
and rough design—my Father's prize when he conquered Arisba;
two large weights of gold; two ritual tripods;
an ancient bowl from Sidon given by Dido.
If Luck allows us in fact to beat the Italians,
to capture scepters and share by lot their possessions,
I'll take the horse and golden weapons of Turnus
270 *out* of the lot—you've seen that stallion, the crimson
crest and shield, Nisus—right now I reward you!
My Father too will give you twelve of the choicest
female captives, males with all of their armor,
and most of all land—Latinus himself is the owner.
Euryalus, in truth you're older than me by a little:
we'll surely revere you now. I'll take you completely
to heart and keep you close on every occasion.
I'll seek no glory in any matter without you.
Advancing peace or war I'll give you my foremost
280 trust in word and act."

A Strong Mother

                          Euryalus answered
in turn: "No length of time will alter or move me
from courage and daring. If only Fortune will follow
and not oppose me! I ask for only one favor
beside all your gifts. My Mother descended from Priam's
ancient people. The land of Troy did not keep her,

nor King Acestes' walls when we sadly departed.
She's unaware now of all of my danger.
I left her without good-byes. Night is my witness
and your right hand: I cannot stand the tears of the woman.
290 I ask your help to console her. She's poor and abandoned.
Let me receive that pledge: I'll go with more daring
and face risk." Trojans were struck by the prayer.

A Pledge to be Fulfilled

Some shed tears, notably handsome Iulus,
touched by a form of his own love for a father.
Then he said,
"You're surely deserving—all your initiative stands out!
Your mother in fact will be mine, lacking Creusa's
name only. No small thanks will await her
for bearing a son. Whatever results from your action
300 I swear as my Father used to swear on my forehead:
all I promised, if things go well and you safely
return, will keep for your mother and family members."
He stopped, in tears, and loosened the sword from his shoulder,
strikingly worked in gold through the skill of Lycaon
of Knossos, ready for use in an ivory scabbard.
Mnestheus gave Nisus the hide stripped from a shaggy
lion, and trusted Aletes gave him a helmet.

Bloodletting at Night

They left at once, well armed. Everyone followed
down to the gates—young men, elders and leaders,
310 many in prayer. A handsome Ascanius joined them,
older in spirit now, weighed with concerns of adulthood.
He offered them many words for his father. But thin air
scattered them all and sent them to clouds. They were futile.
Once outside the two men passed trenches in darkness
and made for the enemy camp, soon to be killing
every man they could see winey or sleeping,
sprawled on grass. On a bank were chariots, front-up;
men dozed by a wheel or harness. Wine-flasks and armor
lay around. First the son of Hyrtacus spoke up:
320 "Euryalus, now it's for real. We *must* be aggressive.
Here's our path. Keep watch so no one behind me
can raise a hand. While you pay careful attention
I'll slash and widen the trail with plenty of killing."

He spoke in a low voice, then drove with a weapon
at proud Rhamnes who happened to lie there on heaped-up
bedding, his whole chest in a labor of snoring.
Turnus had royally welcomed this king as a prophet.
But no prophecy now could prevent him from dying.
Nisus killed three servants thoughtlessly lying
330 nearby among weapons; the armor-bearer of Remus;
a driver close to his team. The blade cut through their dangling
necks. He carried the leader's head off, ignoring
the blood-spurting trunk which darkened and puddled
the ground and bed. Lamus and Lamyrus also,
and young Serranus, a fine figure who'd gambled
a lot that night, his body spread out completely,
oppressed by the Wine-God—if only he'd happily played on
longer, matching day and night with his gambling!
Just as a starving lion will scatter a crowded
340 sheep-pen when mad hunger compels him to bite at and drag off
lambs limp from shock, afraid of bloody and snarling
jaws: Euryalus killed each man in a sweating
rampage. He came on plenty of nameless or common
soldiers, on Fadus, Herbesus, Abaris, Rhoetus—
only Rhoetus knew dimly, watching and fixed on
it all in stark fear next to a wine-urn.
He stood and faced the sword: it sank in his ribcage
completely, then withdrew, covered with dying
blood. He dribbled, coughing a violet mixture
350 of wine and blood, then fell. Euryalus pressed on
in stealth hotly. Close to the friends of Messapus
he saw a last fire guttering, horses
tethered and cropping weeds. But Nisus spoke to him tersely
(he sensed the boy's desire to kill was excessive):
"We'll pause right here. Hostile light is approaching.
We made a way through the enemy. Enough of this killing."

A Dangerous War-Prize

They left behind plenty of weaponry finished in silver,
men's drinking bowls and beautiful carpets.
Euryalus did take Rhamnes' medallions and gold-scaled
360 sword-belt—the wealthy Caedicus once had released them,
a gift for Remulus, making friends from a distance.
When Remulus died he told a grandson to have them;
after that man's death Rutulians took them in battle.
Euryalus vainly strapped the belt on a sturdy

shoulder then donned Messapus' fine helmet and crested
crown. They left the camp and headed for safety.

Spotted and Chased

Horsemen meanwhile sent from the town of Latinus
(though part of the force had lingered in fields in formation)
were riding to Turnus, their prince, bearing dispatches.
370 All three hundred had shields; their leader was Volcens.
Nearing the camp now and skirting the earth-works,
they saw two men on a trail to the left in the distance.
A helmet glittered in darkness—glinting reflections
exposed in the night a thoughtless act of Euryalus.
Volcens took close notice and called from the vanguard,
"Hold it, you men—why are you armed and about there?
Where are you headed?" The Trojans gave him no answer
but hurriedly ran for the woods and trustworthy darkness.
Horsemen galloped here and there to the junctures
380 they knew of, and watched and blocked all of the exits.

Separated in the Woods

The forested patch bristled with bushes and swarthy
holm-oak. Dense thorn-trees filled it completely.
Tracks were obscure, a path visible rarely.
Branches and darkness hampered Euryalus, weighted
with booty. Fear and the area's footpaths confused him.
Nisus escaped. Unthinkingly now he had slipped from
hostile ground (afterwards known as Albanus,
from Alba's name—Latinus had high stables at that time):
He stopped and searched for his missing friend. It was futile.
390 "You miserable boy, Euryalus, where did I leave you?
How can I trace you back and unwind the perplexing
trails of all these woods?" He turned and examined
footprints at once. He roved through thickets in silence.
He heard horses—he heard a noise of pursuers—
and not long after a cry came within earshot.
Soon he saw Euryalus taken, surrounded,
confused by the dark locale and enemy uproar,
held and pinned. He fought intensely but vainly.

A Prayer to the Moon Goddess

What could Nisus do? What force or daring, what weapon
400 could save the boy? Should he charge the enemy center,
die some splendid death from the wounds he would fall on?

Cocking a spear with his arm he impulsively turned it,
looked to the high Moon and prayed to that Goddess:
"Stay close, Latona's daughter, help in my struggle.
You are the stars' pride, the forest-protector:
if Hyrtacus ever brought a gift to your altar
for me, his son, if my own hunting augmented your honor,
my hanging sacred gifts on your dome and your door-top:
guide my spear through the night-wind to scatter that cordon."

Spears Out of the Darkness

410 He stopped, tensed each nerve for the spear-throw,
and hurled: cutting through shadowy darkness, the weapon
came from behind at Sulmo and cracked when it jolted
the backbone—splintered wood passed through the stomach.
The man groveled, spitting a warm flow from his belly,
he shivered—the body shook with continual spasms.
Men glared around. And look: Nisus already
had poised another sharper spear by his earlobe.
While enemies worried, that spearpoint ground through the
        temples
of Tagus and stuck there, warmed by the brain it had punctured.

Euryalus' Life is Threatened

420 Volcens madly fumed, unable to pinpoint
the spear's thrower. Where could he charge in his fury?
"You'll pay me with warm blood," he said, "in the meantime—
one life for both." He drew a sword from its scabbard
and made for Euryalus. Nisus utterly panicked,
shouting wildly, unable to hide in the darkness
any longer, he suffered absolute torment:
"I'm here, I did it, turn on me with your weapons,
Rutulians! I tricked you all, that boy is unable
to dare a thing, I swear by the sky and starlight that know you.
430 Only his love for a sorry friend was excessive."
But just as he spoke the blade drove at Euryalus,
broke through the white chest and punctured the ribcage.
The boy crumpled, dying, his beautiful body
running with blood. The neck went limp on a shoulder
the way a violet hangs when cut by a ploughshare,
its life lost; or the weak stem of a poppy,
dangling its head when chance rain overwhelms it.

The Rage of Nisus

So Nisus charged dead center, striving for Volcens
most through them all: he focused only on Volcens.
440 Enemies clustered densely around him on this side and that side;
repulsed, Nisus drove harder, whirling a bolt-like
sword till it sank deep in the screaming Rutulian's
face. He took the enemy's life as he perished
himself, repeatedly stabbed. He fell on his lifeless
friend, in peaceful rest at last as he died there.

In Memory of Two Soldiers

Lucky pair: if my song retains any power,
no day will ever forget you. Time will remember,
so long as the house of Aeneas remains by the solid
Capitol's rock and a Roman father governs the empire.

Rutulians Mourn Their Dead

450 Rutulians took back stolen belongings in triumph,
but carried the dead Volcens back to his quarters
in mourning: mourning in camp too when the bloodless
Rhamnes was found and all those leaders lost in a single
slaughter—Serranus, Numa—hundreds of people
ran to the place, fresh with death and the half-dead,
still warm men, blood filling and foaming the river.
People recognized booty which hard sweat had recovered—
Messapus' dazzling helmet and chest decorations.

Two Heads on Spears

In time early Dawn sprinkled the landscape
460 with light, leaving the saffron bed of Tithonus.
When sunlight soon poured out, already revealing
the world, Turnus roused men for the battle
and armored himself. Bronze-clad troops were aligned by each
     leader
for war. Various rumors had sharpened their anger.
In fact they stuck two heads (a horrible specter)
on raised spears and followed them yelling and screaming:
"Euryalus, Nisus!"

A Mother's Extreme Grief

Aeneas' durable men formed a defense-line
by walls on the left—the river guarded their right side.
470 They lined deep earthworks or stood on top of a tower,
dejected—they knew too well whose heads were uplifted.
The grey and bleeding faces shocked and dismayed them.
Rumor meanwhile put on wings in the worried
camp and hurried with news to the ear of Euryalus'
mother. Warmth drained from her sad bones in an instant.
Her hand pushed off the shuttle, unrolling the weaving.
She ran outside to a joyless howling of women.
She tore out hair and senselessly made for the front-line
troops and defense-works, forgetting the danger and weapons
480 of hostile forces. She filled the sky with her protest:
"I see your face, Euryalus? How could you leave me
old and alone—you, my only consoler,
so cruel? They sent you to face horrible danger:
you spared no time for a last good-by to a miserable mother?
Now you're given to Latin dogs and vultures to plunder.
Sprawled in a foreign land, your wounds unwashed by your
        mother,
your eyes not shut, your corpse not part of a death-march.
This robe won't cover you now—I hurriedly wove it
night and day, easing my old concern with some weaving.
490 Where will I follow? What ground will hold your dismembered
body and torn flesh? All you could offer
is *that*, my son? On land and sea, the face I have followed?
Stab me, if anyone's kind! Rutulians, hurtle
all your spears—kill me first with your weapons!
Or you, our Gods' majestic Father, have pity:
thrust my despised face into hell with your lightning.
Otherwise how can I break from this bitter existence?"
Her grief stunned them. A moan somberly drifted
through all, their fighting spirit flaccid and breaking.
500 Pain so consumed her now that Idaeus and Actor,
warned by Ilioneus and mourning Iulus,
took her between themselves to rest in a shelter.

Memories of Troy

A sound of brass: the trumpet's call in the distance
blared out terror. Shouts followed, the heavens re-echoed
and Volscians all charged in shielded formations,

ready to fill trenches and dislocate ramparts.
One group probed a gate or wall, scaling with ladders
where chinks of light revealed a thin line of defenders
and men were not so crammed. Against them the Trojans
510 pushed with hard poles and poured out sundry bombardment—
accustomed through long war to defending a city.
Stones were rolled down, too, lethally heavy,
sometimes able to break up covered formations.
Closely ranked, the attackers took on every missile,
some now falling: Trojans had rolled an enormous
stone where a large mass threatened: it rushed down
and sprawled Rutulians broadly, smashing their armored
protection. They cared no longer to fight such a battle
blindly. Rutulians eagerly pelted the ramparts
520 instead with arrows.
Elsewhere Mezentius, waving a torch of Etruscan
pine, charged in smoke and fire—a harrowing vision—
while Neptune's child, Messapus, that breaker of horses,
tore at a wall's timber and called for some ladders.

Help from the Muses

You Muses, Calliope: I pray for your breath in my music.
What deaths took place? Which men were finished by Turnus'
sword? How did he send them down to the Hell-God?
Unroll the conflict's whole extent to my vision.
Remember it, Goddesses: truly *you* can remember.

An Embattled Tower

530 A high tower looked out far from its walkways
and stood on crucial ground. Many Italians
contended with all their force and equipment to take it
or wreck it. Trojans countered by dropping more boulders
and hurling dense volleys of spears from the windows.
Turnus, the leader, threw up a firebrand whose burning
flame stuck to one side: winds were increasing:
the fire held on, consuming planking and doorframe.
Trojans inside were in turmoil. They wanted to bolt from
the fire but could not. They turned and crowded together
540 in parts less plagued by the heat. But the tower abruptly
fell foward, heavily crashing like thunder from heaven.
Half dead on the ground in the huge pile-up that followed,
impaled on their own spears, chests punctured by hardwood,

many came to an end. Helenor and Lycus
alone escaped, but hardly—Helenor the younger,
secretly borne to a king of Maeonia once by Licymnia—
a slave who'd sent him to Troy's war, though his father
forbade it. With light sword and bare shield undistinguished,
he saw himself ringed by a legion of Turnus,
550 Latin lines closing on this side and that side.
Just like a beast closely surrounded by hunters,
growling at spears, knowing death is approaching,
will fling itself in a final leap at the weapons:
Helenor could also see he would die in that hostile
mob and he rushed in, charging where weapons were densest.

Turnus like the Wolf of the War-God

But Lycus was much more quick on his feet and he sprinted
past enemy armor straight for the heights of a rampart.
His hands clawed for the top and he reached to his comrades
but Turnus had chased him—close behind with a weapon
560 now he triumphantly chided: "You hoped to be able
to slip from my hands, fool?" He instantly grabbed him
though Lycus hung on, detaching a big section of earth-works:
much like Jupiter's eagle lifting a rabbit
or white swan with hooked talons and heading for cloud-bank:
or Mars' wolf snatching a lamb it wants from the mother's
pen while she baas and baas. Everywhere cheering
went up as Rutulians rushed and filled up the trenches
with dirt while others hurled fire-brands at wall-tops.

Defenders Kill and Are Killed

Ilioneus' massive rock—a chunk of some mountain—
570 killed Lucetius nearing a gate and carrying torches.
Good with a spear, Liger flattened Emathion.
Asilas killed Corynaeus with arrows, unseen from a distance.
Caeneus beat Ortygius. But Turnus defeated
Caeneus, Dioxippus, Promulus, Clonius, Itys,
Sagaris, Idas, who stood on top of a tower.
Capys finished Privernus: the light spear of Themillas
had hurt him first, his hand madly discarding
a shield to reach for the wound: an arrow came winging,
fastened the hand to the left side, sank in and deeply
580 punctured the chest: that wound in his lung would be fatal.

Mezentius' Prey

Arcens' boy stood tall in exceptional armor,
a sheen of Iberian iron, the chlamys embroidered:
a standout figure. His father Arcens had sent him;
his mother had raised him in groves around the Symaethus
River close to the altars of rich and tranquil Policus.
But now Mezentius, dropping a javelin, whistled
a sling three times overhead, stretching the leather,
and flung a water-quick shot at the enemy's forehead
and split it. The young man sprawled on a pile-up of gravel.

Taunting the Trojans

590   And this was the first time (they say) that Iulus
aimed a fast arrow in war (scaring and hunting
beasts before), handily downing the sturdy
Numanus. Named Remulus also, he'd taken
the younger sister of Turnus lately in marriage.
He'd just now marched to the front line and had hollered
remarks, unseemly and seemly, throwing a newly
royal chest out, striding hugely and calling,
"Embarrassed again, Phrygians? Trapped in your bulwarks,
imprisoned twice? And stalling death with some earthworks?

600   Look at the men who demand our wives and a battle!
What God or madness drove them to Italy? Ulysses,
that phrase-painter, is not here, nor Atreus' children:
our people are rooted and hard: we carry our children
first to the river for fierce cold and a toughening current.
Our boys keep watch. They hunt and wear out the forest.
They tame horses for play! And they level their arrows.
Our men get used to work, to a pittance, to patience.
They break ground with hoes or they shake towns in a battle.
Our lives are bruised by iron. The hides of our oxen

610   are chafed by flattened spears. And aging comes slowly:
it takes no strength from our mind and changes no vigor—
we clap helmets on grey-hairs! We constantly relish
gathering new war-loot and living off booty.
And you? In your shiny prints of yellow and purple?
Your hearts are dull. You like to indulge in your dances,
wearing tunics with sleeves, headdresses, neckbands—
Phrygian *women* for sure, not men! Go back to the two-stop
flutes you're used to twiddling on Dindymus Mountain.
Cybele's calling, your mother on Ida, with timbrels

620   and boxwood. Leave arms to *men*. And yield to our iron."

The Odds Against Numanus

Ascanius could not stand such threatening language
and sing-song talk. The Trojan leveled an arrow
point-blank, arms apart, stretching the horse-hair.
He paused to pray humbly to Jupiter, vowing:
"All-powerful Lord, favor my daring
start: I'll bring annual gifts myself to your temple.
I'll station a gold-horned bullock in front of your altar.
He'll carry a shining head high like his mother's,
the horns butting already, hooves kicking up gravel."
630 The sky's Father heard him. It thundered in cloudless
blue on his left while the lethal bow-string was twanging:
the drawn-back arrow flew through the air with a chilling
sound and struck Remulus' head, cracking the temple
with steel. "Go on, make fun of our strength with arrogant
        speeches!
Captured twice, Rutulians? Trojans have sent you an answer."
Ascanius cut short words but otherwise Trojans
gladly shouted, their spirits raised to the star-heights.

A Warning from the Sun-God

By chance from a tract of sky long-haired Apollo
had watched. He noted the fort, the Ausonian war-lines,
640 and spoke from a throne of cloud to the winner, Iulus:
"A fine new strength, young man. Stars will receive you,
a God's son, and your sons will be Gods. By law in the future
every war will end under Assaracus' people.
Troy could not contain you." Even while speaking
he sprang from the highest air and parted the winds' exhalations
to head for Ascanius. Changing in form he resembled
old Butes, who'd carried the arms of Anchises
at Troy once and loyally guarded his doorway;
later Aeneas had made him Ascanius' comrade. Apollo
650 became the old man in every way—in complexion,
speech, white hair, and the barbarous clank of his armor.
He said these words to a heated Iulus:
"Enough, son of Aeneas. Your weapon has safely
killed Numanus. Great Apollo has granted
your first distinction; he doesn't envy your weapons.
But no more battling, young man." Apollo was finished
and gone from men's eyes in the midst of that warning:
he vanished from view in thin air in the distance.

Dardan leaders recognized the God and those godlike
660 arms—they heard, when he flew, a rattling quiver.
They therefore checked, at the word and will of the Sun-God,
Ascanius' war craving. They entered the battle
again themselves, throwing lives into manifest danger.

Bitias and Pandarus at the Gate

Shouting passed through all the wall-top defenders.
They stretched bows keenly and twisted their spear-thongs,
all the ground was a sprawl of weapons, colliding
helmets and shields clanged: fighting grew fiercer,
rising the way an immense storm from the western
horizon strikes the ground with rain from the Kid-stars,
670 hail falling from clouds at sea, Jupiter bristling
with Southwinds, twirling waterspouts, bursting clouds in the
        heavens.
Bitias and Pandarus, sons of Alcanor in Ida,
raised among Jupiter's groves by the Wood-Nymph, Iaera,
men like tall young oaks in their fatherland's mountains,
opened a gate assigned by command of their leader.
Sure of their arms they boldly invited Rutulians to enter!
They stood there, right and left, each by a tower,
belted in iron, crests flashing high on their helmets:
paired like trees growing in breezes together
680 beside some stream like the gently flowing Athesis,
or high on a Po bank, lifting their uncut
hair to the sky, each crown nodding and swaying.
Seeing the open gate, Rutulians rushed in
rapidly and Quercens, a finely armored Aquicolus,
Tmarus (a headstrong character), Haemon (a son of the War-
        God),
either were turned back with all their supporters
or lost their lives right there at the entrance.
Anger swelled: minds went mad at that moment,
Trojans gathered as well, crowding the same place,
690 some of them dashing far out boldly in hand-to-hand combat.

Turnus Exploits an Opening

To lordly Turnus, all rage in another
sector and routing defenders, word came that the Trojans,
flushed by the latest killing, had opened an entrance.
He stopped what he'd started. Intense fury compelled him

to rush that enemy gate and those arrogant brothers.
He speared Antiphates first, the first to confront him,
his mother a Theban, his father a tall one, Sarpedon.
The hard-thrown spear downed him, the shaft of Italian
cornel flying through light air and thudding the stomach,
700 gone deep in the gut. The wound, dark as a cavern,
foamed with blood, spear-point warmed by the innards.
Turnus killed Meropes next, Aphidnus and Erymus.
Now Bitias: vision burning, brain in an uproar,
the Trojan would fall to no spear, not by a spear-throw:
a massive bludgeon came twirling and whistling from Turnus,
thrown like a thunderbolt. Neither Bitias' double
bull's-hide shield nor the gold-scaled breastplate he trusted
held up. The huge thighs weakened and gave out.
Earth groaned when his big shield toppled like thunder
710 and struck him: as piled-up boulders fall at times on Euboean
beachsand near Baiae: dropped and heaped in the water
in great masses earlier, now they are thudded
forward or dragged down to lie in the tumblers
of mixed-up sea or to stir dark sand on the bottom.
Procyta's highland shakes at the sound, and Aenaria's
hard bed, where Jupiter's order sentenced Typhoeus.

A Blunder of Pandarus

So here the war-strong Mars contributed spirit
to Latin strength, twisting a sharp spur in each breastbone.
He scattered desire to escape and dark fear among Trojans.
720 Rutulians massed, provided with plenty of fighting
room, and the War-God drove their spirits.
Pandarus, knowing blood had poured from his brother,
that Luck had changed place and Chance went against him,
with all his strength, working ponderous shoulders,
turned the gate on its hinges. Plenty of Trojans
fighting hard outside the wall were abandoned.
Others rushed to get back and Pandarus took them—
madman! He'd failed to see the Rutulian leader
dash inside surrounded by soldiers. Locked in the camp-ground
730 he looked like a huge tiger with slow-moving cattle.
A strange light immediately glinted in Turnus'
eyes and he banged a frightening shield. On his helmet
the crest quivered, blood-red. The shield flickered like lightning.
Aeneas' men knew that massive and hateful
form and a few abruptly panicked. But Pandarus leaped out,

a tall figure, hotly enraged at his brother's
death. "This is no house of your bride or Amata,
Turnus. No Ardean walls of your father contain you.
It's hostile ground you see—with no power to leave it."

Paying Dearly for a Mistake

740   Turnus chuckled. He told Pandarus calmly,
"Start it. Try your hand if you're willing and manly.
Then go tell Priam you found another Achilles."
He stopped and Pandarus, summoning all of his power,
hurled a spear with knots and bark still on the hardwood.
It picked up a breeze but Juno, the daughter of Saturn,
deflected its wounding course. It slammed in a gate-post.
Turnus told him, "You won't escape from my weapon:
it comes from a strong right hand, a maker of really
wounding blows." And rising high for a sword-swing,
750   he chopped: the blade cut through brow and both temples,
dividing the young cheeks—a horrible mangling.
Loudly the huge bulk of Pandarus pounded the gravel,
arms limp, brain and blood on the armor.
He sprawled on the ground dying, the evenly severed
head slumping here and there on each shoulder.

Terror Inside the Fort

Trojans turned, ran in fear and confusion.
If just one thought had now occurred to the winner,
to open the gates by hand and usher his friends in,
that day would have marked the war's end and the Trojans'.
760   But frenzy consumed Turnus: a mad craving for slaughter
drove him against the enemy.
He took on Phalaris first, then severed a hamstring
of Gyges. He seized their spears and threw them at fleeing
Trojans. Juno supplied him with spirit and sinew:
he killed Halys, their friend; Phegeus, right through the buckler;
men on a wall working for Mars, unsuspecting;
Alcander next; Halius, Noeman, Prytanis.
Lynceus, moving against him, called for companions.
But Turnus, with sword flailing, deftly mounted a rampart
770   and took him, a single close-range sword-swipe removing
the helmeted head—it lay at a distance. The next one
to die was a fierce hunter, Amycus—no one was better
at smearing metal tips of arrows with poison.
A son of Aeolus died—Clytius. A friend of the Muses—

Cretheus: every Muse had loved his continual singing,
the lyre in his heart: tuning and playing on harpstrings,
he'd sung about men's armor, horses and warfare.

A Desperate Rallying Cry

Finally Trojan chiefs—they'd heard of the slaughter—
joined forces. Mnestheus and lively Serestus
780 looked on scattered friends and their enemy, walled in.
Mnestheus asked them: "Where will you run or escape to?
Beyond that wall what other walls do you own here?
A single man completely enclosed by your earthworks,
you men: how can he shed such blood on your campground
safely, sending dozens of fine young men to the Hell-God?
What laggards! You feel no shame? Or regret for your ancient
Gods, our strong Aeneas, your suffering people?"

Closing in on the Lion

His language burned them. They stopped running and tightly
closed ranks. Turnus checked his aggression
790 briefly, and made for a part of the fort guarded by water.
Tougher now, Trojans crowded and pressed him,
loudly yelling the way tribesmen will threaten
a fierce lion with hostile spears: although he is frightened
he'll glare wildly and snarl: fury and daring
prevent his turning tail, while men and their spearpoints
prevent his moving against them, much as he wants to.
That's how Turnus backed off doubtfully, taking
slow steps, burning inside with resentment.
Even now he attacked the enemy center
800 twice, forcing columns back to the walls in disorder.
But soon the whole camp's forces massed in a body.
Juno, Saturn's daughter, could not dare to supply him
with strength to fight them: Jupiter sent down
Iris from windy skies with a stern warning for Juno:
Turnus must yield this high ground to the Trojans.
The man was therefore powerless. Neither a sword-hand
nor shield could stop them: hard-thrown missiles from all sides
drubbed him. The cavernous helmet was constantly ringing
around his temples. Boulders dented the solid
810 bronze, knocked the crest from its crown, and the pelting
threatened the shield's boss. Trojans doubled their spear-throws,
Mnestheus himself like a stormcloud. The whole body of Turnus
flowed with sweat, a grimey and seeping moisture. His breathing

slowed and weakened. His frame shook in exhaustion.

Into the River

Leaping headlong finally in all of his armor,
he dove in the river. The tawny flow of the Tiber
received his fall and gentle currents returned him
to friends. Blood washed off, the man was contented.

X

THE RETURN AND RAGE OF AENEAS

Gods Gathering

Meanwhile the house of the strongest Olympian opened.
Mankind's King and the Gods' Father called an assembly
there in the starlit throne-room: from there he could survey
every land, the Latin people and Trojan defense-works.
Seats filled in the two-doored hall. Jupiter started:
"Majestic Sky-Gods, why this change in your purpose,
this deep unsettling of spirit? Why the reversal?
I disapproved of war—of Italians jarring with Trojans.
What discord thwarts my command? What fear has convinced you
10   to whip one side or another to war and to weapons?
The right time for fighting will come: don't hurry the future:
Carthage will test Roman defenses ferociously.
The Alps will open and send down massive destruction.
Then you may hate and fight—then you may ravage—
But now no more. Be glad to settle a peace-pact."

Goddess Against Goddess

So Jupiter's words were few; but those of the gold-haired
Venus were not:
"My Father, man's and the world's permanent Ruler—
indeed who else can we pray to now or acknowledge?—
20   You see those leaping Rutulians? And Turnus on horseback
riding high through their midst, galloping proudly,
the War-God behind him? Meanwhile Trojans lack the protection
of closed walls: they fight at the gates, on a rampart
or wall itself: their blood saturates trenches.
Aeneas is absent and unaware. Will you never

allow this siege to be lifted? Enemies threaten
the walls of a young Troy again—another attack-force,
a new Diomedes looming from Arpi, the Aetolian village,
to duel with Troy. New wounds await me, I'm certain,
30   your own daughter stopping the spear of some human.
If Trojans made for Italy lacking your favor,
spiting your will, let them pay for their evil:
don't help them. If Trojans however have followed
the signs given by Sky-God and Hell-God, how can some person
now subvert your rule? Why make novel pronouncements?
Need I recall the burned fleet on Eryx's beaches,
the mad gale at sea which the Aeolian storm-king
dared to create, then Iris dispatched from a rain-cloud?
Now even Underworld beings—resources
40   not yet tapped—are stirring: Allecto is packed off
suddenly, crazing Italian hamlets on orders from heaven.
I think nothing of empire. I hoped for an empire
when Luck lasted. The one you choose is the winner.
If no country exists your hard wife will apportion
to Trojans, Father, I plead—on the smoldering wreckage
of ruined Troy—that you send Ascanius safely
from battle. Or let me: give my grandson survival.
Let unknown waters toss even Aeneas,
take him whatever way Fortune may offer;
50   but help me shield and guide that boy from the horror of battle.
I have Amathus, high Paphos, Cythera,
a home in Idalia. Let him relinquish his armor
and age there quietly. Give your order divinely
that Carthage level Ausonia: nothing will hinder
Tyrian cities. But how has it helped us to slip from
war's plague, to run from Greeks in a fire-storm,
worn out on desolate land and dangerous water,
Trojans looking to rebuild Troy in Latium country?
To sit in their last homeland's ashes was better—
60   the dirt where Troy stood. Bring back the Xanthus
and Simois, Father! I ask that the miserable Trojans
re-live Troy's destruction.''

Divine Retaliation

                    But Queen Juno responded,
driven by rage: "Why do you force me to break from
long silence and tell my sorrows in public?
Who among Gods or men pressured Aeneas

to start this war, to move on King Latinus in battle?
Fates told him to make for Italy? Granted:
a raving Cassandra forced him! Did Juno persuade him
to leave camp, commit his life to a Southwind,
70   trust walls and the war's crux to a youngster,
meddle with peace and the faith of Tuscany's people?
Which God compelled him to lie? Where is the cruel
power of Juno here, Iris dispatched from a cloud-trail?
Shameful, yes! Italy circling your newborn
Troy with fire, Turnus defending lands of his fathers—
Pilumnus' grandson—his mother a Goddess, Venilia.
What of the Trojans' fire and soot harming the Latins,
plowing strangers' land and pirating booty?
What if they pick then tear girls from their fathers and husbands,
80   offering peace with one hand, arming ships with another?
Venus may spread some mist or blank wind where a man was,
leading Aeneas from Greek clutches in battle,
Venus may change a whole fleet into Sea-Nymphs;
but *our* helping any Rutulian is wicked!
Aeneas is gone, unaware? He should remain so.
You have Paphos, Idalia, the heights of Cythera:
why incite harsh crowds and a war-heavy city?
Did we attempt to rip up Troy from its drifting
foundations? We? Or the man who threw your despondent
90   Trojans at Greeks? What was the reason that Europe
and Asia rose in war, secretly breaking a peace-pact?
Did I command a Trojan lecher to capture that Spartan?
Did I supply spears or foment longing for battle?
You might have feared for your children then; now your
          complaining
is late and unlikely. You raise invalid contentions."

Divine Neutrality

All the Gods assented when Juno was finished,
resembling a mixed murmur of wind in a woodland,
caught first by some trees then muttering darkly
and grumbling, warning sailors a storm may be coming.
100 Now the strongest Father—the first force in the cosmos—
began to speak, hushing the high house of the Sky-Gods.
Earth trembled profoundly, steep heavens were quiet,
the Westwind diminished and waves on the ocean subsided.
"Take my words to heart now and retain them.
What with Troy and Ausonia clearly prevented

from peaceful union, with all your constant dissension,
let each side take what luck and hope this day will provide you.
I'll look on both Rutulian and Trojan as equal,
whether the camp's besieged through Fates of Italians
110 or Trojan mistakes or malice, some wrong word or prediction.
I'll bind Rutulians too, the same struggle for each man
and his own luck. They'll all have Jupiter ruling.
Fates will find a way." He swore by his brother's
river—the Styx's pitch-black banks and its chasm.
He nodded: the nod rumbled all of Olympus.
Talk had ended. Jupiter rose from the golden
throne, ringed and escorted by Gods to the threshold.

The War Goes On

Rutulians meanwhile drove at the gates of the Trojans.
Men sprawled and bled. Walls were circled by torches.
120 Aeneas' men, kept within the embankments,
had no hope of escape. Sadly they stood on a tower's
height or ringed a wall like a thin crown; they were helpless.
Asius (Imbrasus' son), Thymoetes (Hicetaeon's),
the two called Assaracus, old Thymbris, and Castor
were ranked in front, joined by two of Sarpedon's
brothers, Clarus and Thaemon, from Lycian hilltops.
The hulking Acmon, who came from Lyrnesos, contorted
his whole body to lift a massive chunk of some mountain—
tall as his father Clytius, his brother Mnestheus.
130 One man tried defending with boulders, another with lance
          throws;
some built fires or fitted bowstrings with arrows.
Look at the Dardan boy himself, right there in the middle—
Venus was right to worry—his fine forehead uncovered:
the way a gem framed in gold shines in adorning
the neck or head, or just like dazzling ivory
when skilled craftsmen inlay it with Orican boxwood
or terebinth. Hair fell to his welcoming milkwhite
neck and a golden clasp loosely contained it.
And you, Ismarus, watched by your big-hearted people,
140 dipping reads in venom, aiming and wounding:
you'd come from a house of Maeonians, men who extracted
wealth from the soil and gold from the Pactolus River.
Mnestheus too stood near. He'd driven out Turnus
yesterday; now he walked high on the ramparts in honor.
And Capys—his name would lead to the city of Capua.

Return Journey at Night

While those men bore the hard struggle of battle,
Aeneas cut through the river's channel in darkness
after leaving Evander's camp. He reached the Etruscan
king's banks and told of his name and his nation,
150 what he required and brought himself. He told of the army
Mezentius gathered for war and the violent passion
of Turnus. Aeneas warned and variously pleaded
for trust in human affairs. Instantly Tarchon
struck a pact to join his force: a Lydian people
escaped doom by trusting this foreign commander.
They launched a fleet with Gods in command and Aeneas'
ship leading. Its prow had Phrygian lions
above and Ida below—what joy to a Trojan
in exile! Aeneas grandly presided; he pondered
160 the war's mixed outcome. Pallas was nearby,
just to his left. He often asked about starlight
and course on such dim nights, about country and ocean
        maneuvers.

A Prayer to the Muses Once More

Open Helicon now, you Muses, and quicken
my song: what groups from Tuscan beaches were joining
Aeneas and arming ships to sail on the water?

The Grand Fleet

Massicus' bronzed *Tiger* cut through the current,
leading a thousand men who'd come from the cities
of Cosae and Clusium. Their weapons were quivers and arrows,
light on their shoulders—Death rode on the bow-wood.
170 Abas had joined them, a fierce one, all his ranks in distinguished
armor. The Sun-God gleamed in gold on their stern-deck.
He led six hundred men, Populonia's children,
young but skilled in war; three hundred from Ilva,
too, the Chalybes' Island. lavishly rich in deposits.
The third, an augur for God and men, was Asilas.
Innards of beasts and stars in heaven obeyed him;
Birds' language and lightning fire told him the future.
He'd gathered a thousand close-ranked men bristling with lances:
Pisa commanded their loyalty—Alph's town at the outset,
180 later a Tuscan city. Behind them was Astyr,
a sure and handsome horseman in colorful armor.

Three hundred men, all of one mind, were behind him:
sent from Caere, farms near the Minio River,
from ancient Pyrgi and coastal, fog-bound Gravisae.
And you, Cinyrus—bravest Ligurian war-lord—
I won't omit you. Nor you, with your handful of helpers,
Cupavo—a swan's plumage rose from your helmet,
a sign of your father's change (a fault of the Love-God):
Cycnus, they say, your father, despairing of Phaëthon's
190   love, sang in the leafy shade of a sisterly poplar,
trying to soothe the pain of love through his music,
when soft feathers appeared, he whitened and grew old:
gone from the earth, his voice follows the starlight.
The son, matched by a crowd of shipboard companions,
moved the massive *Centaur* forward by rowing.
She leaned on waves like a hugely threatening cliffside.
A long and deep wake was cut by her keel-line.

Mantua

Ocnus had also called up troops from his fatherland's coastline—
his father the Tiber, his mother a prophetess, Manto—
200   giving to you, Mantua, walls and the name of a mother.
Mantua: rich in your parents, not all from a single
family: from three, with four clans in each household.
Mantua headed the clans, her blood strong as the Trojans'.

The Rest of the Armada

Next came five hundred to march on Mezentius,
led on the waves by an angry pinewood River-God, Mincius—
Lake Benacus, wreathed in blue-grey sedge, was his father.
Aulestes rode in a heavy ship that surged when its hundred
oars churned the water, lashing and bubbling the surface:
He sailed the immense *Triton,* alarming the wave-crests,
210   a blue-black conch on her prow, with a human and shaggy
swimmer out front whose form below was a sea-snake's—
the half-wild chest foamed and hissed through the water.
So thirty chosen leaders moved in some thirty
ships to help Troy. Bronze cut through the salt-field.

Sea-Nymphs

Day had already passed from the sky and a kindly
Moon's night-wandering chariot beat by Olympus:
Aeneas, his body never relieved from its worry,
had taken the wheel himself, then tended a mainsheet,

when look: halfway back to the fort he was met by a friendly
220 circle of water-dancers, the Nymphs whom Cybele warmly
had told to change from ships into Nymphs, to have power
at sea. They swam together and cut through the water—
the same number of bronze bows which had stood on the shore-
    line.
They knew their king from a distance and ritually circled.
One of them, well trained in speech, Cymodocea,
followed the ship, grasped the stern with her right hand
and lifted herself while her left hand paddled the gentle
seas, and said to a puzzled Aeneas, "You're watching,
son of the Goddess? Watch—and pay out canvas for running.
230 We all were pines on the holy mountain of Ida—
once your fleet—now we are Sea-Nymphs. Rutulians rashly
and wrongly came to attack us with torches and axes:
we broke your cables against our will and we sought you
at sea. Our Mother pitied and gave us our sea-forms,
made us divine, to pass our time in the water.
Now for your boy Ascanius: Latins bristling for battle
have trapped him in earthworks and trenches: they pelt him with
    arrows.
Your cavalry, strong Arcadians teamed with Etruscans,
hold the position you ordered; but Turnus decided
240 firmly to stop all riders from reaching the campsite.
Up now, move! Dawn is approaching: order your comrades
to arm first then take the matchless shield which the Fire-God
himself gave you, his gold border around it.
Tomorrow's light—don't think my words are unlikely—
will see an immense heap of Rutulian bodies."

A Prayer to Cybele

Her hand pushed at the high stern when she finished,
knowing exactly how, and the vessel rushed through the water
quick as a spear or an arrow abreast of an Eastwind.
Sister ships kept pace while the Trojan son of Anchises,
250 confused and amazed, felt spirits raised by the omen.
Briefly he looked to the arched sky and invoked it:
"Caring Mother of Gods, of Dindymus, Ida,
of tower-supporting towns, your team a bridling of lions:
lead me now in this war. Stand by your omen
rightly. Walk with your Trojans, Goddess, be present."

Trojans Reunited

That's all he asked. The sky meanwhile was turning,
ripe daylight already dispelling the darkness.
He told each friend first to follow the signals,
armor their hearts and prepare themselves for a battle.
260 Soon he could see his own camp and the Trojans.
Standing high astern he lofted the gleaming
shield by hand: Trojans who saw it from wall-tops
raised a shout to the sky. Hope addled their anger:
they hurled spears dense as cranes on the Strymon
River that sail under dark clouds calling each other,
loudly urging their flock to run from the Southwind.
The scene astonished all the Ausonian leaders
and Turnus, until they turned and saw an invasion—
the sea filled with ships approaching the shoreline.
270 Aeneas' helmet and crest burned like a fire-light.
The broad shield glowed fiery and golden
just like a comet burning bloody and somber
some humid night, or white-hot Sirius rising
to bring on drought, dismay and sickness in people,
troubling the eastern sky with its ominous luster.

Another Way of Reading the Gods

But daring and self-trust hardly departed from Turnus:
he'd take those beaches first and stop the arrivals from landing!
He spoke out, lifting spirits and adding a challenge.
"All you prayed for is here—to smash them in person!
280 Let Mars himself be your power. Let each man
think of his wife and home now. Remember our signal
Fathers' acts and awards. Make a stand in the shallows,
there, when they first step out, off balance and shaky.
Luck will help the adventurous."

Perilous Landings

He stopped to consider which men to lead in the skirmish
and which to trust with the task of blockading the earthworks.
Aeneas meanwhile tried to offload friends on a gangplank
down from his high stern. Many awaited
a gentle backwash of surf, then leaped in the shallows.
290 Others used oars. Tarchon was watching
the beach for calm water, where waves were not breaking,
but seas rolled up unimpeded, the turbulence building.

He suddenly swung the prow and pleaded with shipmates,
"Now, you men I've hand-picked: pull on your rugged
oars and lift us, drive the ship's beak till it splits up
enemy ground: the keel itself will plow us a furrow.
I won't resist wrecking the ship at this juncture—
only get us beached!" When Tarchon had spoken,
all the rowers pulled strongly together,
300 driving the spray-flecked ship at the coast of the Latins.
The whole fleet made it, sitting undamaged
on dry sand, but not the vessel of Tarchon:
flung onto rollers, she hung for a time on a jagged
ridge, unsteady but holding, till breakers exhausted
and split her, dropping the men right there in the water.
Pieces of oars and flotsam of benches impeded
their steps. A swift undertow dragged at their ankles.

A New Battle is Joined

Turnus hardly dawdled. He rode fiercely at Trojans,
a whole cohort attempting to keep them from beachsand.
310 Signals blared. The first to charge at some rustics
and sprawl Latins, an omen of war himself, was Aeneas:
he killed Theron, the biggest man who had boldly
stalked the Trojan. A sword cut through the fittings
of brass, the gold-gnarled tunic, draining an open
side. He struck Lichas next, who'd been cut from a dying
mother at birth—sacred to Phoebus now for escaping
a knife-slash when little. A forceful Cisseus crumpled
for Death nearby, and tall Gyas—both had been downing
men with clubs—but neither Hercules' weapons,
320 their strong hands, nor their father Melampus could help them
(Hercules' friend while earth supplied him with heavy
labor). And look: when Pharus casually taunted,
a twirled spear stopped his mouth and its racket.
Then you, Cydon, who sadly followed your latest
attraction, a youngster with blond fuzz on his cheekbones,
Clytius: Aeneas' hand would have flattened and freed you
from love (as a boy love was your joy) to lie there in sadness
had not your brothers closed ranks to prevent it—
seven sons of Phorcus hurling their seven
330 lances. A few made harmless clangs on the helmet
and shield but some, close to the body, a caring
Venus deflected. Aeneas called to the loyal Achates,
"Bring more spears! None from my hand will be wasted.

Spears from Greek bodies on Troy's fields will be twisted
now in Rutulians'." He gripped and threw an enormous
weapon that zinged at the brazen shield-plate of Maeon
and pierced it, broke through the chest protector and ribcage.
A brother, Alcanor, ran to support his collapsing
brother by hand, but a spear punctured his shoulder
340 and instantly passed on its bloody trajectory, leaving
his arm torn at the socket, hanging by tendons and dying.
Now Numitor pulled the spear from a brother's
body and aimed at Aeneas. He wasn't permitted
to strike him—it grazed the huge thigh of Achates.
Clausus approached next. Coming from Cures and trusting
his youth and strength, from a distance he struck the gullet of
        Dryops,
the rigid spear fatally wedged under the chinbone—
a throat-wound taking voice and life after he cried out.
He fell to the ground face-first, coughing up blood-gouts.
350 Three more from Thrace, of the high clan of the Northwind,
and three from Ismara, their homeland, with Idas, their father,
were variously killed by Clausus. Halaesus approached him
with grouped Auruncans. The son of Neptune, Messapus
(known for his horses) helped. This side and that side
strained and drove back, they fought on Ausonia's threshold
itself the way discordant winds in a far-flung
sky will struggle and rise, matched in momentum and vigor,
unyielding among themselves in the clouds, on the ocean,
all fixed on a long fight—the end undecided.
360 Latin and Trojan forces charged in the same way,
leg locked against leg, this man at that man.

A Young Warrior Rallies his Men

On other ground where rocks were tumbled and scattered
by rushing water, where trees on banks were uprooted,
Pallas watched his Arcadian horsemen, not used to
fighting on foot, turn and run from the Latins:
rough terrain this once had forced them to jump from
their mounts. The only hope in that desperate moment
now was to plead—harsh words might heat up their courage—
"Where are you running, my friends? I swear by your bravest
370 acts, the wars you've won, the name of your leader, Evander,
my hopes that rise now and rival praise from my Father:
don't trust your feet! Cut your way through the Latins
with metal! There, where men are most crowded,

Pallas will lead you back. Your country demands it.
No Gods beset us: we humans are driven by human
power, with no more hands or spirit than *we* have.
Look at the sea, a wide barrier blocks you,
we lack land for escape—would you head for Troy or some
     ocean?"

The First Blood Spilled by Pallas

He stopped and charged, head-on, the enemy center.
380 Lagus faced him first (impelled by some unfair
Fate): he tried hoisting a ponderous boulder
but Pallas' lance found a gap in his ribcage
halfway down the back: the spear-tip, extracted,
pulled out bone. Hisbo, hoping to catch him
next from behind, failed. The merciless killing
of Lagus had made him rage unthinkingly and Pallas
received his charge and swollen chest—on a sword-point.
He struck at Sthenius; the old bloodline of Rhoetus,
     Anchemolus—
once he had dared to defile a stepmother's bedroom.
390 You twins also died on Rutulian war-ground:
Larides and Thymber, sons of Daucus, identical children
even to family, pleasantly baffling your parents.
Now Pallas made a hard distinction between you:
he cut off Thymber's head with a sword of Evander
then lopped Larides' hand—still seeking its owner,
the half-dead fingers trembled, re-handled a weapon.
Every word and signal action of Pallas ignited
Arcadians. Mingled shame and guilt armed them for fighting.
When Rhoeteus' chariot fled on by, it was Pallas
400 who speared him—and gained time in that manner for Ilus:
the strong spear had been aimed from a distance at Ilus
when Rhoeteus came between, chased by two brothers,
Tyres and excellent Teuthra. The chariot threw him:
he beat with his half-dead heels on Rutulian fieldgrass.
Just as the right winds come up in the summer
when shepherds have set scattered fires in a woodland,
a line of flame quickly and broadly extending,
the Fire-God crackles through fields and ground intervening,
he looks in triumph down at the flame that exalts him:
410 so valor formed a solid front of your comrades
to help you, Pallas. Halaesus, gathered in armor
himself, moved against you. A vigorous fighter,

he'd butchered Ladon already, Demodocus, Pheres.
He'd flashed a sword, severed Strymonius' fingers
and reached to choke him. His rock had smashed into Thoas'
face, spattering blood and brain tangled with bone-chips.
His father, who sang of the future, had hidden Halaesus
in woods; when death dissolved the man's colorless vision,
Fates took charge and destined the son for Evander's
420   weapon. A willing Pallas pleaded beforehand:
"Tiber, my Father, grant that the steel which I balance
now will travel with luck through the hard chest of Halaesus.
Your oak-tree will own the man's clothing and armor."
The River-God heard him. Halaesus, protecting Imaon,
sorrily exposed a lung to the Arcadian spear-throw.

Two Young Men's Destinies

And here Lausus, a major force in the conflict,
allowed his men no fear of the heavy slaughter, but finished
Abas, who'd faced him first—he'd stalled and knotted the fighting.
Arcadians now sprawled by sprawling Etruscans,
430   and even you Trojans, although the Greeks could not kill you.
Columns clashed, their vigor and leadership well-matched,
rear-guards mashed up front so close that they could not
move hand or sword. Pallas kept pushing and straining
here, Lausus there—both exceptionally graceful,
close in age. But Luck had already denied them
return home. Not that the King of lofty Olympus
would let them charge each other now in the battle:
soon each must wait for death from a greater contender.

Lion and Bull

Turnus, meanwhile, warned by his provident sister
440   to help Lausus, cut through ranks in his chariot swiftly.
Spotting friends he said, "It's time—stop your attacking.
Pallas belongs only to me: I'm moved to confront him
alone. I wish his father himself could be watching."
Followers moved back from the field at that order.
Pallas marveled at all the Rutulians backing,
the proud command and the massive body of Turnus.
He looked back fiercely, watching it all from a distance.
Words of his own opposed the words of that leader:
"Either I'm praised now for taking excellent booty
450   or dying nobly. For either chance my Father is ready.
No more threats." He stopped and proceeded to midfield.

Blood collected and cooled in Arcadian stomachs.
Turnus jumped from the chariot, ready to walk up
close. Like a lion seeing, high on some lookout,
a bull ready to fight on a field in the distance,
then charging: the form of Turnus approached in the same way.
When Pallas thought he'd come within range of a spear-throw
he moved first, hoping chance would support him
in facing greater strength. He called loudly to heaven:
460 "Hercules! Just as my Father's table received you,
a stranger: receive my prayer in this great undertaking.
Let Turnus watch half dead as I strip him of bloody
arms! Let his dying eye behold me in triumph."

The Appointed Time

Hercules heard the man, repressing a heavy
sigh deep in his chest. The tears he shed would be futile.
The Father, Jupiter, spoke to Hercules gently.
"To each his own day. The moment of every
life is unreclaimably brief. To spread one's name through
    achievement—
that's the task of manhood. Many sons of the Sky-Gods
470 fell by the high walls of Troy—even my own son,
Sarpedon, died. Fates of his own will be calling
Turnus, too: he's close to the end of his lifetime."
He stopped and looked away from the fields of Rutulia.

Turnus Kills Pallas

Pallas directed the spear with all of his power
then pulled a gleaming sword from deep in its scabbard.
The spear went flying: it forced its way through the shield-rim
and struck the built-up armor high on the shoulder,
actually grazing the huge body of Turnus.
Now Turnus poised a spear of oak with its iron
480 tip for a moment. He called to Pallas then threw it:
"See if my own weapon will penetrate deeper."
The brass and iron shield of Pallas had various
layers and many bull's-hides protecting his middle.
Yet the wide and shimmering spear-point tore through the
    chest-plate,
slowing somewhat before piercing the ribcage.
Pallas yanked the warmed point in vain from the puncture:
blood and air followed the path of the weapon.
He sank on the wound, his armor clanking around him.

He died on that hostile ground coughing his blood out.

A Fatal War-belt

490   Standing above him,
Turnus called, "Arcadians! Take my words to Evander:
tell him I send back Pallas' corpse—he deserved it.
Whatever comfort or honor a tomb or burial offers
I grant. Making friends with Aeneas has cost him
plenty." He stopped, planted a foot on the lifeless
body, and lifted the ponderous weight of a war-belt,
inscribed with evil: the death of a number of husbands,
beds blood-smeared there on the night of their wedding.
Engraved in gold richly by Clonus, the son of Eurytus,
500   the war-prize belonged to Turnus now and it pleased him.

Another Appointed Time

You minds of men! Blind to the Fates, to the future,
to how your place is kept when Luck is in favor!
The hour was near when Turnus would empty a kingdom
for Pallas' life: he'd hate this day and that war-prize.

Uncontrolled Grief and Rage

Soon friends were mourning loudly for Pallas.
In tears they laid the corpse on a shield and upraised him.
What great pride and grief to return to a father!
The first day that gave him to war had removed him.
Still he'd left a huge pile of Rutulians behind him.
510   Definite word of the deep loss—not a rumor—
rushed to Aeneas now. His men were the thinnest
remove from disaster. Helping Trojans retreating
he hacked with a sword at foes who were closest and hotly
cut a broad path through troops while he headed
for you, Turnus, proud of your recent killing. Aeneas
envisioned Evander and Pallas himself, the table he'd gone to
first as a stranger, the hand he'd taken. He captured
four young sons of Sulmo alive, and as many
reared by Ufens, to kill as Underworld victims:
520   he'd pour the captives' blood on the ashes of Pallas.
He aimed an angry spear at Magus now from a distance.
The man nimbly ducked—the spear went quivering past him.
Reduced to begging, he clutched a leg of Aeneas:
"I ask through your dead father, your hopes for a growing
Iulus: keep me alive for my son and my father.

My home is large, the wealth deep in my cellar—
engraved silver and solid weights of unfinished
and finished gold. A Trojan victory turns on
more than one life. I won't be a major distinction."
530 Aeneas replied, when he stopped, to the contrary, saying,
"All the silver and gold weights that you mention
will keep for your sons. Turnus ended such ransom
in war first and last by the killing of Pallas.
Here is my dead Father's judgment, *here* is Iulus."
He stopped and gripped the helmet, angling the beggar's
neck backward, and drove hard to the sword-hilt.

More Killings

Nearby, the son of Haemon, a priest of Diana
and Phoebus, had wreathed his devoted forehead in fillets
of wool. All his clothing and signal arms were resplendent.
540 Forced into open field he slipped—and Aeneas,
a giant hovering shadow, killed him. Serestus collected
the arms and removed them—a prize for you, royal Gradivus.
When Linus began to re-group with Caeculus, Vulcan's
boy, and Umbro, arrived from the Marsian foothills,
Aeneas attacked them fiercely. He cut off the left arm
of Anxur, the sword detaching a shield he'd been toting.
He'd made some grandiose comment, believing his muscle
could match his mouth—carried away to some heaven,
perhaps, assured he would live long and be grey-haired.
550 Tarquitus paraded too in dazzling armor.
Born to the Nymph Dryope and Faunus the Tree-God,
he faced the heat of Aeneas, who leveled a weapon
and nailed the heavy shield's weight to the breastplate.
He cut off the head, pleading in vain and preparing
a speech there on the ground. Rolling the lukewarm
torso aside, Aeneas proudly and angrily cursed it:
"Lie there now, you terror! No excellent mother
will burden the earth or a family tomb with your body.
I'll leave you to wild birds or throw you in water—
560 waves and hungry fish can lick at your gashes."

Fighting Like Aegaeon

Quickly he ran down Antaeus and Lucas, of Turnus'
vanguard, a rugged Numa, blondhaired Camertes,
a son of the high-spirited Volcens, the richest
Ausonian farmer, ruler of peaceful Amyclae.

The monster Aegaeon, some men say, had a hundred
arms and hands, fire bursting from fifty
lungs and mouths when he challenged Jupiter's lightning
and unsheathed fifty swords that clashed on as many
matched shields: Aeneas, once his blade became blood-warm,
570   beat down men in rage on the field in the same way.
He drove at the chest of Niphaeus who guided a horse-team
and look—the horses veered in fright when they spotted
Aeneas grimly threatening, striding: they trotted
backward, dumped their guide and ran for the shoreline.

Two Brothers Die

Lucagus meanwhile moved up center with Liger,
his brother, who flicked the reins of their chariot's off-white
horses, while Lucagus whipped out a sword and brandished it
        wildly.
Aeneas could hardly stand such fury and frenzy.
Appearing immense with spear at the ready, he faced them.
580   But Liger called out,
"You see no Phrygian field here or Achilles'
or Diomedes' horse. The war and your lifetime
will end on this land." The speech of Liger went flying
around madly. The Trojan leader was ready
but not with a speech: he threw a spear at his rival.
Just as Lucagus leaned forward to slap at a horse-flank,
using the flat of a sword, extending the left foot
and ready for combat, the spear passed through the gleaming
shield's base and pierced his groin on the left side.
590   Struck from the chariot, rolling in gravel, he died there.
Aeneas had done his duty. He bitterly mocked him,
"No sluggish or startled horse-team, Lucagus, tilted
your chariot: no empty enemy shadow reversed them:
you jumped from the team yourself." He stopped and arrested
that team, the brother extending a useless and wretched
hand in prayer when the same chariot dumped him:
"Man of Troy, for your own sake and the parents
who bore you, spare my life. Pity a beggar."
The plea had weight. But Aeneas: "You gave me another
600   speech just now. Die—let brother remain with his brother."
The sword opened his chest where life had been hiding.

The Siege is Ended

And so the Trojan leader distributed killing

throughout that field like a mad torrent of water
or dark tornado. At last Ascanius ventured
from camp with friends: the siege had failed and was lifted.

Juno Pleads for Turnus

Jupiter meanwhile spoke to Juno abruptly:
"Ah, my sister and lovely wife at the same time!
Venus keeps up Trojan power—you thought so,
your judgment's right—not some war-quickened *human*
610 hand or fierce will or patience in danger."
And Juno, subdued: "Why does my beautiful husband
aggravate my hurt? I fear your commands; they depress me.
If all my love had the force now which it once had
and should have still, you'd not deny me the favor,
with all *your* power, of leading Turnus from battle.
Let me keep him safe for Daunus, his father.
If not he'll shed good blood, be punished by Trojans,
despite his tracing a name from our own through Pilumnus,
his great-great-grandfather. Over and over
620 his generous hand has piled gifts on your threshold."

Stalling Death

The King of windy Olympus answered her briefly.
"If all you ask for is time, a stay of impending
doom for a doomed man—I'm sure you see my position—
carry Turnus away from the Fates that pursue him.
You're free to enjoy that much. If a deeper concession
hides under your plea, a design about changing
the whole war, you feed on blank expectations."
And Juno, in tears: "What if you grant in your wisdom
what words deny and the life of Turnus continues?
630 Right now a brutal end waits for a guiltless
man, or I'm far from the truth. If only a put-on
fear were your game! Or you'd change—and you can—what you
    started."

Real and Unreal Aeneas

Hurriedly leaving the heights of the sky when she finished,
wrapped in cloud and driving a storm through the upper
air, she made for the Trojan line and Laurentian campsite.
The Goddess contrived from empty mist a defenseless
Aeneas: thin shadow, a startling wonder to look at,
equipped with a Trojan sword, shield and a godlike

head and crest. She gave it meaningless chatter,
640 mindless noise, and it mimicked the walk of Aeneas.
When death is traversed (they say) such figures will fly there,
or flutter in dreams, deluding the mind of the dreamer.
The figure proudly strode right up to the vanguard
to fluster and goad Turnus with weapons and insult.
Turnus charged: he hurled a spear from the distance
that whirred: the figure turned its back on the combat:
Turnus actually thought Aeneas intended
to yield. Filled with vain hope he addressed it,
"Where do you run to, Aeneas? Leaving the bed you had planned
      on?
650 This hand will give you the land you sought on the sea-ways!"
He chased and yelled at the figure. He brandished a naked
sword unaware that a wind might carry his joy off.

A Wrong Escape

By chance a ship lay moored at the base of a rock-pile.
She stood with open gangplanks and rope-ladders ready,
sailed by King Osinius here from Clusium's coastline.
There the tremulous form of a fleeing Aeneas
disappeared with Turnus quickly pursuing,
hurdling obstacles, leaping high on a gangplank.
He'd scarcely reached the prow when the daughter of Saturn
660 cut the cables, pulled at the ship, and it rolled on a sea-swell.
Aeneas elsewhere had called for the missing Turnus to fight him,
many had faced him, he'd sent each corpse to the Death-God;
his tenuous look-alike, no longer needing to hide out,
flew up high and mingled with darkening stormcloud.
A gale meanwhile carried Turnus to seaward.
He gazed back confused, hardly grateful for safety.
Lifting both hands to the star-heights he cried out,
"All-powerful Father—you think that I merit
shame like this? You want me to hurt and be punished?
670 Where am I borne to? From whom? What course will return me
to camp now to see the walls of Laurentum?
What of all the men who followed my war-flag?
I left each troop—it's cursed and criminal—dying
back in that field. I picture them scatter and tumble,
I hear their groans. What can I do? Where is the deepest
earth to consume me? You Wind, show me some pity—
run me aground. Turnus willingly begs you:
break up the ship, drive it on truculent sandbanks

where neither Rumor will know or Rutulian follow."
680 His mind, while he spoke, wavered this way and that way:
whether to fall, so badly disgraced, on a weapon,
madly forcing the crude steel through his ribcage,
or leap right now in the sea and swim for the winding
beach—return once more to fight against Trojans.
Three times he tried both, but the power of Juno
stopped him. She deeply pitied the man but restrained him.
The ship cut through seas, rushed by a turbulent current,
gliding back to the old city of Daunus, his father.

Headland and Surf

Meanwhile Mezentius, prompted by Jupiter, hotly
690 resumed the war, charging jubilant Trojans.
Tuscans counter-charged—all of their hatred
and weapons in fact volleyed and aimed at that single
man. He stood like a headland, a hugely projecting
seawall facing the wind's rage, bare to the breakers,
living through every threat and force of heaven and ocean.
Remaining unmoved he knocked to the ground Dolichaeon,
the son of Hebrus. Latagus fell, and a runaway Palmus:
he struck Latagus' face and mouth with a boulder,
a big chunk of some mountain; Palmus he hamstrung
700 and left there slowly writhing. (Lausus was given
the arms to shoulder, plumes to stick on his helmet.)
He killed Euanthes too, a Phrygian; Mimas,
a friend and equal of Paris: the same night that his mother
Theano brought him to light for his father Amycus, Paris
was born to the queen—she'd feared she carried a fire-brand.
Paris was buried near Troy, his homeland; Mimas, in unknown
Laurentian soil. Now, like dogs that snap at and drive from
the mountain heights a boar hidden for years in the pinegroves
carried by Vesulus Mountain, or gorged for years in some reedy
710 Laurentian bog: after he runs in the netting
he stops and fiercely snorts, bristling his shoulders,
no one brave enough to approach or arouse him,
preferring to taunt with spears and shouts from a distance:
so Mezentius, justly hated by Tuscans,
found no one with spirit and bare sword to engage him.
They irked him with loud yelling and spears from a distance.
Still unafraid the man stalled them on all sides,
grinding his teeth, the shield fending each lance off.

Lion and Prey

A man had come from ancient Corythus' border—
720 Acron, exiled from Greece, engaged but not married.
Mezentius eyed him scattering ranks in the distance,
decked in purple nuptial plumes for his lady.
The way a starved lion, prowling through highland
retreats, compelled by maddening hunger, will happen
to see a doe dash out or a stag with burgeoning antlers:
he snarls with immense pleasure, backhair erected,
he clutches that flesh in a crouch, his jaws a revolting
and bloody slaver:
Mezentius rushed at the massed enemy fiercely
730 and Acron went down, sadly, heels beating the greyish
dust where he died, the broken spear in his own blood.

Hard Sleep

Mezentius even disdained to flatten a running
Orodes by wounding the man with a spear from the blind side:
he ran and faced him soldier to soldier directly,
killing him not through stealth but stronger exertion.
He stepped on the fallen chest to pull out his weapon:
"A tall one lies here, men, with no small role in the battle—
Orodes!" Glad friends joined in the war-cry.
And dying Orodes: "I'll have vengeance, whoever
740 you are: you won't rejoice for long, conqueror. Equal
Fates are watching. Soon you'll lie on this war-field."
Mezentius bridled. He answered and smiled through his anger:
"First *you'll* die. The King of men and Father of Sky-Gods
will see to me." He stopped, yanked the spear from the body,
and hard quiet pressed the eyes of Orodes:
iron sleep darkened and closed them forever.

Mourning Distributed Equally

Caedicus killed Alcathous now; Sacrator, Hydaspes.
Rapo killed Parthenius, then the powerful Orses.
Messapus killed Ericetes (the son of Lycaon) and Clonius:
750 the second thrown to the ground by a horse with no bridle,
the first on foot. Where a Lycian, Agis, was walking,
Valerus cut him down—he lacked none of his fathers'
courage. Salius killed Thronius; but Salius
died by the skilled Nealces' bow from a distance, unnoticed.
The grave War-God now distributed mourning

and death equally. Both sides, winning or losing,
charged and were killed. No one saw an escape-route.
Gods in Jupiter's hall pitied their futile
rage, the intense labor of people on both fronts.
760 Here Venus watched; there, the daughter of Saturn.
Tisiphone fumed, pale and surrounded by thousands.

The Domination of Mezentius

Mezentius moved on the field like a storm-wind and brandished
a truly immense lance. Huge as Orion
cutting a wake stride by stride through the deepest
ocean marsh and taller than waves by a shoulder:
or hauling an old ash-tree down from some mountain,
his feet on the ground, his head obscured in a raincloud:
Mezentius walked that tall with his ponderous weapons.
Aeneas had watched him move the length of a column,
770 preparing to face him. Mezentius fearlessly stood there,
his own mass, awaiting a high-minded rival.
He watched and guessed the distance a spear-throw would cover.
"You God in my own hand and the weapon I balance:
stay close and help me. I vow Lausus will buckle
that armor himself. I'll steal from the corpse of a stealer,
Aeneas." He stopped and flung a spear from the distance
that hissed as it flew but clanged off the shield of Aeneas—
it pierced Antores, an excellent man, in the belly.
Antores, arrived from Greece, Hercules' comrade,
780 had lived in a town of Italy close to Evander.
He lay in anguish now, mistakenly wounded and gazing
to heaven, remembering lovely Argos, and dying.

A Disabling Wound

Then Aeneas prayed and hurtled: his weapon
pierced the convex shield, three layers of bull's-hide,
linen and brass, and sank low in Mezentius'
groin but not too deeply. Quickly Aeneas
pulled the sword by his thigh, glad to have spotted
Tuscan blood. He charged the shaken man in a frenzy.

Praise for a Soldier

But Lausus cried aloud watching the action,
790 his face in tears from the deep love for his father.
A hard death would come from your eminent conduct:
if ancient time sustains faith in your action

I surely won't be silent, memorable soldier.

Father Defended by Son

Mezentius yielded ground as if hamstrung and useless.
Retreating, he pulled the enemy's lance from the shield-rim.
Lausus hurried and mingled himself in the fighting:
just as Aeneas' hand rose for the death-blow
Lausus parried the stroke himself and Aeneas
was checked. Friends loudly cheered and supported
800 the son, whose buckler protected the father's withdrawal:
they hurled weapons and drove the enemy well back
with missiles. Aeneas fumed but stayed under cover.
The way a black stormcloud pours out its headlong
rain and hail, scattering every planter
and plower afield, travelers hunching safely in shelter
close to a stream-bank or high in the arch of a cliff-side—
the earth gets drenched so people can work in the daylight
once the sun returns: that's how the war-storm
covered Aeneas. Weapons thundered on all sides;
810 he bore it. He scolded Lausus and threatened the young man,
"Where will you run to die? Your daring surpasses
your strength: your love makes you careless." But Lausus
went on, gloating madly. Fiercer resentment
rose in the Dardan leader. The Fates had collected
Lausus' last threads: the hard blade of Aeneas
thrust in the youth's belly and vanished completely,
its point passing through buckler, armor (too light for such
        menace)
and tunic, woven in soft gold by his mother.
All his front bloodied, he sadly relinquished
820 life to the air, giving a corpse to the Death-world.

An Enemy's Loss Mourned

The son of Anchises, in fact, watching the dying
man's face with its strange manner of greying,
deeply sighed and held out a pitying right hand—
love for his own father had troubled his vision.
"Wretched man, what can the love of Aeneas
give you now to match your laudable instincts?
Keep the armor you took such pride in. I'll send you
back, if it's any concern, to the spirit and ash of your fathers.
You died, sadly. One fact may lessen the sadness:
830 you fell by the great hand of Aeneas." Upbraiding

some timid friends of Lausus, he knelt on the ground and he
    raised him,
the usually braided hair now bloodied and dirty.

A Son's Loss Mourned

The father meanwhile had reached a bank of the Tiber.
He rinsed his wound in water, resting his body,
leaned against a tree-trunk. Nearby the bronze-plated helmet
hung from a bough; his heavy arms lay still in a clearing.
Hand-picked men were around him. Wheezing and sickly,
resting his neck, beard sprawled on his chest and dissheveled,
he asked all about Lausus, often dispatching
840 a man to recall him, or bring worried words from his father.
But friends brought him the dead Lausus in mourning
high on a shield, a great man now, wounded and beaten
greatly. The father had sensed grief: his heart had expected
the worst. Dusting his hair repeatedly, raising
both hands to the sky, he clutched the body and cried out,
"How could so great joy in living possess me,
my son? To let you withstand the enemy's right hand—
you, my son! Your wound rescued your father:
you're dead, I live. Oh, but what pain to be exiled
850 now, what misery stings me, how deeply that wound goes!
I sullied your name, my son. I'm guilty of evil,
driven in shame from the scepter and throne of our Fathers.
I should be punished: my fatherland's people despised me.
I should be given to all these deaths: I deserved them.
Instead I'm alive, yet to abandon daylight and people.
But now I will." He raised himself on an aching
leg while speaking. Though deep hurt had diminished
his strength he was hardly crushed. He called for a graceful
comfort in war, his horse—the one he had always
860 ridden in triumph. He spoke to the animal sadly:
"We've lived a long time, Rhoebus—if anything earthly
lasts long. Today we'll return either in triumph,
with bloody spoils like the head of Aeneas in vengeance
for Lausus' pain, or make no way with our power
and both go down. I can't believe that your strongest
heart will yield to foreigners' rule and be mastered by Trojans."

Taunts and Spear-Throws

He stopped, took his usual place on the horse's
back and filled both hands with fine-pointed lances.
Bronze helmet gleaming—the crest was of horsehair—
870 he rode to the front quickly. Shame had engulfed him,
mixed with grief in his heart verging on madness.
He knew his valor, but love had made him fanatic.
Now he called out loud three times for Aeneas.
The Trojan recognized that voice. He prayed with a relish,
"Father of Gods, let it happen. Highest Apollo,
let this combat begin."
He said no more but moved with a poised spear to confront him.
Mezentius called out, "How could you scare me, you savage?
Son-killing—that was the only way you could wound me.
880 But I don't panic at death, or care for your Sky-Gods.
Enough! I came to die—and to bring you some presents
first." While speaking he twirled a spear at his rival,
another spear and another, throwing while circling
widely around him. The gold shield-boss withstood them.
He galloped from right to left three times in a circle,
flinging lances, the Trojan champion turning
three times, the bronze shield an overgrown forest.

A Final Strategy

When everything dragged on, weary of yanking
so many spears out, the fight's unfairness compelling
890 him now to mind all options, finally Aeneas
threw, with a leap, a spear at the war-horse's temple.
The animal reared up, lashed the air with its hoof-swings
and dumped Mezentius. Tumbling itself on the rider
headlong, it tangled and pinned him, throwing a shoulder.
Trojans and Latins burned the sky with their outcries.

Bared Throat

Aeneas ran up, pulling a sword from its scabbard,
and spoke down to him: "Where is Mezentius' fury
and wild strength now?" The Tuscan regarded
man and sky, gasping for air when he answered,
900 "Sour enemy, why do you threaten and taunt me?
Kill me, it's no great crime. I came here for combat:
Lausus made no peace-pact for *me* with a Trojan.
I ask one thing—if enemies humor their victims—

let my body be buried. I know I'm surrounded by bitter
people who hate me. I ask that you fend off their fury:
let me lie close in a tomb to the body of Lausus."
After speaking he consciously bared his throat to the weapon.
Life ran out in a flow of blood on his armor.

XI

MOURNING, DEBATE, AND
THE DEATH OF CAMILLA

A Dead Warrior's Arms

Meanwhile Dawn rose, leaving Ocean behind her.
Aeneas, though pressed to take time for the careful
burying of friends, though deeply disturbed by the killing,
thanked and pledged to the Gods at first light for his triumph.
He stood the trunk of a large oak on a barrow,
stripped it of branches and hung it with glittering armor,
the spoils of a leader, Mezentius—gifts for the potent
War-God now. He attached the blood-dripping head-crest,
the man's broken lances, the breastplate (with punctures
10   in twelve places), the shield of brass on the left side.
The ivory-hilted sword hung from the neck-place.
Then he began to encourage men who had crowded
closely around him, all the leaders who cheered him:
"The greatest work's been done, men. All your remaining
fear can vanish. Here are the spoils of a once-proud
king, the first fruits of my hand: Mezentius lies here!
Now we'll march on the Latin king and his ramparts.
Be spirited, hopeful. Be ready with arms for the forthcoming
      battle.
No one will stall or confuse us. Flags will be pulled up,
20   Gods will approve, our men will be led from the campground:
no sluggish thoughts or worries will stop or delay us.
First we'll commit our friends' unburied bodies
to earth—the only honor they need in Acheron's death-world.
Go and adorn with your last rites their excellent spirits.

They made a pact of blood to win us this country.
Let Pallas be sent first to the town of Evander
in mourning. The man was never lacking in courage.
A black and bitter day killed and removed him."

Mourning for Pallas

He stopped, in tears, turned and walked to an entrance.
30   Pallas' lifeless body lay inside and Acoetes,
an old man who'd carried the arms of Evander
back in Arcadia, kept watch. He'd gone with that foster
child he loved into war, but signs had opposed them.
Servants gathered now, a large number of Trojans,
women of Troy, accustomed to grief, letting their hair down.
Indeed when Aeneas himself moved through the doorway
mourners beat their breasts and lifted a raucous
cry to the stars. The building groaned with their sorrow.
Aeneas, regarding the snow-pale features of Pallas,
40   the propped head and the smooth chest with its open
wound from a spear of Ausonia, wept and addressed him,
"Pitiful boy. Fortune came to me smiling;
why did she envy your life, stop you from seeing
our kingdom, from riding home to your father in triumph?
This was not the promise I gave to your father,
Evander, on leaving. The day he embraced me and gave me
general command he feared and warned me of danger:
fierce and robust men would confront us in battle.
Perhaps right now your father is taken with empty
50   hope, making vows at altars laden with presents,
just as we follow your dead body—indebted
to none of the Gods now—in rites that seem empty.
Joyless father, to see a son's heartrending death-march,
not the return he hoped for, none of the triumph
or great promise I made. Still, these wounds are not shameful.
Evander, you'll see no son run off like a coward
for mere safety. You'll crave no vile death as a father.
And yet what strength Ausonia's lost and Iulus is lacking."

Funeral Procession

When done lamenting he ordered the pitiful body
60   raised. He sent a thousand picked men from the army
to follow the corpse—a final procession for Pallas—
to share the father's grief: limited comfort
for so much loss, but owed to a suffering father.

Men skillfully wove the frame of a gentle
bier from oak withes and shoots of arbutus.
A pile of spread-out leaves covered the pallet.
The youthful body then was placed high on the rustic
litter, as though a blossom picked by virginal fingers—
a drooping hyacinth maybe or delicate lilac,
70   still retaining its own figure and brilliance
though Earth, its mother, no longer strengthened or fed it.
Now Aeneas brought out two garments of purple,
stiffened with gold stitching: Dido of Sidon
had made them once by hand, happy to do it,
weaving the fine gold herself in the fabric.
He spread one robe on the body, a final adornment,
and sadly covered the hair, soon to be ashes.
He also built a pile of Laurentian war-wealth;
he ordered the prizes lead on in the drawn-out procession.
80   He added weapons taken from enemies, horses;
he tied the hands of men behind, to be sent to the lower
darkness as victims, their blood to sprinkle the death-fire.
He ordered leaders themselves to carry some tree-trunks
clapped in armor, with enemies' names attached to the breast-
      plates.
Acoetes followed along, joyless, weakened by old age,
now smearing his face with a fist or a cheek with a finger,
then throwing his whole frame on the ground in prostration.
Bloodstained Rutulian chariots were also included.
Aethon followed behind, the war-horse of Pallas,
90   shorn of trappings. Large tears wetted his cheekbones.
Two men carried the helmet and spear; but Turnus, who'd killed
      him,
had claimed the rest. A dismal retinue followed:
Trojans, Arcadians, all the Tuscans, reversing their weapons.

Farewell to a Good Soldier

After the long line of people had traveled a distance,
Aeneas halted. He sighed deeply and told them,
"Grisly deaths in the same war call me to others'
grief now. I salute your greatness, Pallas, forever.
Good-by forever." He said no more but directed
himself back to the high earth-works and campsite.

Peace for the Living as Well as the Dead

100 Envoys already had come from the town of Latinus,
     their temples wreathed in olive. They asked for the favor
     of bodies returned which were wounded and lying
     afield, permission to cover the dead with an earth-mound:
     no one fought with beaten, unbreathing men, and Aeneas
     could help someone he'd once called host and an in-law.
     Aeneas kindly allowed the truce they requested—
     he'd hardly refuse—he also questioned, and answered.
     "What undeserved luck involved you men of Latinus
     in such a war? Why did you run from the friendship I offered?
110 You want peace for men deprived of the War-God's
     luck, for dead men? I'd gladly concede—for the *living*.
     I'd never come here lacking God's word for a throne-room.
     I don't wage war with you people: your king has abandoned
     my friendship, trusting himself to the army of Turnus:
     Turnus himself should face death, in all fairness.
     To end the war by hand, to drive out the Trojans,
     he should be ready to clash with the arms of Aeneas.
     A man should live by his own right hand and by heaven.
     But go now. Cremate your pitiful citizens' corpses."

An Enemy's Praise

120 After Aeneas finished the envoys were quiet
     and stunned. They all glanced at each other in silence.
     Shortly Drances, an old man who had always
     reviled and hated the young Turnus, answered Aeneas
     in turn: "Man of Troy, you're widely reputed—
     more widely in war. How shall I praise you and rank you
     with heaven? Admire your justice more or your war-work?
     We'll gladly bring your word to the town of our fathers.
     If Fortune offers a way in fact we will join you
     with King Latinus. Turnus can look for another arrangement.
130 We'd even enjoy raising the mass of your destined
     walls, hoisting Trojan blocks on our shoulders."
     All the rest, when he stopped, voiced their agreement.

Time of Mourning

     Twelve days were agreed on. Peace was between them.
     Trojans harmlessly mixed with Latins in forests,
     wandering ridges where two-edged axes were thudding,
     felling tall ashtrees and pines that reached to the star-heights.

They worked at cutting scented cedar and chopping
oak into wedges. Carts groaned carrying rowan.

A Father's Grief

Rumor already had flown with a story of sorrow
140 that filled Evander's house and the town of Evander
(and Rumor had just now said that Latium's *victor* was Pallas).
Arcadians rushed to the gates. Following ancient
custom they held torches. The long line of a death-march
lit up the road, dividing broad fields with its fire-glow.
Trojan marchers met them; they merged in a single
loud cortege. Soon as mothers could see them
close to home, they inflamed the sad city with outcries.
Now no force could hold Evander back from the body.
He entered the crowd, the bier of Pallas was lowered,
150 he fell forward and clutched him, weeping and sighing.
Grief opened a way for his words finally, weakly:
"Pallas, this is not what you promised your father.
If only you'd trusted the savage War-God with caution!
I hardly doubted the novel glory of battle
would please you at first and you'd take pride in your weapons;
but oh, what first fruits of this too-close war, what a bitter
beginning: a cursed young man and none of my prayers
or vows heard by Gods. You're lucky now to be buried,
my sacred wife, saved from anguish like this one.
160 But I'm still living. I beat some Fate; a survivor,
the father who's left. If only I'd followed our Trojan
friends, speared by Rutulians, giving my life up:
this grim march might have brought the *father* home and not
         Pallas.
I don't blame Troy or the pact we agreed on,
hands we joined in friendship; misfortune was owed to
our old age. And if early death was awaiting
my son at least he killed a thousand Volscians beforehand—
that helps: he died in Latium leading the Trojans.
I cannot give you a worthier funeral, Pallas,
170 than kindly Aeneas will, and those great Phrygian leaders,
Tuscan captains, all of Tuscany's army.
They carry superb trophies from men you gave to the Death-God.
You too would stand here now, Turnus, a gruesome
tree-trunk in armor, if Pallas had matched you in muscle
and years. But why keep Trojans from war with my sadness?
Go back—and remember to bring a charge to your leader:

my hateful life drags on since Pallas has fallen:
your own right hand owes the killing of Turnus
to son, you see, and to father. The only place for your service
180 and luck is there. For me I seek no pleasure in living;
it's not right. I'll reach my son deep in the Death-world."

Around the Pyres

In time the Dawn-Goddess brought nourishing daylight
back to these wretched people. And brought back struggle and
     hardship:
Aeneas, a father, heaped up pyres now on the winding
beach, along with Tarchon. Every family carried
its own dead (their fathers' custom). Fires were ignited.
Smoke obscured the sky's depths with its darkness.
They circled redhot pyres three times dressed in resplendent
armor. They rode three times on horseback around them,
190 watching the sad death-fire and loudly lamenting.
Tears sprinkled the ground; they sprinkled the weapons.
Cries of people rose to the sky with a rasping of trumpets.
Soldiers threw spoils on the fire pulled from the bodies
of dead Latins: helmets, elegant sword-blades,
bridles, heat-scarred wheels, familiar tokens,
the men's very own shields and comfortless lances.
Many bodies of bulls fell for the Death-God.
Stiff-haired swine and sheep taken from every
field were bled and burned. Mourners who witnessed
200 their friends' cremation along the shoreline protected
the charred remains—not turning away till the humid
night transformed sky into glittering star-fire.

More Days of Sorrow

No less grief elsewhere afflicted the Latins.
They built countless pyres and buried the bodies
of many men in the ground. Others they carried
to nearby fields, or sent back to their cities.
The rest they burned—a mixed-up, immense heaping of dead men
lacking distinction and number. Everywhere ravaged
plains glowed with clustered fires as though they competed.
210 A third Dawn parted the cool shadows of heaven
and still they mourned, scraping the deep ashes and jumbled
bones from pyres. They heaped up warm earth for a death-mound.

New Hatred of War

But truly in homes of the rich town of Latinus
the wailing was most drawn out, the mourning extremest.
Mothers and bleak young wives, affectionate sisters,
their hearts drained, boys deprived of their fathers
all damned the appalling war and the engagement of Turnus.
His own sword, they demanded, should settle the conflict:
he'd claimed honor first and Italy's kingdom.
220 Drances fiercely riled them: "The call is for Turnus
alone: we only want Turnus in combat."
But plenty of people expressed other opinions:
for Turnus the great name of the queen was a safeguard;
he'd earned prizes in war and fame could support him.

The Wrong News

But now, in the midst of all that heat and commotion,
look: sullen envoys brought back word from the city
of great Diomedes that all their work was for nothing.
Gifts of gold, intense pleas, all of that labor
and cost had done no good: the Latins must look for
230 help elsewhere, or make peace with the Trojan commander.
King Latinus himself slumped. Distress overwhelmed him.

A Major Gathering

Angry Gods had willed and warned that Aeneas
was fated to come. Seeing fresh gravesites before him,
the king summoned a major council. Heads of the people
were called; they came to the high house by his order,
bustling through crowded streets to assemble
in royal halls. Latinus sat in the center,
extremely old; sceptered, but hardly contented.

Ill Tidings Repeated

He told the men just back from the Aetolian city
240 now to say what they'd heard, insisting on all the responses
in proper sequence. Conversation was silenced.
Venulus started speaking, complying with orders.
"My countrymen, after we conquered or worked through
every danger we saw the camp of that Greek, Diomedes:
we grasped a hand that blasted Ilium's country!
He'd won some land in Apulia now and was building
a town, Argyripa, named for his fatherland's people.

After he gave permission to speak in his presence
we set forth gifts and told him the name of our country,
250 described our attackers, and why we'd come to his campsite.

Sufferings of the Conquerors

"Having quietly heard us out he responded,
'Ah, you happy men of the kingdom of Saturn,
ancient Ausonians! What Luck has troubled your peaceful
realm and provoked you to start a war so uncertain?
Every man whose blade polluted a Trojan
plain, not counting losses in fights near the cliff-steep
walls—the Simois buried those men—all of us suffered
unspeakable pain through the world: we paid for our evil.
Even Priam would pity our band! Consider Minerva's
260 grim star, avenging Caphereus, cliffs of Euboea—
after the war we were driven to one shore or another.
Atreus' son Menelaus was exiled far as the pillars
of Proteus. Ulysses faced the Cyclops of Etna.
Why recall dethroned Pyrrhus or routed
House-Gods of Idomeneus, Locrians living on beaches
of Africa? Agamemnon himself, that leader of hardy
Greeks, fell at his own door by the hand of a vicious
woman—adultery ambushed the winner of Asia!
Gods prevent me too from seeing my homeland,
270 the altar and wife I desire, and Calydon's beauty.
Even now signs and visions alarm and pursue me—
friends lost, climbing for air while they wander
a river as birds on the wing—how horribly punished
are all my people!—they screech on crags as if weeping.
What else can I hope for now, from the moment
I madly swung my sword at the form of a Goddess?
I went for Venus: I wounded her hand with my weapon.
No: never drive me back to such fighting.
I'll wage no war with Trojans after uprooting
280 Troy. I don't recall the old malice with pleasure.
The gifts you bring me here from the land of your fathers
might go to Aeneas. I faced his dangerous weapons,
I fought him by hand, trust my experience: standing
high by a shield he'll twirl that spear like a whirlwind.
Indeed if Ida's country had borne two more like Aeneas,
Trojan force would have reached Inachus' city,
Fates would have turned around, and Greece would be mourning.
Each time we stalled at a hard wall of the Trojans,

there was the hand of Aeneas or Hector, obstructing
290 Greek triumph. They held us back for a decade.
Both were known for outstanding armor and spirit;
Aeneas, for reverence first. Join in a treaty
if luck provides. Beware of fighting that army.'
Now you've heard the king's answer, my peerless
King, and what he thinks about war on a grand scale."

Hope for Compromise

A worried and restless murmur ran through the Latin
crowd when the envoy finished: the way that a river,
blocked or slowed by rocks, may turn into grumbling rapids,
the nearby banks a noisy growling of water.
300 Soon as the anxious talk lapsed into silence
the king prayed to Gods on the high throne and responded,
"To settle this urgent matter before had been better,
my fellow Latins. I wish we'd done so—not to be calling
a council now with enemies camped by our city.
My people: this war is outlandish, the nation we fight with
descended from Gods, invincible, never exhausted
in battle—when beaten they can't let go of their weapons!
You held out hope for aid from Aetolian forces:
drop it. And self-trust? You see how it's thinned out:
310 the rest of our cause lies piecemeal or wasted
before your eyes; your hands can touch all our resources.
I blame no one. Everything manhood was able
to do was done. The whole kingdom's body was tested.
Now, though things are doubtful, here's the judgment I lean to,
briefly explained. Give me all your attention.
I own some old land close to Tuscany's River,
running far west beyond the Sicanian border.
Rutulians plow those hard hills, and Auruncans
work to plant them. It's harsh country for grazing.
320 The whole region of high plain and pine-covered mountain
can go in friendship to Troy. We'll ratify treaties
fair to us both. We'll call them friends of our kingdom.
They'll settle and build walls if they greatly desire to.
Or, if they plan to capture the land of another
people, we'll help them set sail from our country:
we'll build them twenty ships of Italian oakwood—
more, if they're able to man them—plenty of timber
lies by the water. They'll outline the manner and number
of ships; we'll furnish bronze, workmen and boatyard.

330 To give my word as well and firm up the treaty
     I'm pleased to send a hundred envoys from Latium's
     finest families, hands extending the branches
     of peace and presenting gifts: gold and ivory talents,
     a throne and white robe, signs of our kingship.
     Think it all through. Help us. Our state is exhausted."

Turnus Challenged

     Drances now stood up. Resentful of Turnus'
     glory—bitter spurs of envy had pricked him—
     the man was wealthy and skilled in speech. Though his war-hand
     had cooled, people valued his leadership highly.
340 Strongly rebellious, taking pride in his mother's
     noble birth (what he took from his father is unclear),
     he burdened the council with words and built up their anger:
     "You ask advice on a matter that's puzzling to no one,
     my good king. We need no speech, everyone knows it:
     Luck's come down on our land, though we say it in whispers.
     That man with the wrong omens and contrary manner
     should let us talk freely and stop his hot-airing.
     (I speak in spite of a sword, his threats to destroy me.)
     Scores of our sun-like leaders we see are collapsing,
350 a whole city sunk in grief; he jabs at the Trojan
     camp, sure of escape, scaring the sky with his weapons!
     My excellent king, you can add one more to the many
     gifts you've pledged and ordered sent to the Trojans—
     don't let one person's violence rule you—
     your own daughter. As father give her a splendid
     wedding, the man she deserves, and join in a permanent peace-
          pact.
     But now, if deep terror holds our thoughts and emotions,
     let's call on the man himself: we beg your indulgence!
     Yield, renounce these claims to kingdom and country.
360 Why throw such miserable people so often at open
     danger? *You're* the cause and crown of Latium's trouble.
     War won't save us: peace is everyone's prayer,
     Turnus, peace, and a single definite promise.
     I'll be the first—you think I'm hateful, it may be,
     let's not stall there—I'll beg humbly: pity your people,
     drop this rage, you've lost, leave it. We've witnessed
     enough death and bloodshed, enough farmland abandoned.
     If glory concerns you still, if plenty of power
     remains in your arm, if you set your heart on a princess's dowry,

370 trust that heart, dare to advance on Aeneas.
     What if a royal bride matters to Turnus—
     our lives are worthless? A mob of unmourned and unburied
     dotting the plain? You, if strength is inside you,
     a trace of your fatherland's War-God, face your provoker and fight
       him.''

To Fight On

     Drances' words ignited the fury of Turnus.
     He'd moaned and grunted; now he passionately answered,
     "Plenty of words, Drances, you're always orating—
     when war demands fists. When elders are summoned
380 you're here first; but councils should not be filled with the chatter
     you fly on grandly and safely, not while bulwarks are staving
     enemies off, while blood's filling our trenches.
     Go on with your usual thundering eloquence, charge me
     with fear, Drances—you, a stacker of corpses
     yourself among Trojans, gilding the field with your welter
     or trophies! Whatever real strength can accomplish
     you're free to try; indeed the enemy's close by,
     don't look far, he circles the walls in abundance.
     Why put it off, charge right in! Is your War-God
390 forever a windy speech and a pair of escaping heels?
     So I'm 'defeated.' You dirt, will anyone fairly
     prove I'm beaten? Look at the Tiber cresting with Trojan
     blood, a whole branch and root of Evander's
     family fallen, Arcadians stripped of their armor.
     Hulking Pandarus hardly found me 'defeated,'
     or Bitias, faced and dispatched with a thousand in one day
     to Hell's God—and Trojan earthworks had me surrounded.
     'The war's not healthy'? Sing that brainless song to a Trojan
400 ear or your own. You always persist in unsettling
     men with your pompous fear. You upgrade the power
     of people conquered twice and *down*grade arms of the Latins.
     Myrmidon chiefs are afraid of war with the Trojans
     now, Diomedes and Larisaean Achilles are shuddering,
     the Aufidus River turns back from the wavy Adriatic!
     Or else a play-acting liar pretends to be frightened
     at all my wrath; he spices deceit with his trembling.
     Don't move back! My hand will never deprive you
     of life. Live with yourself and your petty emotion.
410 I turn now to the deep concern of my Father.
     If you no longer have much hope in our army,

if we're so friendless after losing a single
skirmish, drained and wrecked, our luck irreversible,
sue for peace. Extend your hand and be passive.
Still, if only our true courage were present!
I'd hold that man outstanding in spirit, blessed in his labor
before all others, who'd hate to see such a failure,
who'd sooner grovel in dust, bite it and die there.
If we're still strong, therefore, with healthy resources,
420 Italian cities and people remaining to help us;
further, if Trojans gained glory through much of
their own bleeding and dying—all of us entered
that war-storm; why be ashamed and recoil on the very
doorstep? Why should we quail right now, when the trumpets
have not yet sounded? The struggle and change of a single
day can improve much. Fortune may toy with a people
then set them on solid ground again when she alters.
So. 'No help from Diomedes and Arpi.'
Still Messapus will help, and Tolumnius gladly.
430 Many people have sent their leaders, and ample
renown follows each man picked from Laurentine and Latin
fields. Camilla too commands an excellent cohort,
Volscian columns of bronze-flowering riders.
And what if the Trojans want me alone in a combat?
Do I alone obstruct the common good and your pleasure?
Victory never hated or ran from these fingers:
I won't stop striving, hoping for this: I will test him,
I'll charge Aeneas with verve, let him equal Achilles
in size or strap on armor crafted by Vulcan's
440 hands! I've sworn my life to my Father, Latinus.
I am Turnus, second to none of our leaders
in courage. Aeneas wants me alone? I *ask* him to call me!
And Drances? He'd rather not appease with his own death
Gods who are angry. If honor and strength are required, he won't
     bear it.''

New Cries of War

So they argued together, raising a number
of doubts. But Aeneas had broken camp and was moving,
a messenger rushed to the royal palace, an uproar
rose that filled the city with great consternation.
Trojans had formed ranks and stood by the Tiber,
450 Tuscans had come downhill, a battlefield filled up.
Minds were instantly stunned. Hearts of the people

quavered; hard spurs prodded their outrage.
Men nervously scrambled for swords. "Weapons!" they shouted.
Fathers muttered and mourned them sadly. A tumult
everywhere surged through the air, loud disagreements
resembling flocks of starlings that happen to settle
in deep groves, or swans on the fish-filled Padusa
River, gabbling hoarsely and loudly through marshes.
"Yes, you people"—Turnus wrested the moment—
460 "counsel and plan things, praise a peace-pact and sit here
while armed men assault your kingdom!" He'd finished
with talk: he left the high hall in a hurry.
"You, Volusus: arm your Volscian detachments,
lead the Rutulians," he said. "Equip your horsemen, Messapus.
Cover the broad plain, Coras—you and your brother.
Some of you block the city gates: take to the towers.
The rest follow my lead and charge when I tell you."

Rushed Defenses

People immediately ran from the whole town to the wall-tops.
Latinus, the father himself, abandoned the council.
470 A sorry hour had disturbed the high design he had worked with.
He often blamed himself for not accepting Aeneas
before the city, and calling the Trojan son-in-law freely.
Now trenches were dug near gates. Boulders were hauled up
with stakes. The hoarse and brazen signal for bloody
war sounded. Boys mingled with mothers
ringing the wall—everyone called to the desperate struggle.

The Mothers' Curse

The queen, too, borne by a large body of women
high uphill to the fortress and temple of Pallas,
offered gifts, her virgin daughter Lavinia close by
480 (a cause of the grave crisis), her eyes becomingly downcast.
Mothers entered the temple, filled it with incense
smoke, and grim prayer poured through the eminent doorway:
"Our strength in war, Protectress, Virgin of Triton:
crack the spear of that Phrygian bandit and sprawl him
flat on the ground. Splatter his blood on your portals."

An Unconfined Horse

Turnus equipped himself for war in a frenzy:
already he'd clapped on the auburn breastplate that bristled
with scales of bronze, and greaves were his leg-guards.

Head still bare, tying a sword at the hipbone,
490 he rushed from the fortress heights like a gold coruscation,
spirits leaping with hope in advance of his rival,
just like a stallion that snaps a tether and gallops
free of the stall at last, reaches an open
field, heads for a herd of mares in a pasture
or swims a well-known stream, familiar water,
then leaps back out, neck held high in a whinny
of pleasure, hair playing on nape and on withers.

Exceptional Courage

Camilla galloped to meet him, the Volscian cohort
around her, right to the very gates, where the war-queen
500 dismounted. Her whole company followed by jumping
down from their horses. Then she addressed him:
"Turnus, if confidence rightly belongs to the bravest,
I promise to charge Aeneas' cavalry boldly,
to go and confront alone Tuscany's horsemen!
Let my hand be first in testing the danger of battle;
you should stand by the wall protecting the city."

Battle Assignments

Turnus stared at the fearsome girl and he answered,
"Virgin pride of Italy! How can I thank you,
what return can I offer? For now, a share in this conflict,
510 because your spirits outleap everything, truly.
Scouts have returned, reports are firm that Aeneas
has brashly sent some light cavalry forward
to rattle the plain. Mounting a steep and deserted
ridge himself, he'll march down on the city.
I plan a surprise attack in some canopied forest:
I'll block both of the path's escape-routes with soldiers.
You take out the Tuscan horsemen, combining
your flag with tough Messapus, the men of Tiburtus,
and Latin troops. Assume the cares of a leader."
520 He stopped, encouraged Messapus to fight in the same way,
rallied friends and leaders, then left for Aeneas.

Taking the High Ground

A valley curved sharply: good for an army's
ambush or ruse from dense cover, the darkened
and narrow trail was flanked and crowded on both sides;
a tight entrance led to a dangerous outlet.

Level ground lay far above on the mountain
ridgeline, less marked but safe for a lookout,
whether battle be joined from the left or the right side,
or heavy stones rolled from a stand on the hilltop.
530 Turnus marched up here by familiar trail-signs.
He halted in treacherous bush and held his position.

A War-queen's Past and Future

Diana meanwhile spoke from her throne in the heavens
to Opis, an agile girl in her friendly and sacred
company. Sad words came from Latona's
daughter: "My girl, Camilla enters a cruel
war wearing our armor now, though it's futile.
She's dearer than any other. It's not an impulsive
love of Diana, some novel sweetness that moves me.
When Metabus left the old town of Privernum,
540 expelled for his hated rule and insolent power,
he fled with this child. He dodged fights in the city
and took this friend into exile. He altered Casmilla
slightly, her mother's name, and called her Camilla.
He carried her close to his own heart while he headed
for lonely woods on a long ridgeline. Everywhere weapons
fiercely pressed them, Volscians hurriedlly tried to surround
       them,
and look: a river blocked their escape—the Amasenus,
bubbling and spilling over its high banks from a heavy
downpour. Ready to swim, he paused out of anxious
550 love for the child, his dear burden. With everything turning
inside him he made an abrupt and reluctant decision.
By chance he carried a large spear in his forceful
warrior's hand, of oakwood, knotty and seasoned.
He wrapped his daughter in corktree bark and he lashed her
tight to the weapon, cinching the two at the middle.
His huge hand poised, he prayed to the heavens:
'Dear virgin Diana, protector of forest,
I give, as the father himself, this child: the weapon she clings to
first and humbly is yours. She runs from the enemy: take her,
560 Goddess, I beg you. She trusts a wind now which is doubtful.'
He finished, cocked his arm and lunged—and the weapon
arched over the roar and swirl of the water:
Camilla sadly flew on a whistling javelin.
Metabus, now with a large crowd pressing him closely,
threw himself in the river. He crossed it and pulled from

a grassy bank the spear and the girl, his gift for Diana.
No house or walled city now would accept him.
Nor would the wild nature of Metabus want one:
he passed the time in lonely mountains with sheep-men.
570 Camilla lived in woods near frightening wolf-dens.
He nursed her with milk from the mare of a feral
herd, squeezing the teats for the soft lips of his daughter.
The child no sooner had taken first steps on her tender
feet but he placed a sharp lance in her fingers
and hung from her small shoulder a bow and some arrows.
No gold in her hair, no long robe for her clothing:
her head and back were draped with the skin of a tiger.
Already her soft hand might hurtle a youngster's
lance or whirr overhead the lean thong of a slingshot,
580 downing a white swan or Strymonian egret.
Many mothers in towns of Tuscany vainly
longed for this daughter; she only rejoiced in Diana,
preserving her love of chastity, constantly caring
for weapons. How I wish this conflict had never
come to possess her—to try provoking the Trojans!
She'd now be one of our consort, close to a Goddess.
Hurry, my Nymph. Bitter Fates will oppress her.
Glide from the sky, visit the land of the Latins
where grim fighting is joined under contrary omens.
590 Here are my weapons. Take an arrow for vengeance:
whoever profanes or wounds her inviolate body
must pay likewise in blood—Italian or Trojan.
Then in a cavelike cloud I'll carry her wretched
body myself, the armor unstripped, to a tomb in her homeland."

Battle Lines Joined

Opis flew, when she ended, through light heavenly breezes,
shrouded in dark cloud that sounded like whirlwind.
Trojan forces meanwhile moved on the city.
Tuscan leaders, a whole army of horsemen,
formed numbered sections. All of the flatland
600 grumbled when horses pranced and jerked at the tight-held
bridles, turning and twisting. The far field was an iron
bristling of spears. The plain flared with a lifting of weapons.
Nonetheless Messapus and fast-riding Latins,
Coras (his brother) and virgin Camilla's battalion
appeared on the opposite field, moving their right hands
back on long-projecting spears or rattling their arrows.

The sides came closer. Horses whinnied and fretted.
They moved down to a spear-throw distance where each side
paused. A sudden shout: they kicked at their frantic
610 horses and shot forward, everywhere weapons were flying,
thick as the gloom of a snowstorm blocking the sky out.
Tyrrhenus and wild Aconteus, charging, collided
and speared each other right off, the first to go sprawling
and loudly screaming. Their mounts fractured each other,
chest rupturing chest, Aconteus hitting
the ground like a bolt, or a weight flung from a stone-sling,
thrown far and headlong. His life scattered in crosswind.

Pursuers Become the Pursued

Already some Latin ranks were buckling and turning.
Chucking shields they galloped back to the city
620 with Trojan squadrons behind them led by Asilas.
They all approached the gates; but the Latins, reversing
again with a yell, pulled at the soft necks of their horses:
now the Trojans fled, letting their reins out.
The way surf charges and turns into backwash,
one time rushing the beach and leaping on rockpiles,
a wash of swirling foam far up the beachsand,
then it quickly retreats, it seethes and sucks at the gravel,
swishes away from the shore in a sliding of water:
Tuscans drove Rutulians twice to the city
630 and twice were routed, glancing back with their shields up.

Fierce Infighting

But after a third charge they all were entangled
in close fighting. Man picked out man from each column.
Now truly the wounded and dying groaned in a sloshing
of blood; weapons and human bodies were jumbled
with writhing half-dead horses. Fighting grew fiercer:
Orsilochus hurled a spear at Remulus' stallion
(afraid to attack the man), lodging the weapon
behind an ear. Mad from the blow, the animal reared up
high, chest out, frantically thrashing with forelegs—
640 Remulus struck the ground and rolled there. Catillus
cut down Iolla and then Herminius, massive
in body and armor, imposing in spirit, with shoulders
and blond head bare. Wounds had not scared him:
he'd openly faced each weapon. The quivering javelin
drove through his broad shoulders: the man knotted in torment.

Dark blood everywhere gushed. Soldiers inflicted
death with swords or looked themselves for honorable death-
    wounds.

Amazonian War-work

An Amazon right in the center thrived on the slaughter.
Wearing a quiver, baring a breast for combat, in one place
650 Camilla heavily rained her flexible lances;
elsewhere she snatched up a strong axe without tiring.
She shouldered Diana's golden bow and her rattling
arrows even when forced back and retreating—
she turned in flight to aim the bow and its arrow.
Hand-picked friends ringed her: the virgin Larina,
Tulla, the bronze axe-wielder Tarpeia:
Italian girls Camilla had chosen herself like a Goddess,
graceful and fine in peacetime, comrades in wartime.
They looked like Amazons marching to battle in painted
660 armor in Thrace, drumming the Thermodon River,
whether Hippolyta led them or Penthesilea, returning
in Mars' chariot, raising tumultuous welcome
with crescent shields, women leaping in columns.

The Killings of Camilla

Who was the first and last to fall by your weapons,
bitter virgin? How many dead did you litter the ground with?
Euneus, Clytius' son, first confronted your spear-shaft:
its length pierced his open chest and he coughed up
bloody dribble. He fell in some red-spattered gravel
and bit it, the wound fatal: he groveled and died there.
670 Liris next and Pagasus: one of them clinging
to reins when a stricken horse pitched him, the other
coming to lend an unarmed hand to a struggling
friend—they both went headlong. She added Amastrus,
Hippotas' son. She chased, pressed from a distance
and speared Harpalycus, Tereus, Demophoön, Chromis.
Whenever the girl's hand hurtled a weapon
a man of Phrygia fell. Ornytus, far off
and strangely armored, rode an Apulian horse like a hunter.
A hide peeled from a bullock covered the soldier's
680 broad shoulders. The open jaw of a massive
wolf rested its white fangs on his forehead.
He'd armed himself with a farmer's pike to go wheeling
around in the crowd, by a whole head taller than others.

Camilla caught him (his column had turned, it was easy)
and stabbed him. She spoke down to him, angrily taunting:
"Tuscan! You thought you were chasing deer in some forest?
The hour has come to cancel your bragging—a woman's
weapon has done it! At least you'll carry a signal
name to your father's grave: you fell by the spear of Camilla."
690 Butes died next and Orsilochus—two of the biggest
Trojans. She drove a spear from behind into Butes'
neck, by the back-guard and helmet, that glistened
with sweat—by the small shield that hung from one shoulder.
She raced from Orsilochus, widely tracing a circle,
then fooled him by circling within: she pursued her pursuer.
She rose up high to double the force of an axe-blow
right through the armor, through human bone, while he pleaded
and begged. Warm brain spattered his face-wound.
The soldier son of Aunus met her and stopped short,
700 abruptly afraid at the sight. An Appenine dweller,
hardly the last (if the Fates allowed) Ligurian liar,
seeing no way to escape now from the combat,
no chance to turn aside the onrushing war-queen,
he planned to trick her. He started a clever deception,
saying, "What's so special? A woman relying
for strength on a horse? Trust yourself as my equal:
don't ride off, fight me alone, armed and on foot here.
Then we'll know whose glory is breezy or shallow."
The speech burned and enraged her. Bitterly smarting,
710 she handed her horse to a friend and fearlessly stood there,
shield unmarked, sword bare, a match for her rival.
The man figured the trick had worked and he quickly
took off by flicking the reins and digging the metal
spurs in his mount: he rode away like a coward.
"Ligurian fool! Your spirits are proud and elated
for nothing: you've tried an oily trick of your country,
but lies won't return you safely to Aunus, that bluffer."
The girl spoke while she ran, quick-footed, fire-like,
crossing the path of his mount and arresting the bridle:
720 she faced the man and took her toll of enemy bloodshed,
the way the Sun-God's hawk on the wing will easily follow
a flapping dove from its high cliff into cloudbank,
seize, pin it and tear the flesh with its talons—
bloodied and ripped-out feathers drift in the breezes.

Tarchon Harangues his Men

The Father of Gods and men however was watching
all this closely, seated high on Olympus.
Jupiter stirred the Tuscan, Tarchon, to battle
fiercely: the hard spurs of the God trebled his fury.
Tarchon drove a horse straight at the carnage:
730 where lines yielded he called to the wings, he harangued them
each by name and reformed ranks scattered in battle.
"Never ashamed, you Tuscans? Forever inactive?
What fear, what gross laziness comes to your spirits!
Some *woman* wrecks your lines and gets you to scatter!
Why then carry your swords, your impotent weapons?
You're not so lazy at night grappling with Venus,
dancing with Bacchus when curved flute-songs invite you!
You like looking for sweets, the full goblets and tables
you crave and admire, some willing seer announcing
740 your rites in a deep grove with fat-dripping victims."

Eagle and Snake

He stopped and spurred his horse at the enemy center,
expecting to die there. Charging Venulus madly,
he yanked the man from his mount; he managed to hold him
close to his chest with all his strength as he rode off.
A cry rose to the sky from all of the Latins,
who turned and watched while Tarchon raced like a brushfire,
bearing the armed man through the field. Breaking the metal
spear-tip of Venulus, Tarchon probed for an open
spot for a mortal wound. Venulus fought back,
750 holding the hand from his throat, muscle to muscle.
Just like a golden eagle clutching a serpent
in high flight, gripping the prey with its talons:
the wounded snake writhes and maneuvers its body,
erecting bristly scales it struggles to hold up
its hissing mouth, but the bird rips it as keenly
with hooked beak, the air lashed by its wingbeats:
that's how Tarchon carried his prize from Tiburtine
lines, exulting. Maeonian sons followed their leader's
example, trusting the outcome, and charged.

Watching for a Chance to Kill

                                          Now it was Arruns
760 in debt to the Fates. Shrewdly he circled ahead of Camilla,

so quick with her lance. He took no difficult chances.
Wherever the woman madly charged at a cluster
there was Arruns calmly watching her movements.
Wherever she won, leaving some rival behind her,
the young man jerked his reins calmly and quickly.
Approaching her here, then there, he traveled through every
arc of a circle. His dead-sure spear maliciously quivered.

Fascination with Gold

By chance a priest once devoted to Cybele, Chloreus,
gleamed in outstanding Phrygian arms in the distance.
770 He rode a froth-flecked horse covered in scaly
pelts of brass linked with gold and looking like feathers.
The man shone in far-fetched purple and dusk-blue;
he aimed his Lycian bow with Gortynian arrows.
He sported a prophet's helmet of gold and a golden
bow on one shoulder; he'd gathered the shimmering folds of a
     saffron
linen chlamys together using a sun-gold
clasp. His tunic and leggings were wildly embroidered.
Now whether to fasten Trojan spoils to a temple
or capture and wear a priest's gold on her person,
780 Camilla blindly trailed him, hunting the one man
through every skirmish and brawl. It was careless:
a girl's love for prize fashion had fired her.

A Prayer to the Sun-God

Arruns at last would seize the moment. In hiding
he shook a spear and prayed Gods for their guidance:
"Apollo, highest Lord and holy Soracte's protector,
we paid you worship first by heaping our burning
pinewood and walking across, upright and trusting,
stepping on glowing embers to show our devotion.
All-powerful Father, help me to wipe out
790 shame on our army. I don't crave a trophy of armor,
no booty for beating a girl—other achievements
will bring me prizes—but till this frightening menace
falls wounded, I go to my Father's town in dishonor."

The God Complies Partly

Phoebus heard the prayer and decided to grant it
in part; the rest he dispersed in a hurrying crosswind.
He gave his nod to a sudden and violent killing,

Camilla's death; he gave no nod to Arruns' returning
to see his high homeland—that prayer turned into Southwind.

A Frightened, Escaping Wolf

Then Arruns gave a spear to the wind and it whistled,
800 turning every Volscian head sharply to look at
the war-queen. Camilla herself was thinking of nothing,
neither the wind nor the weapon's approach and its whirring—
until the spear struck. It clung to her naked
breast and deeply drank the blood of the virgin.
Friends ran to the queen in a turmoil and caught her
fall. Arruns fled in absolute terror:
elation mixed with fear but he dared not rely on
arms clashing further with arms of the virgin.
The way a stray wolf will escape, disappearing
810 in high mountains before some hostile weapons pursue him
after he's killed a large bullock or shepherd:
aware of the rash act he heads for a thicket,
tucking that shivering tail under his belly:
Arruns restlessly hid from sight in the same way,
content to escape by losing himself in the army.

A Last Word for Turnus

Camilla was dying. Her hand tugged at the weapon.
The steel tip lay deep, through the bones of her ribcage.
She paled and slumped. Her eyes, caught in a death-chill,
were downcast; her once ruddy color had left her.
820 She breathlessly spoke to Acca, one of her equals,
the one before all others Camilla was sure of,
sharing concern. "Acca, my sister," she told her,
"my strength held out till now. The end is a bitter
wound—everything greyed or blackened around me.
Hurry and take a final order to Turnus:
succeed, fight hard—keep Troy from our city!
Good-by—already." While speaking, letting some reins go,
she slipped to the ground, resisting, but gradually colder.
Her whole body slackened; Death was arresting
830 the limp neck and propped head. She gave up her armor,
sighed, protested. Her life ran out among shadows.

Intensified Struggle

Now an enormous cry went up to strike at the golden
stars. Fighting increased with the fall of Camilla.

The entire Trojan force charged, together with Tuscan
leaders' close-ranked groups and Arcadian wings of Evander.

A Goddess Takes her Revenge

All this time Opis had sat high on a mountain.
Diana's observer had watched the fighting unruffled.
After seeing the grim wounding and death of Camilla,
the noise of outraged men in the distance around her,
840   she sighed and spoke with deep pity and caring:
"You paid too much, young girl—too cruelly punished
for having tried to provoke Trojans in battle.
It did no good to worship Diana in lonely
woods or carry her arrows high on your shoulder.
Still, your queen won't leave you disgraced in the final
hour of life: your name will last among nations
after your death: they'll know your pain was avenged here.
Whoever profaned and wounded your body will suffer
the death he deserves." At the base of a prominent mountain,
850   shaded by dark oaks, lay a huge earthen construction,
the tomb of Dercennus, an ancient king of Laurentum.
The lovely Opis lightly leaped on the barrow
and paused, eyeing Arruns first from that death-mound.
Seeing him there in high spirits and foolishly gloating
she said, "Why do you wander off? Approach me and die here!
Step up close: take your proper reward for destroying
Camilla. You'll die in fact by the bow of Diana."
She spoke like a Thracian girl, pulled from the golden
quiver a feathered arrow and angrily drew back,
860   stretching the bow so much that its end-points were almost
touching, her hands on a line, her left at the iron
tip, her right on the string close to her nipple.
Arruns instantly heard the whizz of that weapon,
the stirring of air. Metal drove in his body.
A final groan and gasp. Followers left him
there in the ignorant dust of the field—they forgot him.
Opis rose on her wings to the air of Olympus.

A City Imminently Threatened

Her light horsemen had run off first at the loss of Camilla.
Rutulians broke and ran; a bitter Atinus
870   and disjoined leaders fled, deserting their sections,
turning their mounts: they made for the city and safety.
No one could hold back Trojans who pressed them

and brought on death, no one's weapons could stop them.
Slack-stringed bows hung from lagging Rutulian shoulders.
Hooves of their horses beat on the crumbled ground at a gallop.
A dark dust-cloud swirled and rolled to the city
gates. Mothers beat their breasts when they looked out.
Cries of women rose to the sky and the star-heights.
Men who came back first in a rush for the open
880　gates got mixed in the crowd and crush of enemy soldiers:
they faced a miserable death right there at the entrance,
close to a wall or secure home of a father,
stabbed and dying. Other people were locking
the gates, not daring to open the town any longer
to take in pleading friends—which led to a horrible slaughter
of soldiers guarding a gate or charging at weapons.
Those outside, their parents watching and weeping,
were driven headlong down into trenches and rolled there.
Others paid out reins of their mounts and insanely
890　smashed into gates or posts, though all were durably bolted.
Mothers even tried to help from the wall-top,
moved by genuine love of country, recalling Camilla,
their trembling hands hurling weapons of hardwood,
hurriedly making do with planking or tempered
stakes for spears. They wanted to die first for the city.

News of Reversals

What bitter news meanwhile spread through the woodland
where Acca reported extreme reversals to Turnus!
Volscian ranks wiped out, the fall of Camilla,
furious enemy charges, the War-God behind them,
900　seizing it all: terror bore down on the city.
Turnus fumed. The cruel power of Jupiter forced him
to leave those rugged hills, the ground he'd obstructed.

Aeneas Arrives Before the City

He'd hardly gone from view, making for level
ground, when Aeneas, our Father, arrived in the open
pass, mounted the ridge and emerged from shadowy forest.
Both were therefore moving fast on the city
with all their power, neither far from the other.
Aeneas glimpsed a smoking, dusty plain in the distance.
He saw Laurentine troops at the same moment that Turnus
910　recognized the furious arms of Aeneas—he almost
heard the approaching hooves and snorting of horses.

A Day's and a Battle's End

They might have tried at once to skirmish or battle
had not the Sun-God reddened, his tired chariot touching
Iberian water. Day had lapsed; Night was returning.
Both sides camped by the city and fortified earth-works.

XII

SINGLE COMBAT

A Wounded Lion

Turnus could see the War-God against him. The Latins
were drained or broken: they eyed him now and demanded
the single combat he'd promised. Still he was fire-hot,
spirits peaked and implacable: just like a lion
speared in the chest by hunters in Carthage's country,
turning at length to fight, gladly unruffling
the knotted mane on his neck and fearlessly snapping
the spear that sneaked in and stuck there, his mouth bloody and
     growling:
Turnus' violence burned and swelled in the same way.
10 Shortly he found the king and excitedly told him,
"Turnus is not for stalling. Aeneas' cowards
have not one word to retract, no pact they agreed to:
I'll meet him. Start the rites, Father. Draw up a treaty.
Either this hand will send that Trojan deserter of Asia
down to the Underworld—Latins will sit there and watch it,
my sword alone will remove that shame on our people—
or let him win. Concede Lavinia's wedding."

Is Combat Necessary?

Latinus answered Turnus with level emotion.
"Your spirits excel, young man; the more your aggressive
20 courage mounts, the more I must be impartial,
reflecting, cautiously weighing all of the hazards.
You claim the realm of your father Daunus, the many

towns you've taken by hand, the backing and gold of Latinus.
But Latium's fields and Laurentum have other unmarried
girls of decent family. Let me speak to you bluntly,
intrigue aside: take what I openly tell you.
I never had the right to marry my daughter
to any former suitor: every God and seer proclaimed that.
But won by your love, won by familiar bloodline,
30   grieved by a wife's weeping, I broke each law that constrained me:
I tore that bride from her groom, I engaged in impious conflict.
Since then, Turnus, you've seen what setbacks have followed
in war. You've suffered first and worst in the struggle.
Twice we've lost major engagements, we barely
protect Italian hopes in the city, we warm up the Tiber's
flow with blood, we turn our wide plains to a bone-white.
I've wavered so often. What madness altered my thinking?
With Turnus killed am I ready to join with new allies?
Then why not end the struggle while Turnus is healthy?
40   What will Italy say, your Rutulian kinsmen,
if I consign you to death—let Luck cancel that word out!—
and after you've sought the hand of my daughter in marriage?
Consider the war's turnarounds; pity your father,
old and sad now in Ardea's distant
country."

Honorable Death

The speech hardly altered the rashness
of Turnus: efforts to cure him *worsened* his illness.
No sooner able to speak to the king he insisted,
"Don't worry for me, excellent Father: I ask you
to set aside fear. Let me exchange death for some honor.
50   Our hands too have showered weapons; our spear-throws were hardly
feeble; blood flowed from the wounds we inflicted.
The Goddess-Mother who hid that coward in female
mist will hide in the empty shadows far from Aeneas."

Another Royal Plea for Peace

Ah, but the queen, dreading the chance of new fighting
(and soon to die herself), wept and clasped the ebullient
Turnus: "I weep for you. Does any regard for Amata
touch your spirit? You gave my miserable old age
the only secure hope. It's all in your hands now:
the proud rule of Latinus, a whole tottering household.

60 I ask one thing. Avoid this fight with the Trojan.
Whatever risk awaits you now in such combat,
Turnus, awaits me also. I'd sooner surrender my hateful
sight than be captured, to look on a son like Aeneas."
Lavinia felt the tearful stress of her mother.
Her cheeks were wet and flushed, stippled with redness
where deep warmth of feeling had rushed to the surface.
The way a man might dye Indian ivory
with crimson streaks, or mix roses with lilies,
pink among white: Lavinia's color had altered.

Hard Determination

70 Desire moved Turnus. He stared at the face of the virgin
and yearned to fight still more. He briefly answered Amata,
"Please don't cry. Don't make some terrible omen
follow me now in this hard hour with the War-God,
Mother. To stall death is no option for Turnus.
Idmon: take a message—it's hardly a sweet one—
to Phrygia's master: soon as Aurora has reddened
the morning sky in her chariot ride from Phoenicia,
let no one lead a Trojan against a Rutulian:
with both armies at peace we'll settle the war with our own blood,
80 seeking Lavinia's hand right there on the war-field."

Horses and Tools of War

After speaking he quickly left for his quarters.
He called for horses, glad to watch as they snorted:
Orithia'd given the horses herself, a reward for Pilumnus
because they were whiter than snow and faster than Northwind.
Trainers bustled about them, slapping a hollow
chest with an open palm or brushing a mane out.
Turnus now clapped his shoulders in armor
of pale copper and stiff gold. He fitted a sword on,
fitted a shield, and the horned, red-crested helmet.
90 The Fire-God himself had styled that sword for his father,
Daunus; he'd dipped it, hot, in Underworld water.
Next the sturdy spear which stood in the central
hall, leaned on a huge column: Turnus forcibly seized it.
A prize of Auruncan Actor, he rattled and shook it,
yelling, "Now—I've never called on my weapon
in vain—now is the time! Mightiest Actor
first gripped you and now Turnus: I pray we can sprawl him.
My strong hand will pull at the Phrygian sissy's

breastplate and strip him. I'll smear dust in the hair-curls
100 he frizzles with warm irons and sprinkles with myrrh-gum!"
Fury drove him, his whole countenance burning.
The sharp eyes flashed and glittered like watchfires.
He looked like a bull frightfully grumbling and snorting
before a charge, horns angrily swinging,
butting an oaktree stump or lashing at breezes,
a hoof kicking up sand to anticipate conflict.

The Prospect of Peace

Aeneas, no less fierce meanwhile in armor
his mother had brought him, anger peaked for the War-God,
would gladly settle the war by the pact he'd agreed to.
110 He calmed fears of friends and a somber Iulus,
recalling their Fates. He sent unambiguous tidings
to King Latinus. Men spoke of the peace-terms.

Armies Not in Conflict

The following Day had hardly sprinkled the mountain
tops with light and the Sun-God's horses were rising
from deep water, nostrils flaring with light-breath,
when men of Troy and Rutulia prepared for the combat
by measuring space near a high wall of the city
and setting hearths and shrines on the grass for their common
Gods. A number of men wearing ritual aprons,
120 their temples wreathed in olive, brought out water and firebrands.
The massed Ausonian army advanced through the crowded
gates, armed with lances. All the Trojan and Tuscan
army faced them, a bustling assortment of weapons,
steel aligned as though the voice of the War-God
had gruffly commanded. Leaders galloped through thousands,
right through the center, proud of their purple and gold trim,
Assaracus' bloodline: Mnestheus, hardy Asilas;
Messapus, that son of Neptune and breaker of horses.
Each man on a given signal withdrew to his own place,
130 drove a spear in the ground and set up a shield there.
Mothers anxiously streamed out, weaponless people,
weak old men; they sat on the roof of a tower
or house; others were standing by high gates of the city.

Faced with a Brother's Loss

On top of a hill now known as the Alban
(then the hill had neither name nor distinction),

Juno closely watched both the Laurentine
and Trojan ranks, the plain and town of Latinus.
Quickly she spoke to Juturna, the sister of Turnus,
Goddess to Goddess (the latter governed some burbling
140 rivers and marsh—Jupiter gave her the honor
as high King of the air when he took her as virgin):
"Joy of my spirit, graceful Nymph of the rivers,
you know I've placed you first among all of the Latin
girls who've climbed in the thankless bed of our great-souled
Jupiter: freely I gave you a place in our heaven.
Don't blame me now if I tell you of sorrow, Juturna.
Where Fortune seemed to allow, when Fates were advancing
the Latin cause, I guarded your city and Turnus.
Now I see the man jars with Fates which are stronger.
150 Some hostile force, a Fate-full hour, is approaching.
My eyes can't watch this fight or witness the peace-pact.
But you—you're closer to Turnus—help if you dare to,
and act: it suits you. Good things may follow on sadness."
She'd hardly finished when tears flowed from the eyes of
      Juturna—
she struck her lovely breasts a third and a fourth time.
"No time to weep," said Juno, the daughter of Saturn.
"Hurry, rescue your brother from death in some fashion.
Start some fight, wreck the pact they agreed to.
I'll back your daring myself." She urged her but left her
160 sadly confused and hurt, her judgment unsteady.

On Parade

Kings meanwhile: the gathered strength of Latinus,
who rode in a four-horse chariot, gold at his temples:
the crown of twelve radiant beams in a circle,
a sign of the Sun, his grandfather. Turnus directed
two white horses and shook a pair of wide-pointed lances.
And there, Aeneas: Rome's first father and founder,
with star-like shield blazing and weapons from Sky-Gods.
Close by, Ascanius rode from the campground—another
hope for a great Rome. A priest in unspotted
170 clothing brought a wooly ram and the young of a bristly
boar. He nudged the beasts to a smoldering altar.

A Prayer and a Pledge

Leaders turned and faced the rising sun while they sprinkled
salt meal and marked the heads of the victims

by cutting forelocks. They poured wine on the altar.
Sword unsheathed, Aeneas dutifully pleaded:
"Sun-God, be present now. Earth, be my witness:
thanks to your help I lived through arduous labor.
Omnipotent Father: and you, his wife and the daughter
of Saturn: be kinder now, I beg you. Eminent War-God:
180 your will, Father, turns and twists all of our killing.
I call on you Springs and Streams, the home of the highest
Air, Powers who live in the blue of the Ocean:
if Chance concedes a win to Ausonian Turnus,
we losers agree to withdraw to the town of Evander.
We'll yield Italian land; the men of Aeneas
will never renew the war or challenge this kingdom with
        weapons.
Still, if our side wins the nod of the War-God—
it's likely, I think, the Gods are likely to want that—
I won't command Italians be subject to Trojans:
190 I want no throne for myself: let both of our nations
be equal, drafting a permanent peace-pact, unconquered!
I offer my rites and House-Gods. My Father Latinus
may keep his accustomed army and power. The Trojans
will build my walls. We'll give Lavinia's name to our city."

The Scepter Will Never Bear Leaves

Aeneas had spoken first. Latinus continued,
lifting a hand to the sky and looking to heaven:
"Aeneas, I swear by the same Earth, starlight and Ocean,
by both of Latona's children, both faces of Janus,
divine Underworld force, the hard shrines of the Hell-God.
200 Jupiter, hear me—you sign peace-pacts with lightning—
I hold the altar, I call on fire and Power around us:
no day will tear up this pact of peace for Italians.
No force will alter my will, whatever should happen—
no, not if a flood should swirl through the country
and wash it to sea, or Sky dissolve into Hell-world.
Just as my scepter"—by chance he was holding the scepter—
"will never provide shade by lightly leafing and branching,
the base removed now from roots in the forest.
It's lost a parent, it's lost hair and limbs to the axe-men:
210 once a tree, now it's plated in splendid
bronze by craftsmen, given to Latium's fathers to carry."
Thus between themselves they strengthened the peace-bond
while leaders around them watched. They ritually slaughtered

sacral beasts by the fire, ripped out the entrails
live and heaped up loaded plates on the altar.

Divine Provocation Once More

Rutulians had looked for a long time on this combat
as lopsided, truly. Mixed feelings confused them,
more so on closer inspection: the two were not equal.
Turnus' quiet walk heightened the tension.
220 With downcast eyes he humbly stooped at an altar,
cheeks gaunt, skin youthful but pallid.
Soon as Juturna (the sister of Turnus) felt a disturbance
increasing, the hearts of people in doubt or discouraged,
she went in their midst in disguise, in the form of Camertus.
(He'd come from an old large household, the name of his father
famous for courage; the man was a vigorous fighter.)
She moved right in the ranks, aware of the crisis,
planting various rumors and asking them frankly,
"Isn't it shameful, Rutulians, exposing a single
230 life for us all? Don't we match them in number
and strength? Look at all the Arcadians, Trojans,
gangs of death-bent Tuscans hostile to Turnus:
if half of us charged we hardly meet opposition!
Turnus may rise to the God whose altar he prays at,
men may keep him alive by telling his story;
we'll be forced to lose our homeland and cower
to insolent rule because we sat in a field and did nothing."

An Eagle Thwarted

That kind of speech inflamed the emotions of people
more, and more muttering crept through the army.
240 Laurentines themselves changed and even the Latins:
men who'd hoped just now for community safety
and rest from war craved weapons and prayed for
a wrecked peace-pact. They pitied the unfair portion of Turnus.
Then Juturna added a worse thing by sending
an omen from high in the sky. Presently nothing
misled and disturbed Italian minds more than this portent.
Jupiter's golden eagle, driving some shorebirds
through dawn-red sky and causing formations to flutter
and screech, suddenly turned, stooped on the water
250 and ruthlessly clamped a superb swan in its talons.
Italian spirits leaped when all of the shorebirds
loudly converged on the raptor—the scene was amazing—

they darkened the sky with feathers, forming a cloudbank
that crowded their enemy down, their weight overwhelmed him
until he wearied: talons tossing the booty
down to a stream, he raced into cloud to escape them.
Rutulians greeted the sign now with an uproar
and showed their fists. A seer, Tolumnius, told them
first, "There, that's what I prayed for so often:
260 I know and accept our Gods. *I'll* be your leader—
seize your weapons, you wretched people! A vicious
foreigner scared you, like impotent shorebirds,
and ravaged your coast: now *he'll* set sail to escape you
on deep water! Close ranks, and together
defend the prince this fight was intended to capture."

Battling Again

He stopped and ran forward to hurtle a weapon
at Tuscans who faced him. The cornel hissed as it cut through
the air, well aimed. Instantly everyone shouted
loudly, hearts were fired, wedge-formations were scattered.
270 The spear went flying where nine handsome brothers were
          standing
by chance on opposite ground—all born by a single
faithful Tuscan wife to Gylippus, the Arcadian native.
It struck one man in the stomach where buckles connected,
where belt stitching chafed and rubbed on the belly:
a man superbly proportioned, in glittering armor,
fell in the tawny dust, his abdomen ruptured.
The brothers grieved and raged. A spirited cluster,
some with swords—the hands of others had lances—
they blindly charged with their steel. Laurentines were marshaled
280 against them and charged. Massed Agyllines and Trojans
again flooded the field, with Arcadians' colorful armor.
One desire possessed them all: to decide it with weapons.
Altars were pulled down. The whole sky was a tumult,
a storm of missiles, a wild downpour of metal.
They bore off hearth-fires and bowls. Even Latinus,
carrying pelted House-Gods, ran off. The pact was demolished.
Warriors bridled chariot teams or they vaulted
on backs of mounts, their swords drawn for a muster.

A Victim for the Great Gods

One man eager to muddle the pact was Messapus.
290 He rode straight at Aulestes, who sported a Tuscan

king's insignia. Rushing away to escape him,
he stumbled miserably backwards over an altar,
banging his head and shoulder. Hot for a spear-thrust,
Messapus dashed up—the man begged—but the heavy and
    post-like
lance struck, the winner high on horseback proclaiming,
"This one's had it! A better victim goes to the Great Gods."
Italians ran up and stripped the body, though still warm.

War's Manglings

Now Corynaeus grabbed a blackened torch from an altar.
When Elysus came and cocked a spear, Corynaeus
300 dashed fire in his face—the big beard was ignited
and smelled burnt—Corynaeus pursued him,
gripped the flustered enemy's hair in his left hand,
kneed him hard, brought him down with a struggle,
and drove the rigid sword in his waist. Podalirius followed
Alsus, a shepherd who ran past spears on the front line:
he threatened the man with a bare weapon but Alsus
swiped with an axe at the face and chopped it from forehead
to chin—blood went flying, streaking the armor.
Hard silence weighed on the sight of the other:
310 iron sleep and endless night sealed up his vision.

A Frustrated Attempt at Order

Aeneas rightly held a weaponless hand up.
Head bare, he tried to shout to the army.
"Where do you run to? What's this surge of sudden disorder?
Control your anger! The treaty now is established,
all the terms arranged: I should be fighting alone here.
Away with your panic! Allow my strong hand to confirm it:
our pact and ritual owe Turnus to *me* now."
But then, as the man tried to address them, an arrow
swished on its wings and look: it's wounded Aeneas.
320 The hand or wind that caused that blow is uncertain.
What God or Chance brought so signal an honor
to men of Rutulia? The act and its glory are hidden:
no one advanced himself for wounding Aeneas.

Exploiting an Advantage

But seeing Aeneas withdrawn from the army
by troubled leaders, Turnus could *hope* suddenly, warmly:
he called for horses and armor, leaped on his chariot

proudly, gave the reins a vigorous shake and he rode off.
Sending scores of dead brave men to the Death-God
(the half dead he rolled aside), chariot trampling
330 through ranks, he seized spears and threw them at fleeing
men like blood-mad Mars himself when aroused by the frozen
Hebrus River: he bangs a shield to intensify combat,
whips maddened horses to race through an open
field and leads the Southwind and Westwind in far-off
Thrace, which grumbles under their hoofbeats, while Anger,
Deceit and a black Terror drive with the War-God, his comrades:
Turnus lashed at sweating horses as fiercely
now in battle. They stamped on wretchedly slaughtered
enemies, clumps of gore scattered by tearing
340 hooves, blood pounded and mixed in the gravel.
He gave Sthenelus soon to Death, and Thamyrus, Pholus—
the first from afar, the others up close. He killed from a distance
Glaucus and Lades, both sons of Imbrasus, who'd raised them
himself in Lycia, clapped them in similar armor
to fight by hand or on horseback, outrunning the Northwind.

New Land for a Corpse

Elsewhere Eumedes drove in the midst of a skirmish.
The son of aging Dolon and famous in warfare,
he'd kept a grandfather's name, a father's muscle and mettle.
Dolon had once boldly demanded, for going
350 to spy on the Greek camp, a chariot prized by Achilles.
But Diomedes had charged him another
price for that boldness: he huffed for the horseteam no longer.
Turnus watched Eumedes now in an open
stretch: he threw a light spear through the clearing that hurt him:
he halted his paired horse-team, leaped from the chariot, hovered
over the half-dead form, pinned with his right foot
the man's neck, snatched a gleaming sword from his victim,
and reddened it deep in the throat. He shouted above him,
"Look at the Western Land you wanted and warred for,
360 Trojan—lie there and measure it! *There's* compensation
for daring to test my sword: raise your walls on your death-
        ground!"

Stormwind at Sea

He sent Asbytes along (as Eumedes' friend) with a spear-throw.
He killed Chloreus, Sybaris, Thersilochus, Darcs
and then Thymoetes, flung from a horse's neck when it threw him.

Just like the breath of a Thracian Northwind that builds up
noise on the deep Aegean and surf on the beaches,
gusts swooping and clouds flitting through heaven:
Turnus cut a path where sections were yielding
ground, turning and running. He rode at his own speed:
370 wind rattled the horse-team and fluttered his head-crest.

Beheading

Phegeus could not stand that hounding and yelling.
He blocked Turnus' chariot: gripping the foamy
bits of the driving horses he angled them downward.
But Turnus caught an exposed flank with a spear-head
as Phegeus pulled and hung on the bridle: it severed
the stitched cuirass but only tore some flesh from the body.
The man could still hoist a shield and turn on his rival:
he made for Turnus, he hoped for help from his dagger,
but axle and wheel rumbled forward and knocked him
380 headlong down to the ground. Turnus pursued him:
between the helmet's base and the top of the breastplate
his sword cut off the head. He left the trunk in the gravel.

Attempts at Healing

While Turnus won in the field, scattering death-blows,
Ascanius now joined Mnestheus and loyal Achates:
they settled the blood-stained Aeneas, propping his every
other step with a long spear, down in their campground.
The man fumed. He tried to extract the head of the broken
arrow. He yelled for the quickest method to help him:
a wide sword might open the wound and uncover
390 the tip inside, sending him back to the fighting.
Iapyx had come already, the son of Iasus.
Phoebus had loved him greatly; possessed by that feeling
the God would have gladly given him talent and favor—
his own vision, fast arrows, and skill as a lyrist.
The man preferred, hoping to stall the death of a father,
knowledge of plant powers: the art of the healer.
He chose a quiet practice and work without glory.
Aeneas stood there, bitterly grumbling and leaning
against a huge spear, a crowd of soldiers around him,
400 Iulus weeping. Aeneas ignored them. Iapyx
rolled up and tied his cloak back like a doctor.
He busied himself applying strong herbs of Apollo.
Nothing worked. He tried extracting the arrow

head with strong iron tongs: it was futile.
Luck revealed no way, nothing Apollo
provided helped—while more and more on the savage
plain terror increased, danger approached, they could witness
dust that stood in the sky now, cavalry charging,
arrows falling thickly in camp. A pitiful wailing
410 rose from warriors falling under the rigorous War-God.

Help from a Mother

So Venus, distressed by the undeserved pain of Aeneas,
brought some dittany now from Crete, from Mount Ida,
the stem and leaves hairy, the blossom a downy
purple—a well-known plant to the wilderness goats there,
when struck on the back by a swift and tenacious
arrow. Venus obscured her form with surrounding
cloud and, using the plant, some water poured in a gleaming
cauldron, she made a secret decoction, including
healthful ambrosia drops and redolent cure-all.
420 Old Iapyx washed the wound with that fluid,
hardly aware that all the pain would abruptly
leave the body. Blood remained now in the puncture.
The arrow emerged with scarcely a tug from the doctor's
hand. Old strength newly returned to Aeneas.
"Hurry and arm the man! Why do you stand there?"
Iapyx called out first, igniting spirits for fighting.
"It's not some human resource, no art of a master,
not my hand that's come to save you, Aeneas:
some great God makes you return to greater achievement."

The Family's Example

430 Eager to fight, Aeneas clapped on the golden
leg-guards left and right. Disgusted with dawdling,
he shook a spear, shield to one side, and fitted the back-plate.
He found Ascanius, hugged him close to the armor,
lightly kissed his lips through the helmet and told him,
"Learn luck from others, my boy; from your father,
real strength and work. My own hand will protect you
now in war and lead you to eminent prizes.
Do all the same, in time, when you grow to adulthood.
Remember: keep in mind parental example.
440 Your father Aeneas and uncle Hector should stir you."

Renewed Spirits and Force

He finished speaking and moved through the gates like a giant,
shaking a huge spear. Antheus joined him,
Mnestheus hurried close-ranked troops from the campsite,
a whole throng flowed out, the field was a blinding
mix of dust and the ground was a stir and tremble of footbeats.
Turnus could see, from a rise, the enemy coming.
Ausonians watched as a chill raced through their marrow
and shook their bones. But even before the Latins, Juturna
had listened and known that sound: she shuddered and left them.
450 Aeneas took to the open plain with a shadowy column
the way heavy weather will veer from mid-ocean
abruptly to land, scaring and saddening farmers:
they know in their hearts the storm will bring them disaster,
flattening crops and fruit-trees, everything ruined—
the roar and flight of the wind tell them it's close to the shoreline.
That's how the Trojan leader motioned his column
straight at the enemy. Pressed together in wedge-form,
they braced him tightly. Thymbraeus stabbed the heavy Osiris;
Mnestheus cut down Arcetius; Achates, Epulo;
460 Gyas, Ufens. Even the seer, Tolumnius,
first to fling a spear at the enemy, crumpled.
An uproar went to the sky and Rutulians, taking
a turn on the dusty field as losers, retreated.
Aeneas disdained the killing of men with their backs turned;
he chased no one who faced him on foot or on horseback
with spear in hand but searched for Turnus alone in the heavy
gloom: he called for combat only with Turnus.

An Evasive Swallow

Fear stunned the mind of the man-like Juturna.
Metiscus had held the reins of the horse-team for Turnus:
470 she dumped him—left him far back of the car-pole—
and drove herself. Shaking the reins in her fingers
she took on the voice and gear, the whole shape of Metiscus.
Then like a black swallow that flits through a wealthy
lord's majestic home, searching for crumbs in the stately
hall and bringing food back to her cheeping
young, now in an empty portico, now at a quiet
pool twittering: so Juturna, drawn by the horse-team
right at the enemy, flew by them all in the chariot swiftly.
She showed her brother here and there to some cheering

480 but never allowed him to fight. She rushed him away in the
        distance.

Rage Provoked

Aeneas however pursued her turns and evasions.
He called loudly through broken ranks, he expected
to face the man. But whenever he spied his opponent
or tried sprinting after the wing-footed horses,
Juturna yanked at the chariot's reins and escaped him.
What could he do? He felt a moiling frustration.
And other concerns called him in other directions:
by chance Messapus jogged forward to face him,
a pair of steel-tipped flexible spears in his left hand.
490 He aimed one of the weapons and carefully threw it:
Aeneas had stopped, gathered himself in the armor,
dropped to one knee, and still the impetuous weapon
caught his helmet's top and cut off some feathers.
Anger really surged in Aeneas: he'd suffered
sneak attacks, he'd watched chariot horses elude him:
he called Jupiter now to witness: the altar and treaty
were broken. At last he charged the enemy center,
the War-God behind him, to wreak indiscriminate, savage
slaughter. He threw off every restraint on his fury.

Killings Mount

500 What God will sing to me now of the barbarous killing
throughout that field, the many leaders expiring,
Turnus driving here, there the Trojan commander?
How could such conflict please you, Jupiter, smashing
people who'd soon join in a permanent peace-pact?
Aeneas wounded the side of Rutulian Sucro
(the first to stand and fight off Trojan advances)
but hardly slowed him down. So a sword brutally punctured
his lung—the fastest possible death—through the ribcage.
Turnus unhorsed Amycus first, then Diores:
510 facing the brothers on foot, he stopped one charge with a
        spear-head;
the other a sword struck down. Cutting the heads off,
he carried and hung them back on his chariot, bleeding.
Aeneas killed Talon, Tanais and headstrong Cethegus—
three in one fight. He killed a somber Onites
(named by Theban people, his mother Peridia).
Turnus killed two Lycian brothers, sent from the Sun-God's

field, and young Menoetes (his hatred of war unavailing—
he'd worked around the fish-filled Arcadian river
at Lerna and lived poor, unfamiliar with wealthy
520 estates, his father renting the farm he had planted).
When fires are set in diverse parts of a forest
they crackle in dry laurel and dash through the thickets:
when rivers build and plunge down from the mountain
heights they rumble and quickly flow to the floodplain,
trailing wreckage behind them: Aeneas and Turnus
rushed through battle here and there in the same way,
blind to defeat, fury surging inside them,
bursting their chests—all their force went into wounding.

The Slaughter Continues

Murranus announced the names now of his fathers,
530 tracing a whole ancient royal Italian bloodline.
Aeneas threw a stone, a cumbersome boulder,
that struck him headlong. The wheels of his chariot rolling,
he fell to the ground under the yoke: dozens of hoofbeats
drubbed him, horses unthinkingly trampling their master.
Turnus met the savagely yelling and charging
Hyllus by throwing a spear at his gold-plated temple:
the weapon pierced his helmet and lodged in the brain-case.
Your hand also failed, Cretheus, one of the strongest
Greeks, to save you from Turnus; and no God covered Cupencus:
540 Aeneas came on driving a sword through the breastplate,
the sorry shield of brass could stall but not stop him.
That same Laurentine plain witnessed your killing,
Aeolus: startling the ground with the size of your backbone,
you fell there. No Greek force had been able to sprawl you,
not even the wrecker of Priam's kingdom, Achilles.
You'd lived on the heights of Ida, your home in Lyrnesus;
your death's mark was here, a tomb in the soil of Laurentum.

Armies Contending

All the Trojans, all those Latin formations
wheeled and bitterly struggled. Mnestheus, Serestus,
550 Messapus the horse-breaker, forceful Asilas,
Tuscan divisions, Arcadian wings of Evander:
each man drove and strained himself to the utmost.
No rest, no stalling: the strife was ravaging, total.

To Turn on the City Itself

And here his beautiful mother prompted Aeneas
to head for the walls: to turn troops on the city
and jolt the Latins fast, threatening sudden disaster.
While tracking Turnus through various battle formations,
circling this way and that, Aeneas had noticed
the city untouched by hard fighting: it rested unpunished.
560 The thought of a major attack immediately fired him.
Calling Mnestheus, Sergestus and forceful Serestus,
he took to a mound with his leaders; the rest of the Trojan
forces ran there, keeping shields crowded and lances
high. Standing tall in the center he told them,
"Let no one balk at my order: Jupiter stands here!
Let no one slouch because my plan is a new one.
That city started the war—the seat itself of Latinus.
Unless they comply and accept our yoke, admit they are done for,
I'll wreck it today: I'll burn and level those rooftops.
570 What, should I wait till Turnus is pleased to allow me
to fight, till he wishes to meet again, though he's beaten?
My countrymen, *there's* the head and height of this blasphemous
     conflict.
Hurry and bring torches—*fire* will insist on a treaty!"
Soon as he stopped they all competed to match him in spirit:
they formed tight wedges and bore down on the city.
Flames and makeshift ladders appeared in a moment.
Some men charged a gate and cut down the guard there;
others launched missiles that turned the sky into shadow.
Among those first at the wall, raising his right hand
580 high, Aeneas loudly faulted Latinus
and called Gods to witness: again he was forced into battle:
hostile Italians now had twice broken a peace-pact.

A Beehive Filled with Smoke

People scurried inside. Dissension was mounting.
One group ordered the city opened to Trojans,
the gates unbarred, the king himself dragged to the wall-top.
Others continued to haul out arms in defense of the city:
as when a shepherd follows bees to their hive in a jumbled
rockpile and forces acrid smoke in the crevice,
insects inside fear for the wax and their building,
590 loudly buzzing and milling, their anger increasing:
the dark stench rolls through their cells and a muffled

drone fills the rocks—some smoke escapes on the breezes.

The Loss of a Queen

More bad luck fell on the weakening Latins,
a grief that shook the whole city's foundations.
The queen in her room had watched the enemy coming,
the walls rammed, torches hurled at the rooftops,
and no Rutulian ranks, no forces of Turnus.
She sadly believed the man had been wiped out in combat
somewhere. Anguish abruptly disordered her thinking,
600 she called herself a crime, the cause of all evil,
she rambled on insanely, angry and wretched,
tearing her purple robe. Determined to end it,
she tightened the knot of an ugly death from a rafter.

New Grief in the City

When luckless Latin women heard of the killing,
first her daughter Lavinia tore at her blossomed
hair and rose-pink cheeks. The rest were around her,
a raving tumult—wide hallways echoed their anguish.
Grim details spread from there through the city.
Resolve sagged. In ripped clothing Latinus,
610 stunned by his wife's death and the city's destruction,
mussed and dirtied his hair, scattering dust there.
He blamed it all on himself for not taking Aeneas
of Troy before and calling him son-in-law freely.

Brother Against Sister

Turnus fought in a distant field in the meantime,
chasing a scattered few, but not very swiftly.
Less and less he enjoyed the rush of his horses.
A sound borne on the wind had tingled his hearing,
mixed cries of blind fear in the city,
a joyless drone—then a roar of mounting confusion.
620 "My God—what grief or horror deranges the city?
What loud and jumbled clamor spreads from the ramparts?"
Maddened, he stopped speaking and drew in the horse-reins.
But here that sister who'd changed to the form of Metiscus,
the chariot driver in charge of the team and its steering,
countered his question: "Turnus, get after the Trojans—
that's the first and clearest pathway to triumph.
Others can man the town roofs and defend them.
Aeneas may charge and mangle Italians in battle

but your hand too can savage and pack off the Trojans.
630 You'll end the fight with no less killing and honor."
Turnus answered,
"I've known for a time it was you, my sister, who plotted
to wreck the pact first and throw yourself into battle.
You fail to hide your godhead now. What force on Olympus
willed you to come down here and endure such a struggle,
to see some brutal death of a miserable brother?
For what can I do now? What luck will ensure my survival?
I saw with my own eyes Murranus—he called me
and called me—no one surpassed the man or was dearer.
640 He's down, a huge man, hugely wounded and beaten.
And wretched Ufens died to keep from beholding
our shame: Trojans own his body and armor.
Now they smash our homes—the last horror remaining.
How can I stand it, and not disprove Drances by fighting?
Will Turnus run off, the nation see him escaping?
In fact is dying so wretched? You Underworld Powers,
be kind to me now, the Overworld Powers against me:
I'll come down to you, free from wrong and unconscious
of evil, never unworthy of grandfathers' greatness."

A Desperate Plea for Help

650 He'd scarcely ended when Saces, riding a foam-flecked
horse from the enemy center (an arrow had wounded
and bloodied his face), rushed up to Turnus and begged him,
"Turnus, our last savior, pity your people.
The arms of a lightning-like Aeneas threaten to break down
Italy's highest fortress and turn it to rubble.
Torches fly at the roofs right now, Latins are turning
and looking to you, even King Latinus is mumbling:
whom should he call son-in-law? Which pact should he yield to?
Besides, the queen—a woman you trusted completely—
660 has killed herself. She madly dashed from the daylight.
Only Messapus and hard-working Atinus are propping
the gates' defenders. A massed division surrounds them
on either side, with bare swords like an iron
cornfield bristling—while *you* wheel horses through desolate
     farmland."

Decision

Turnus, confused and struck by that picture of changing
luck, stood there silent and staring. Shame like a monstrous

fire in his heart mingled with grief and derangement,
love and awareness of courage nettled his anger.
Soon that darkness dispersed. Brighter in outlook,
670 he turned a feverish gaze from the chariot back to the city.
He saw in alarm the great walls of Latinus
enveloped in fire: it rolled and billowed to heaven.
One peak of flame had enveloped a tower—a tower
Turnus himself had once raised with its thickset
planking and wheels, the high gangways he'd set up.
"Fates have beaten me now, my sister. Stop your resistance.
Where hard Fortune and Gods call we should follow.
It's settled: I'll fight with Aeneas, whatever the bitter
weight of death. Juturna, you'll see me dishonored
680 no longer. But give me rage first: I ask for some fury."

A Mass of Rock Down a Mountainside

He stopped, leaped from the chariot quickly and sprinted
past enemy spears in the field. He left a despondent
sister behind. He rapidly broke through the enemy center
much as a boulder rushing headlong from mountain
heights, detached by the wind or a violent downpour,
old and loosened under the passing of seasons:
a damaging mass with its steep and solid momentum
leaps over rough ground and tumbles through forest,
herds and people: Turnus rushed through dividing
690 ranks to the city wall where most of the bloodshed
soaked the soil, the air whistled with spear-throws.
He signaled by hand and called loudly to war-friends.
"Rutulians! Stop now. Master your weapons, you Latins.
Whatever Luck's here, it's mine. Better that one man
pay for breaking the pact. One sword will decide it."
They all backed off and gave him room in the center.

Clearing a Field

After hearing the name of Turnus, Aeneas,
our ancestor, left the high citadel ramparts:
he broke off all that work, delay was discarded,
700 he gladly leaped and banged hard weapons like thunder,
louder than Mount Athos or Eryx when rumbling
and jostling oaks, or even lordly Appenine, grandly
lifting its snowy peak in the air and rejoicing.
Now Rutulians, Trojans and all the Italian army
stared intently—men who had guarded a looming

wall or had struck that wall with rams at the baseline.
Armor slipped from their shoulders. Astonished, Latinus
himself watched the two tall warriors, natives
of different worlds: they'd battle each other, decide it
    with metal.

The Final Combat Begins

710 And they, soon as the field emptied before them,
charged full tilt: they threw spears from a distance
then fought up close, bronze shielding resounding.
Earth itself groaned as the number of sword-blows
mounted, manhood and luck in a scramble together:
like two large bulls that turn and charge in the Sila
Forest or fight enraged on the heights of Taburnus,
foreheads crashing, alarmed herdsmen withdrawing,
heifers lowing, every steer silent and anxious:
who'll command the whole herd and the forest?
720 The bulls powerfully grapple, wounding each other,
horns ram and gore, spattering shoulders
and necks with gouts of blood as woods echo their groaning:
that's how Troy's Aeneas and Latium's leader
collided with shields. Air and sky filled with the uproar.
In fact Jupiter held an evenly balanced
scale that weighed the different fates of the two men:
one would incline, condemning a man to death in the struggle.

A Sword Shatters

And here Turnus leaped out, thinking it safe now,
lifting his whole body high for a sword-blow,
730 and struck. Trojans and Latins anxiously cried out,
both sides on their feet. But the sword disappointed
a flushed Turnus: it treacherously shattered on impact.
Seeing that strange hilt, his hand undefended,
he turned to escape, sprinting faster than Eastwind.
When Turnus first yoked horses for battle, the story
goes, he was hasty, leaving the sword of his father
and hotly seizing a sword of the driver, Metiscus.
So long as he struck down turning and scattering Trojans
the sword sufficed; but hitting the shield of the Fire-God,
740 the man-made edge reacted like ice when you slap it—
it broke up. The dull brown dust gleamed with its fragments.
So Turnus wildly fled over rises and flatland
now this way and that, indecisively circling.

Either close-packed Trojans everywhere ringed him
or rugged walls blocked him, or desolate marshes.

Stag and Hound

Aeneas nevertheless, though slowed by the arrow
wound that sometimes hurt and hampered his running,
followed step by step. Shaking, Turnus was pressured
the way a stag is brought to bay at a river,
750 or scared and driven to snares by violet feathers:
a barking lead hound hunts and presses the quarry
who bolts, afraid of a snare or the riverbank steepness,
and runs this way and that; but the Umbrian staghound alertly
sticks to him, now he clamps or seems to be clamping,
to bite down hard—on nothing: the deer has escaped him.
Soon the uproar was louder, neighboring marshland
and banks echoed, all the sky a thundering tumult.
Turnus ran, he turned to every Rutulian,
each by name, demanding the sword of his father.
760 Aeneas threatened immediate death to the person
who offered help. He scared and confused people; he threatened
(hurt but pursuing) even to ransack the city.
Now they'd completed five circles of weaving
and dodging. Truly the prize they strove for was neither
slight nor sporting: at stake was the life-blood of Turnus.

Help from the Goddesses

By chance a wild olive sacred to Faunus
had stood nearby, leaves bitter but valued by sailors
once who'd thanked, safely ashore, the God of Laurentum:
they'd hung gifts or attached clothes they had promised.
770 But Trojans had felled the tree. Unconcerned about holy
wood, they'd cleared a space on the field for this duel.
The spear of Aeneas had struck one spot, its momentum
thrusting it hard into tangled roots of the olive.
The Dardan leader struggled to pull out the weapon:
he wanted to chase the man with a spear if unable
to catch him. Crazed with fear Turnus was begging
Faunus: "Please have pity: cling to that weapon,
you excellent Earth—if I always honored and praised you—
Aeneas' men have profaned you now with this fighting."
780 The call for a God's help was not to be futile.
Aeneas got stalled for a long time at the stubborn
roots, struggling with all his force, unable to loosen

the wood's bite. While he strained and hotly persisted,
again Juturna took the form of the driver, Metiscus:
she ran to her brother and gave him the sword of his father.
Now Venus fumed at the brashness allowed to a Lake-Nymph.
She went to those deep roots and tore out the weapon.
Both men stood erect, re-armed and recovered,
one trusting a sword, the other a vigorous spear-throw.
790 They stood up close, breath short, to fight for their War-God.

Troy's Name Lost

Meanwhile the all-powerful King of Olympus
spoke to Juno, who gazed on the fight from a golden
cloud. "My wife, what end now is remaining?
Aeneas will master this land—you know it yourself and admit it.
Stars will claim him; Fates will raise him to heaven.
What hope or plot can you cling to there in your chilly
cloud? Is it right that a God be hurt, dishonored by humans,
that Turnus retrieve a lost sword—and Juturna
could do nothing without you—to strengthen the losers?
800 No: stop now. Yield at last to my prayer.
Don't let spite consume you in silence, or gloomy
worry return so often—to lips of such sweetness!
The end has come. On sea and land you've been able
to vex Troy, to ignite this blasphemous fighting,
disgrace a king's house and tangle a marriage in mourning.
I'll block your further efforts." When Jupiter finished, the
      Goddess,
daughter of Saturn, lowered her eyes and responded,
"Jupiter, truly knowing your will and your greatness,
I've left that land and Turnus both—but not freely.
810 You'd hardly see me alone now on this cloudbank,
enduring dishonor and honor: I'd rather be down there,
circled by war and flame, dragging Troy into losing
battle. Yes: I urged Juturna to run to her wretched
brother and take some great risk for his life: I approved it.
But not to bend her bow, to fight with those arrows:
I swear by the Styx's spring, that implacable water—
the only name and oath binding on Sky-Gods.
I do concede now. I'm done with war; I detest it.
I ask one favor. No law or Fate is against it.
820 For Latium now and your own family honor,
when peace is confirmed in a happy marriage—so be it—
when both sides ratify laws and their treaties:

don't let Latins change the old name of their country,
become like Troy, or call their people the Trojans,
or change their own language or alter their clothing.
Let Alban kings and Latium stay through the ages,
a Roman people, strengthened by Italy's courage.
Troy and its name fell. Let them always be fallen."

Nations United

Man's and the world's Maker smiled as he answered,
830 "You *are* Jupiter's sister, the second daughter of Saturn:
what waves of intense rage rush through your body!
But come. Repress this wrath—it was vain from the outset.
I'll grant your wish, I yield, I'm willingly conquered!
Ausonians will keep the ways and speech of their fathers;
their name will remain the same. Trojans will mix in a body
merely and settle. I'll add their rites and their customs
to Latins'; I'll make one language for all of the people.
A nation will rise from the mixed Ausonian bloodlines
above all men, above the Gods in devotion:
840 no other race will match them, you'll see, in honoring Juno."
The Goddess was pleased. She nodded, altered her purpose
and soon withdrew from the heavenly cloud she had stayed on.

A Little Owl

That done, the Father himself considered another
task: sending Juturna away from the army of Turnus.
They say two plagues (people call them the Furies)
were born from Night's sickly womb in a single
birth with hell's Megaera. Tangles of serpents
knotted them all and wind-quick wings were allowed them.
They stay by their king, Jupiter's threshold or throne; when he's
        angry
850 they're ready to point fear and sickness in humans,
whenever the Gods' ruler prepares a revolting
disease, or alarms with war and death towns that deserve it.
Jupiter quickly sent one down from the heavens
commanding she face Juturna, to act as an omen.
Riding a turbulent wind she flew to that country
just like an arrow twanged through mist from a bowstring,
tipped by a Parthian archer with virulent poison
(Cretan and Parthian arrow wounds are incurable),
hissing and passing quickly unseen through the shadows:
860 Night's daughter bore down on the earth in the same way.

After she found the Trojan ranks and the army of Turnus
she suddenly shrank down to the form of a little
owl that squats at times on graves or abandoned
rooftops late at night to drone rudely in darkness.
So transformed the Fury flapped and re-flapped by
Turnus' face—she squawked and struck the shield with her
    wingbeats.
A strange fear numbed and softened his body.
His scalp chilled and tingled. Words stuck in his gullet.

The Loss of a Sister

But soon as Juturna knew the sound of that Fury's
870 wings in the distance, she mussed then tore her hair in her sorrow,
she scratched her cheeks and beat her breasts with a sister's
grief: "Turnus—how can your sister protect you?
Can anything harder await me? What art can continue
to light your life? I cannot withstand such an omen.
Yes, I'm leaving—no need to ruffle or scare me,
filthy bird. I know your wings and that wing-lash,
your death's rattle. Great-souled Jupiter's lordly
command is clear. Here's how he thanks me—a virgin!
Why did he make me immortal? Why is my human
880 condition lost? I'd end such anguish instantly, truly—
I'd rather go as a wretched brother's friend through the shadows—
but no, I'm deathless. What gave me joy will be joyless
without you, brother. What depths of earth will be open
enough, sending a Goddess like me to the Death-world?"
She said that much, covered her head in a blue-grey
shawl, sighed deeply, and hid in the depths of the river.

As Though Running in a Dream

Aeneas closed in. Flashing a weapon before him,
big as a tree, he called with the heart of a savage,
"What stalls you now, Turnus? Why so reluctant?
890 Don't run off—you're bound to fight fiercely with weapons.
Change yourself into any form, gather whatever
spirits or tricks you can, follow the highest
star if you like, block and conceal yourself in some hollow."
Turnus shook his head. "You wildman, none of your fiery
talk scares me. The Gods—Jupiter's enmity scares me."
He said no more but looked around for a ponderous boulder.
A huge old stone happened to lie on the fieldgrass,
used as a landmark to settle disputes among farmers.

The backs of twelve hand-picked men could barely support it—
900 the backs of men the land might yield in our own age.
That leader restlessly gripped it, hefted it higher,
ran with it swiftly and hurled the stone at his rival.
Still he hardly recognized himself as the runner,
hands raised and huge boulder above him:
his knees quavered, the blood congealing and chilling.
Then the boulder itself rolled through an open
space and stopped short. The blow did not carry.
As though in a dream when languid quiet has covered
our eyes at night, we seem full of desire and we struggle
910 to run, eager but helpless, weak in the midst of our efforts:
we slump, speech unavailing, our usual muscle
strength fading, and words we form do not follow:
so with Turnus. However he strove to demonstrate courage,
a stern Fury denied the advance. His heart was a welter
of mixed feelings; he looked at the town, his Rutulians.
Slowed by fear—a fatal spear threatened—he trembled.
He saw no escape, no force to use on his rival.
He saw no chariot now or the driver, his sister.

Hard as a Siege Missile

While he delayed, Aeneas kept flashing the deadly
920 spear. He spotted a chance: he threw from a distance
with all his force. Stones from siege-slings have never
roared or smashed at a wall, nor has lightning and thunder
cracked so hard: appearing dark as a whirlwind,
bearing its grim conclusion, the spear went flying and broke
        through
the corselet's edge, the seven-fold shield at the bottom,
grinding, and tore through thigh. Turnus was buckled.
His massive knee was forced to the ground by the impact.
Rutulians moaned and leaped up. Every foothill around them
echoed the moan; deep forest answered the outcry.

Hesitation

930 Turnus, humbled, raised a look and extended
a hand: "I did deserve this. I won't be a beggar,"
he said, "use your chance. If care about wretched
fathers can touch you—you had such a father, Anchises—
I ask your pity for Daunus. My Father is aging.
Return me to family, alive or stripped of the daylight
if that's your choice. You've won. The loser's hand is extended.

Ausonians watch us. Now you can marry Lavinia.
Don't stretch hatred further." Armored and trenchant,
Aeneas stood there. He looked around, restraining his
    swordhand.

A Fatal War-prize

940 More and more those words had begun to deter him
when there and then, high on a shoulder of Turnus,
a painful sword-belt appeared, studs familiar and shiny:
young Pallas' belt. Having wounded and sprawled him
Turnus had killed him—then sported the enemy's prize on a
    shoulder.
After Aeneas looked at the prize and absorbed its recalling
bitter grief, a crazed and frightening anger
burned him. "You—wearing a prize from my comrade—
you want to escape? Pallas will kill you: let Pallas
take your blood, a price for the crime you committed."
950 He stopped and buried the sword in his enemy's ribcage
hotly. Turnus slumped, a chill in his members.
Sighing, protesting, his life left for the shadows.

Edward McCrorie's poems, translations and prose have appeared in a wide variety of magazines, newspapers and anthologies. His first book of poems, *After a Cremation,* was published in Berkeley in 1975 by Thorp Springs Press. His Virgil appeared in a collector's edition in 1991 in New Hampshire from Donald Grant Press. He is currently working on another book of poems, and on a translation of Homer's *Odyssey.*

At Providence College he teaches in a Western Civilization program that is team-taught and features the work of Sappho and Homer as well as Virgil. He finished graduate work at Brown in 1970, where poetry style was his main focus, and he regularly teaches the poets of nineteenth- and twentieth-century England and America.